T0207305

Lecture Notes in Computer Science 14705

Founding Editors

Gerhard Goos
Juris Hartmanis

Editorial Board Members

The series Lecture Notes in Computer Science (LNCS), including its subseries Lecture Notes in Artificial Intelligence (LNAI) and Lecture Notes in Bioinformatics (LNBI), has established itself as a medium for the publication of new developments in computer science and information technology research, teaching, and education.

LNCS enjoys close cooperation with the computer science R & D community, the series counts many renowned academics among its volume editors and paper authors, and collaborates with prestigious societies. Its mission is to serve this international community by providing an invaluable service, mainly focused on the publication of conference and workshop proceedings and postproceedings. LNCS commenced publication in 1973.

Adela Coman · Simona Vasilache
Editors

Social Computing and Social Media

16th International Conference, SCSM 2024
Held as Part of the 26th HCI International Conference, HCII 2024
Washington, DC, USA, June 29 – July 4, 2024
Proceedings, Part III

 Springer

Editors
Adela Coman
University of Bucharest
Bucharest, Romania

Simona Vasilache
University of Tsukuba
Tsukuba, Japan

ISSN 0302-9743   ISSN 1611-3349 (electronic)
Lecture Notes in Computer Science
ISBN 978-3-031-61311-1   ISBN 978-3-031-61312-8 (eBook)
https://doi.org/10.1007/978-3-031-61312-8

This Springer imprint is published by the registered company Springer Nature Switzerland AG
The registered company address is: Gewerbestrasse 11, 6330 Cham, Switzerland

If disposing of this product, please recycle the paper.

Foreword

This year we celebrate 40 years since the establishment of the HCI International (HCII) Conference, which has been a hub for presenting groundbreaking research and novel ideas and collaboration for people from all over the world.

The HCII conference was founded in 1984 by Prof. Gavriel Salvendy (Purdue University, USA, Tsinghua University, P.R. China, and University of Central Florida, USA) and the first event of the series, "1st USA-Japan Conference on Human-Computer Interaction", was held in Honolulu, Hawaii, USA, 18–20 August. Since then, HCI International is held jointly with several Thematic Areas and Affiliated Conferences, with each one under the auspices of a distinguished international Program Board and under one management and one registration. Twenty-six HCI International Conferences have been organized so far (every two years until 2013, and annually thereafter).

Over the years, this conference has served as a platform for scholars, researchers, industry experts and students to exchange ideas, connect, and address challenges in the ever-evolving HCI field. Throughout these 40 years, the conference has evolved itself, adapting to new technologies and emerging trends, while staying committed to its core mission of advancing knowledge and driving change.

As we celebrate this milestone anniversary, we reflect on the contributions of its founding members and appreciate the commitment of its current and past Affiliated Conference Program Board Chairs and members. We are also thankful to all past conference attendees who have shaped this community into what it is today.

The 26th International Conference on Human-Computer Interaction, HCI International 2024 (HCII 2024), was held as a 'hybrid' event at the Washington Hilton Hotel, Washington, DC, USA, during 29 June – 4 July 2024. It incorporated the 21 thematic areas and affiliated conferences listed below.

A total of 5108 individuals from academia, research institutes, industry, and government agencies from 85 countries submitted contributions, and 1271 papers and 309 posters were included in the volumes of the proceedings that were published just before the start of the conference, these are listed below. The contributions thoroughly cover the entire field of human-computer interaction, addressing major advances in knowledge and effective use of computers in a variety of application areas. These papers provide academics, researchers, engineers, scientists, practitioners and students with state-of-the-art information on the most recent advances in HCI.

The HCI International (HCII) conference also offers the option of presenting 'Late Breaking Work', and this applies both for papers and posters, with corresponding volumes of proceedings that will be published after the conference. Full papers will be included in the 'HCII 2024 - Late Breaking Papers' volumes of the proceedings to be published in the Springer LNCS series, while 'Poster Extended Abstracts' will be included as short research papers in the 'HCII 2024 - Late Breaking Posters' volumes to be published in the Springer CCIS series.

I would like to thank the Program Board Chairs and the members of the Program Boards of all thematic areas and affiliated conferences for their contribution towards the high scientific quality and overall success of the HCI International 2024 conference. Their manifold support in terms of paper reviewing (single-blind review process, with a minimum of two reviews per submission), session organization and their willingness to act as goodwill ambassadors for the conference is most highly appreciated.

This conference would not have been possible without the continuous and unwavering support and advice of Gavriel Salvendy, founder, General Chair Emeritus, and Scientific Advisor. For his outstanding efforts, I would like to express my sincere appreciation to Abbas Moallem, Communications Chair and Editor of HCI International News.

July 2024   Constantine Stephanidis

HCI International 2024 Thematic Areas
and Affiliated Conferences

- HCI: Human-Computer Interaction Thematic Area
- HIMI: Human Interface and the Management of Information Thematic Area
- EPCE: 21st International Conference on Engineering Psychology and Cognitive Ergonomics
- AC: 18th International Conference on Augmented Cognition
- UAHCI: 18th International Conference on Universal Access in Human-Computer Interaction
- CCD: 16th International Conference on Cross-Cultural Design
- SCSM: 16th International Conference on Social Computing and Social Media
- VAMR: 16th International Conference on Virtual, Augmented and Mixed Reality
- DHM: 15th International Conference on Digital Human Modeling & Applications in Health, Safety, Ergonomics & Risk Management
- DUXU: 13th International Conference on Design, User Experience and Usability
- C&C: 12th International Conference on Culture and Computing
- DAPI: 12th International Conference on Distributed, Ambient and Pervasive Interactions
- HCIBGO: 11th International Conference on HCI in Business, Government and Organizations
- LCT: 11th International Conference on Learning and Collaboration Technologies
- ITAP: 10th International Conference on Human Aspects of IT for the Aged Population
- AIS: 6th International Conference on Adaptive Instructional Systems
- HCI-CPT: 6th International Conference on HCI for Cybersecurity, Privacy and Trust
- HCI-Games: 6th International Conference on HCI in Games
- MobiTAS: 6th International Conference on HCI in Mobility, Transport and Automotive Systems
- AI-HCI: 5th International Conference on Artificial Intelligence in HCI
- MOBILE: 5th International Conference on Human-Centered Design, Operation and Evaluation of Mobile Communications

List of Conference Proceedings Volumes Appearing Before the Conference

1. LNCS 14684, Human-Computer Interaction: Part I, edited by Masaaki Kurosu and Ayako Hashizume
2. LNCS 14685, Human-Computer Interaction: Part II, edited by Masaaki Kurosu and Ayako Hashizume
3. LNCS 14686, Human-Computer Interaction: Part III, edited by Masaaki Kurosu and Ayako Hashizume
4. LNCS 14687, Human-Computer Interaction: Part IV, edited by Masaaki Kurosu and Ayako Hashizume
5. LNCS 14688, Human-Computer Interaction: Part V, edited by Masaaki Kurosu and Ayako Hashizume
6. LNCS 14689, Human Interface and the Management of Information: Part I, edited by Hirohiko Mori and Yumi Asahi
7. LNCS 14690, Human Interface and the Management of Information: Part II, edited by Hirohiko Mori and Yumi Asahi
8. LNCS 14691, Human Interface and the Management of Information: Part III, edited by Hirohiko Mori and Yumi Asahi
9. LNAI 14692, Engineering Psychology and Cognitive Ergonomics: Part I, edited by Don Harris and Wen-Chin Li
10. LNAI 14693, Engineering Psychology and Cognitive Ergonomics: Part II, edited by Don Harris and Wen-Chin Li
11. LNAI 14694, Augmented Cognition, Part I, edited by Dylan D. Schmorrow and Cali M. Fidopiastis
12. LNAI 14695, Augmented Cognition, Part II, edited by Dylan D. Schmorrow and Cali M. Fidopiastis
13. LNCS 14696, Universal Access in Human-Computer Interaction: Part I, edited by Margherita Antona and Constantine Stephanidis
14. LNCS 14697, Universal Access in Human-Computer Interaction: Part II, edited by Margherita Antona and Constantine Stephanidis
15. LNCS 14698, Universal Access in Human-Computer Interaction: Part III, edited by Margherita Antona and Constantine Stephanidis
16. LNCS 14699, Cross-Cultural Design: Part I, edited by Pei-Luen Patrick Rau
17. LNCS 14700, Cross-Cultural Design: Part II, edited by Pei-Luen Patrick Rau
18. LNCS 14701, Cross-Cultural Design: Part III, edited by Pei-Luen Patrick Rau
19. LNCS 14702, Cross-Cultural Design: Part IV, edited by Pei-Luen Patrick Rau
20. LNCS 14703, Social Computing and Social Media: Part I, edited by Adela Coman and Simona Vasilache
21. LNCS 14704, Social Computing and Social Media: Part II, edited by Adela Coman and Simona Vasilache
22. LNCS 14705, Social Computing and Social Media: Part III, edited by Adela Coman and Simona Vasilache

47. LNCS 14730, HCI in Games: Part I, edited by Xiaowen Fang
48. LNCS 14731, HCI in Games: Part II, edited by Xiaowen Fang
49. LNCS 14732, HCI in Mobility, Transport and Automotive Systems: Part I, edited by Heidi Krömker
50. LNCS 14733, HCI in Mobility, Transport and Automotive Systems: Part II, edited by Heidi Krömker
51. LNAI 14734, Artificial Intelligence in HCI: Part I, edited by Helmut Degen and Stavroula Ntoa
52. LNAI 14735, Artificial Intelligence in HCI: Part II, edited by Helmut Degen and Stavroula Ntoa
53. LNAI 14736, Artificial Intelligence in HCI: Part III, edited by Helmut Degen and Stavroula Ntoa
54. LNCS 14737, Design, Operation and Evaluation of Mobile Communications: Part I, edited by June Wei and George Margetis
55. LNCS 14738, Design, Operation and Evaluation of Mobile Communications: Part II, edited by June Wei and George Margetis
56. CCIS 2114, HCI International 2024 Posters - Part I, edited by Constantine Stephanidis, Margherita Antona, Stavroula Ntoa and Gavriel Salvendy
57. CCIS 2115, HCI International 2024 Posters - Part II, edited by Constantine Stephanidis, Margherita Antona, Stavroula Ntoa and Gavriel Salvendy
58. CCIS 2116, HCI International 2024 Posters - Part III, edited by Constantine Stephanidis, Margherita Antona, Stavroula Ntoa and Gavriel Salvendy
59. CCIS 2117, HCI International 2024 Posters - Part IV, edited by Constantine Stephanidis, Margherita Antona, Stavroula Ntoa and Gavriel Salvendy
60. CCIS 2118, HCI International 2024 Posters - Part V, edited by Constantine Stephanidis, Margherita Antona, Stavroula Ntoa and Gavriel Salvendy
61. CCIS 2119, HCI International 2024 Posters - Part VI, edited by Constantine Stephanidis, Margherita Antona, Stavroula Ntoa and Gavriel Salvendy
62. CCIS 2120, HCI International 2024 Posters - Part VII, edited by Constantine Stephanidis, Margherita Antona, Stavroula Ntoa and Gavriel Salvendy

https://2024.hci.international/proceedings

Preface

The 16th International Conference on Social Computing and Social Media (SCSM 2024) was an affiliated conference of the HCI International (HCII) conference. The conference provided an established international forum for the exchange and dissemination of scientific information related to social computing and social media, addressing a broad spectrum of issues expanding our understanding of current and future issues in these areas. The conference welcomed qualitative and quantitative research papers on a diverse range of topics related to the design, development, assessment, use, and impact of social media.

A considerable number of papers this year focused on research on the design, development, and evaluation of social media, exploring topics such as opinion data crawling, crowdsourcing, and recommendation systems, and delving into aspects related to user experience and user behavior. The undeniable influence of Artificial Intelligence on the technological landscape has prompted numerous works focused on the use of AI and Language Models in social media, investigating their multifaceted impact in the field, such as for the identification of malicious accounts and deepfakes, the improvement of search capabilities, the recognition of emotions and detection of human values, as well as the development of improved recommendation systems. The power of social media and its positive impact across various application domains inspired contributions regarding education and learning, culture, business, eCommerce, as well as computer-mediated communication. In the context of learning, the topics explored include academic writing, learning experience, ethics in education, specialized social networks for researchers, platforms for students with disabilities, and the impact of AI in education-related social media and platforms. In business and eCommerce, papers delve into aspects related to branding, consumer behavior, as well as customer experience and engagement. Finally, appraising the role of social media in fostering communication, strengthening social ties, and supporting democracy, contributions explored novel interpersonal communication approaches, hybrid working environments, opinion analysis, media memory shaping, disaster management, social learning, and online citizen interaction. As editors of these SCSM proceedings volumes, we are pleased to present this unique and diverse compilation of topics offering valuable insights and advancing our understanding of the current and future issues in the field.

Three volumes of the HCII 2024 proceedings are dedicated to this year's edition of the SCSM conference. The first focuses on topics related to Designing, Developing and Evaluating Social Media, User Experience and User Behavior in Social Media, and AI and Language Models in Social Media. The second focuses on topics related to Social Media in Learning, Education and Culture, and Social Media in Business and eCommerce. Finally, the third focuses on topics related to Computer-Mediated Communication, and Social Media for Community, Society and Democracy.

The papers in these volumes were accepted for publication after a minimum of two single-blind reviews from the members of the SCSM Program Board or, in some cases, from members of the Program Boards of other affiliated conferences. We would like to thank all of them for their invaluable contribution, support, and efforts.

July 2024   Adela Coman
                                                                   Simona Vasilache

16th International Conference on Social Computing and Social Media (SCSM 2024)

The full list with the Program Board Chairs and the members of the Program Boards of all thematic areas and affiliated conferences of HCII 2024 is available online at:

http://www.hci.international/board-members-2024.php

HCI International 2025 Conference

The 27th International Conference on Human-Computer Interaction, HCI International 2025, will be held jointly with the affiliated conferences at the Swedish Exhibition & Congress Centre and Gothia Towers Hotel, Gothenburg, Sweden, June 22–27, 2025. It will cover a broad spectrum of themes related to Human-Computer Interaction, including theoretical issues, methods, tools, processes, and case studies in HCI design, as well as novel interaction techniques, interfaces, and applications. The proceedings will be published by Springer. More information will become available on the conference website: https://2025.hci.international/.

General Chair
Prof. Constantine Stephanidis
University of Crete and ICS-FORTH
Heraklion, Crete, Greece
Email: general_chair@2025.hci.international

https://2025.hci.international/

Contents – Part III

Computer-Mediated Communication

Closing the Gap Between Long Distance Couples via Asynchronous Remote Touch Communication

Angela Chan[(⊠)] [ID], Francis Quek[ID], Joshua Howell[ID], and Ting Liu[ID]

Texas A&M University, College Station, TX 77840, USA
angela.tze.chan@tamu.edu

Abstract. Remote touch, like natural touch, is ambiguous and can convey a range of affective effects. Prior research demonstrated that remote touch during emotionally tense conversations reduced emotional arousal. This study investigates how remote touch impacts affective experience of positive messages between long-distance couples. Participants interacted asynchronously through paired devices that could transmit various degrees of touch pressure. Participants sent video/audio messages of pleasant memories to their partners in which they could embed touches. Their partners can receive the touch-embedded recordings while wearing a touch device that replays the touches. This study compared the affective response of the recipient under four conditions: video with and without touch, and audio with and without touch. We measured affect through electrodermal recordings and facial expression analysis. Results revealed enhanced affective response and a greater preference in communication when remote touch is used. This study can inform the design and use of affective interactive devices in telecommunications and media settings.

Keywords: Asynchronous Remote Touch Communication · Remote Touch Communication · Affective Remote Touch

1 Introduction

Touch is one of the earliest senses humans develop and allows us to experience and interact with the world around us [1]. To illustrate the importance of touch, one can imagine a life without vision, hearing, smell, or taste. A total loss of touch, however, is "both exceedingly rare and devastating for normal human existence" [1]. Although touch is such a vast field of study that encompasses tactile sensing, instrumental touch, therapeutic touch, etc., our area of interest is in affective social touch.

Affective touch can strengthen the connection between people [2] and creates a form of intimacy that can be better expressed without the use of language [3]. Touch is also ambiguous in that identical touches can convey a range of affective meanings-- a simple upper arm squeeze can serve as comfort in sorrow and congratulations in success. However, for touch to become meaningful, context such as accompanying speech is needed to further shape touch's meaning [4]. This is also true for remote touch [5].

© The Author(s), under exclusive license to Springer Nature Switzerland AG 2024
A. Coman and S. Vasilache (Eds.): HCII 2024, LNCS 14705, pp. 3–16, 2024.
https://doi.org/10.1007/978-3-031-61312-8_1

In situations where in-person interaction is not possible, remote interpersonal touch can be used to support affective communication and foster connectedness [6–8]. For individuals who are living away from their loved ones (e.g., long distance couples, first year university students, deployed military, etc.), remote touch interaction may serve as a critical channel of support. Previous works such as [9–11] have already begun the investigation of remote touch interaction in a synchronous communication setting. Research in asynchronous remote touch communication, however, is still lacking.

Asynchronous communication such as short videos, voice messages, etc. has revolutionized the way we connect with people in social networking [12]. This motivates our research with respect to: (a) how mediated touch can effectively communicate in a similar manner and (b) how *asynchronous* touch can be used to augment and enrich other forms of communication.

As previous work showed remote touch can have a 'comforting effect' in stressful/emotionally charged conversations (reducing biophysical indicators like EDA, heart rate) [9, 10], a question remains as to the impact of remote touch in a broader affective range – to include pleasant, happy, or even excited messages.

We recruited 29 long-distance romantic couples who had been together for at least one year. One research subject in each pair created personalized video and audio messages (with and without embedded remote touch) of pleasant memories for their partner to experience. We measured affective response of the recipient through subjective questionnaires, electrodermal (EDA) recordings and facial expression recognition analysis.

2   Background and Related Works

Affective touch plays a crucial role in social interaction and has been shown to foster intimacy [13], alleviate stress [14, 15] and provide emotional support [16] (among other benefits). Beyond these social benefits of in-person touch, affective touch has been shown to affect the physiology of receivers as well. Goldstein et al., for example, found that, with respect to romantic partners in which one partner was subjected to a pain stimulus, hand-holding helped to reduce pain [17]. Additionally, López-Solà et al. found that in-person hand-holding (when compared to holding a rubber device) "significantly mediated reductions in pain intensity and unpleasantness." [18]. Finally, touch has been shown to reduce anxiety [19], lower heart rate and decrease stress [20]. While these effects—which, in the psychological literature, is often referred to as "lowered arousal"—can, to some degree, be demonstrated when dyads are strangers, these effects are more pronounced when dyads are couples in a committed romantic relationship.

Mediated touch—which Haans et al. defines " as the ability of one actor to touch another actor over a distance by means of tactile or kinesthetic feedback technology" [5]—in many ways mimics the affective benefits of in-person touch. One notable work is Chan's study that showed their remote touch devices were used in a variety of communicative and affective ways to enhance the interaction between romantic pairs during a video call. In their study, couples were provided with the touch devices to use during conversations that contained emotionally-charged moments. The results showed that more remote touches were exchanged during moments of the conversation that contained negative sentiment. Furthermore, remote touches elicited an instantaneous reduction in emotional arousal, measured by heart rate variability and electrodermal activity response (EDA) [9, 10]. Consistent with Chan's findings on the rich range of touch messages, Price's dyadic study using haptic mitts demonstrated the ambiguity of remote touch interaction – Participants used the touch technology to communicate various types of messages with their partners in a nuanced way and no distinguishable patterns were found in the intended meanings associated with the touches [21].

Mediated touch in remote communication such as video telecommunication has demonstrated its ability to enhance social telepresence and overall emotional connectedness between two people. Singhal et al. designed the "Flex-N-Feel" vibrotactile gloves that allow couples to feel the flexing of their remote partners' fingers [11]. In their study, they observed how dyads spontaneously used their system in a 10-min audio and another 10-min video telecommunication. The dyads appropriated the gloves to feel their partner's presence, engage in playful interactions, and share actions together. Their results revealed that overall communication and feelings of emotional connectedness were enhanced. Although this paper showed results in how the gloves were appropriated in communication, couples were not able to use both the "Flex" glove and the "Feel" glove at the same time. Zhang et al. introduced the "Kissenger" system, which allows dyads to exchange kissing sensations through their mobile devices [22]. While [23] did find that the Kissenger system, in combination with Skype, to create a more intimate experience between couples than Skype alone, Samani tested a very narrow array of possible affective responses in a very specific setting.

The works discussed so far have focused on mediated touch in synchronous communication. Research in remote touch in asynchronous communication and its affective impact is understudied. However, there are a few notable exceptions. Wang and Quek demonstrated that communicative touches received co-verbally with verbal storytelling elicited a greater sense of closeness and empathy toward the narrator's perspective [24]. They also found that touch had the capacity to both significantly reduce sadness and increase (though not significantly) joviality. Chan et al. showed that mediated touch, when used in conjunction with a piece of music, can amplify or dampen the mood of the music [6]. In their study, romantic partners were separated into different rooms. One partner listened to a happy and sad piece of music that was augmented with mediated touches that were either generated by a music performer or their partner. The results of the study showed that if the "touch media" was created by their partner, then the mood of the music was amplified (i.e., happy songs felt happier, and sad songs felt sadder). However, this effect was reversed if the belief was that the "touch media" was created by the touch performer (i.e., happy songs felt less sad, and sad songs felt less sad).

As shown, most of the prior research in the field of remote touch communication mainly focused on synchronous communication. Very few studies have been conducted that explore the affective benefits of remote touch in an asynchronous communication setting. This study aims to provide one of the initial steps to inform the design and use of affective interactive devices in asynchronous telecommunications and media settings.

3 Technology Design

3.1 Embedding Touch in Messages Quasi-Synchronously

For this study, touch is embedded synchronously with video and audio, but the packaged media files are experienced at a different time/place.

As it was unpractical to ship any physical devices to our participants (and install device drivers on their computers) who were not co-located with the researchers, we developed a simple interface on a website (see Fig. 1) for embedding touches into the recordings. While the colors on the graphic slider indicate an ordinal description of squeeze intensities (yellow represents a soft intensity, orange is a medium intensity, and red is a hard intensity), the value at the end of the graphic slider indicates a numerical description of the touch intensities (ranging from 0 to 100). As the slider is moved further to the right, the intensity of the squeeze will increase, which will be indicated by an increasing numerical value. Participants may also hold squeezes by keeping the slider in its position. Releasing the slider will release the squeeze. A pilot study was conducted to compare user preferences between a vertical and horizontal slider design. Most users preferred the horizontal slider as it was more natural for them to use.

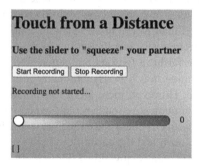

Fig. 1. An illustration of the online graphic slider used to embed touches

3.2 Receiving Touches Generated by an Armband Device

Participants experienced remote touches that were generated by an armband device similarly used by [9, 10]. The device simulates squeezes through applied pressure around the upper arm. Pressure transmission, as informed by [25, 26], offers a range of affective conveyance, and the upper arm supports a rich semantic range of interaction that is appropriate for different types of social contexts [4].

Squeezes are simulated by a servo motor that controlled the tightening and releasing of the fabric armband around the user's arm (see Fig. 2 Left and Fig. 2 Right). A fail-safe mechanism was implemented to prevent any over-squeezing due to mechanical failure. A pressure sensor was mounted inside the device's enclosure and underneath the armband fabric to measure the force of the squeeze between the fabric and the user's arm. The force measurements were used to define the thresholds of different squeeze intensities.

Fig. 2. Picture of the armband touch device components **(Left)**; and an example of a user wearing the armband device during a touch-embedded video message **(Right)**

4   Study Design and Procedures

We used the university's bulk email service to recruit 26 long distance romantic couples (58 total participants) who have been in their relationships for at least one year. The ages of the participants ranged from 19 to 27.

Each partner was assigned to participate in one of two sessions: a virtual session via Zoom session (for the partner who is not co-located with the researcher) and an in-person session (for the person who is co-located with the researcher).

In this within-subjects experiment, we counterbalanced four types of conditions: audio without touch (AN), audio with touch (AT), video without touch (VN), and video with touch (VT). The duration of the experiment was approximately two hours long (one hour for each session). Our study design and procedures were approved in advance by the institutional review board to comply with institutional and government-mandated guidelines for ethical research.

4.1   Virtual Session

Prior to the start of the experiment (after obtaining consent to participate in the study), participants completed questionnaires that surveyed for basic demographic data and details about their relationship (e.g., how long have they been together, how often do they see each other, etc.).

At the start of the session, participants were instructed to list their top four favorite memories that they share with their partners. These personal narratives primarily contain positive sentiment.

Before the start of each recording trial, participants were given five minutes to brainstorm and write notes on what they wish to say in their recordings for their partners.

Participants were introduced to the "touch website" that contained the graphic slider for embedding touches, but they were not instructed on how to use the graphic slider for their recordings—just whatever felt the most natural to them.

Participants were given five minutes to record their messages to their partners while using the graphic slider to embed the touches. The recording order of the media type (i.e., video or audio) was randomized, but counterbalanced for all Zoom participants. A two-minute practice session was provided for the participants to familiarize themselves with the experiment configuration and the graphic slider before the start of the trial.

When it was time to start the recording, participants pressed "start recording" on the touch website while the researcher recorded the Zoom call. This enabled all touches from that point on to be recorded to a.csv file. During the five minutes, the researcher stepped away from the computer to give participants privacy during their recordings. After five minutes, the researcher stopped the Zoom recording while the subject pressed "stop recording" on the touch website, which generated a.csv file of timestamped touches.

After recording all four messages, the recordings and their respective touch files were saved and used for the in-person session of the experiment.

4.2 In-Person Session

At the start of the in-person session participants completed questionnaires that surveyed for basic demographic data, details about their relationship (e.g., how long have they been together, how often do they see each other, etc.). In addition, biometric signals were measured using the Empatica E4 wristband worn by the participants. The participants' facial expressions were also recorded for the duration of each trial.

Participants completed four trials–in each trial, they experienced one of the four 5-min recordings that were created by their partner. The touch output device was worn in only the AT and VT conditions. Prior to each with-touch condition, the touch output device was calibrated to react to the subject's own interpretation of what a "soft", "medium", or "hard" squeeze feels like coming from their partner.

The order of the four media files was randomized and counterbalanced. A semi-structured interview was conducted at the end of the session to survey for preference of media type, whether participants tried to guess the intention of the touches, and any other thoughts on receiving the augmented touches in their audio and video messages.

5 Data Methodology

5.1 Affective Experience, Measured by Arousal

Increasingly researchers study how electrodermal activity—the changes in conductivity of human skin as one sweats—to assess one's emotional arousal [28–32]. [33] accounts for the popularity of EDA over other physiological measures because EDA is provides a "relatively direct and undiluted representation of sympathetic activity, more so than most other psychophysiological parameters." Additionally, EDA data may be more easy to analyze than other physiological data because, according to Finset et al., there is a "linear increase from before to after stimulation, rather than a curvilinear pattern with a post-stimulation decrease before subsequent increase seen in the cardiac response." [33].

Affective interaction is not just a time series, but it is also affected by what is being said and at what time. To understand how the speech (accompanied or not accompanied with touch) impacted participants' EDA response in real-time, we first employed a discourse analysis approach to break down the participants' discourse into individual utterances. After transcribing each media file, we segmented the discourse into timestamped purpose-level utterances (discourse segments with an overall purpose, as described by [34]). For this portion of our analysis, we only used the media files that contained touches (i.e., AT and VT conditions). Our dataset of 26 couples comprised audio-video data of 26 individuals (only using data from the "sender"), yielding 130 data minutes (5 min per condition). Our purpose-based discourse coding produced a dataset of 2,186 utterances.

To measure the instantaneous changes in affective experience when the mediated touches were received, we conducted a fine-scale analysis using the EDA data within utterances of the AT and VT conditions. We used [9, 10].'s approach of averaging two second windows of EDA measurements before and after each utterance to measure the affective changes in response. We offset the "before utterance" measurement window by two seconds after the utterance's start time to account for reaction time [35]. The average of the EDA measurements that fall within a window of two seconds was considered a statistical representation of an EDA state. Our chosen window size is supported by [36], who found that the average duration of skin conductance response to a stimulus was less than two seconds.

5.2 Affective Experienced, Measured by Facial Experiences

As EDA is a reliable measure of emotional arousal [37], it does not provide information on the valence of one's emotion. Therefore, we measured recipients' facial expressions to provide additional information of their emotional states. Facial expressions provide real-time insights into emotional responses and reactions, enabling researchers to obtain a more comprehensive understanding of human communication and interactions. For this portion of the analysis, we removed two participants' data from our dataset due to one participant wearing a face mask and a corrupted video file for another participant.

For analysis, we collected a total of 96, 5-min long Zoom video recordings from 24 receivers. To understand the correlations between video streams and EDA data, we aim to split the video files into image frames with the corresponding timestamps to the EDA data and analyze the facial expressions frame by frame. Figure 3 illustrates our procedures of processing facial expression data.

Frame Extraction. To get image frames with exact timestamps, we used FFmpeg [38], an open-source multimedia framework which supports various operations on a wide range of audio and video files in different formats, codecs, and protocols, to extract individual frames from video files. At this stage labeled B in Fig. 3, we experimented with different frame rates for the frame extraction and found that 20 FPS gives the most feasible results of facial expression recognition. Extracting more frames will result in blurry faces which could not be recognized while less frames will potentially lead to missing the frame which has the most accurate facial expression. Therefore, we decided to split each second of the video into 20 frames. Depending on the length of the video, about 5,000 to 7,000 frames can be extracted from each video file.

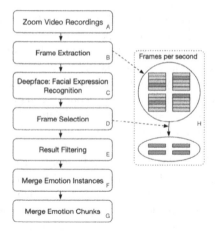

Fig. 3. Facial Expression Recognition Process

Deepface Facial Expression Recognition. To recognize the facial expressions from extracted frames, we applied a robust facial expression recognition system called Deepface [39]. At the stage labeled C Fig. 3, we utilized the high-performing and lightweight Deepface package provided by OpenCV that covers both face recognition and facial attribute analysis to perform the analysis of facial expressions. By applying the Deepface facial attribute analysis on previously extracted frames, we were able to get the facial expression result for each frame along with an expression score which is a percentage that indicates the accuracy of the prediction. We recorded the top two expression results for each frame and thereby had 20 frames of results per second. But we only needed 4 frames per second to match the EDA timestamps (the interval is a quarter second). To get more reliable predicted results, we selected the best frame from every five frames that had the highest expression score (labeled D and H in Fig. 3). These expression results were used to contextualize our EDA findings.

6   Findings

6.1   Received Touches

Figure 4 and Fig. 5 depict an overview of the number of soft, medium, and hard touches for the AT and VT conditions. As shown, the number of each type of touches received varied per each subject.

For the AT condition, the number of soft touches ranged from 0 to 82 (mean = 14, median = 8), 0 to 90 for the number of medium touches (mean = 13.72, median = 7), and 0 to 72 for the number of hard touches (mean = 9.97, median = 6). For the VT condition, the number of soft touches ranged from 0 to 40 (mean = 12.14, median = 10), 0 to 83 for medium touches (mean = 13.14, median = 10), and 0 to 68 for hard touches (mean = 9.31, median = 5). When comparing the total number of touches received, no significance was detected between conditions (U = 410.5, p = 0.876).

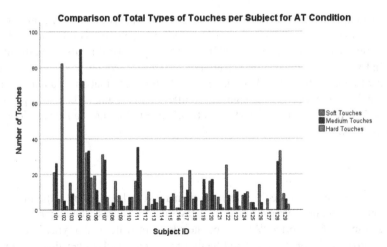

Fig. 4. An Overview of Touches Received in AT Condition

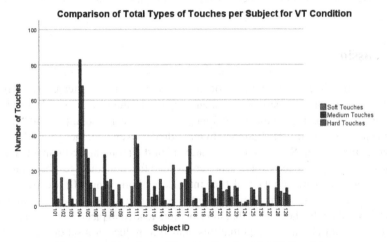

Fig. 5. An Overview of Touches Received in VT Condition

6.2 Affective Measure Findings

In AT, 1176 utterances did not contain any touches, while 303 utterances (~20% of the total number of utterances) contained at least one touch. In VT, 1229 utterances did not contain any touches, while 258 (~17% of the total number of utterances) contained at least one touch.

Our results revealed that the changes in EDA measurements were significantly different between NT utterances and WT utterance for only the VT condition ($U = 173870$, $p = 0.014$). The changes in EDA between NT and WT utterances for AT, however, only approached significance (190714, $p = 0.058$).

When comparing the detected facial expressions that accompanied the utterances in VT, we found significant differences in EDA measurements between NT and WT utterances for only happy facial expressions ($U = 10912$, $p = 0.005$). More specifically, the change in EDA measurements for WT utterances that elicited a happy facial expression response was greater than the EDA change in NT utterances that elicited a happy facial expression. We did not detect any significant differences for angry ($U = 422$, $p = 0.61$), fear ($U = 561$, $p = 0.267$), neutral ($U = 36869.5$, $p = 0.283$) and sad expressions ($U = 3031.5$, $p = 0.422$).

6.3 Overall Preference

When asked to rank each media type from their most to least favorite, the majority of participants (18 out of 26) rated VT as their favorite. In contrast, the majority of participants (23 out of 26) reported "AN" to be their least favorite media type. Interestingly, most participants (25 of 26) preferred having mediated touch rather than no touch in the video and audio messages. Participants reported that receiving mediated touch with their messages allowed them to feel "closer" to their partners and added an "extra layer of engagement".

7 Discussion

Our findings strengthen the importance of context in remote touch interaction. As remote touch may impact entire experiences that encompass the duration of a told story [24] or the performance of a piece of music [6], touch interaction can also impact the "moment-by-moment" instances in conjunction with individual spoken utterances in a telecommunication setting [9, 10]. Situating this research as in the moment-by-moment space but asynchronously experienced – there is no real avenue for immediate feedback and adaptation of interaction based on the real-time interaction. Following [40], we measured the impact of the touch within the framework of speech utterances as the temporal unit of analysis. In their study, they found that interlocutors tended to place their touches during negative sentiment utterances, and that this tended to reduce arousal or EDA/heartrate etc. response. This brings into the question the general use of this technology as a conduit of human interaction.

Research has shown that touch can reduce other negative responses such as fear and pain [41–43]. One could argue that the amelioration of negative affect in [9]'s work is a purely physiological response and not a psycholinguistic one in conjunction with the meaning of the discourse. However, they showed a reduction in arousal only after utterances that were accompanied by touches that were judged to have an affective intent. This shows that the fact of physical touch alone did not produce the affective impact divorced from the discourse context in which the touch is applied.

Thus far we have discussed remote touch to be relevant for negative sentiments. However, using remote touch this way would limit its general usability. Where [9] found a significant reduction in EDA during stressful or emotionally-tense moments, we found significant increase in EDA during more positive moments that elicited happy facial expressions. Our findings show that remote touch has the capacity to influence affect and is not limited to calming functions for negative sentiments, providing a greater emotional breadth and broader range of use for remote touch technology to enrich affective experience.

This work has implications for new research and applications, especially in asynchronous communication. As the explosion of asynchronous short messages/videos in social applications such as Instagram, TikTok, SnapChat, and WhatsApp shows the effectiveness and interest in such interactive technology, enriching such exchanges with an affective touch channel has the potential to add significantly to this interaction landscape. In a future world where touch devices are as ubiquitous as mice and trackpads, one can imagine a connecting a Bluetooth touch input device to augment asynchronous short messages to send to friends or loved ones.

In future work, we plan to investigate the affective experiences of asynchronous remote touch communication over longer periods of time. As each media in our study was five minutes long, it did not provide sufficient time to collect subjective affective reports such as PANAS-X to detect changes in affective response between conditions. However, that the majority of our participants reported a preference of experiencing mediated touch rather than no touch in their video or audio messages may motivate future research in asynchronous remote touch interaction.

8 Conclusion

Previous work showed remote touch can have a 'comforting effect' in stressful/emotionally charged conversations. A question remains as to the impact of remote touch in a broader affective range – to include pleasant, happy, or even excited messages. This study investigated the affective impact of touch-augmented video and audio messages that contained positive memories. Affective response of the recipients was measured through subjective questionnaires, electrodermal activity, and facial expression recognition. Our findings revealed that mediated touch-augmented videos enhanced affective experience during moments that elicited happy facial response. Most of our research participants also preferred to experience mediated touch over no touch in the video and audio messages. Our findings demonstrate the promise of remote touch interaction and invites new research directions and HCI applications to support asynchronous communication between individuals who cannot physically interact.

Acknowledgments. This research is partially supported by NSF grant IIS-1619291.

Disclosure of Interests. The authors have no competing interests to declare that are relevant to the content of this article.

References

1. Fulkerson, M.: The First Sense: A Philosophical Study of Human Touch, MIT press (2013)
2. Debrot, A., Schoebi, D., Perrez, M., Horn, A.B.: Touch as an interpersonal emotion regulation process in couples' daily lives: the mediating role of psychological intimacy. Pers. Soc. Psychol. Bull. **39**(10), 1373–1385 (2013)
3. Maclaren, K.: Touching matters: Embodiments of intimacy. Emot. Space Soc. **13**, 95–102 (2014)
4. Jones, S.E., Yarbrough, A.E.: A naturalistic study of the meanings of touch. Commun. Monogr. **52**, 19–56 (1985)
5. Haans, A., Ijsselsteijn, W.: Mediated social touch: a review of current research and future directions. Virtual Reality **9**, 149–159 (2006)
6. Chan, A., Zarei, N., Yamauchi, T., Seo, J., Quek, F.: Touch media: investigating the effects of remote touch on music-based emotion elicitation. In: 2019 8th International Conference on Affective Computing and Intelligent Interaction (ACII), pp. 1–7 (2019)
7. Papadopoulou, A., Berry, J., Knight, T., Picard, R.: Affective sleeve: wearable materials with haptic action for promoting calmness. In: Streitz, N., Shin'ichi Konomi (eds.) Distributed, Ambient and Pervasive Interactions: 7th International Conference, DAPI 2019, Held as Part of the 21st HCI International Conference, HCII 2019, Orlando, FL, USA, July 26–31, 2019, Proceedings, pp. 304–319. Springer International Publishing, Cham (2019). https://doi.org/10.1007/978-3-030-21935-2_23
8. Nakanishi, H., Tanaka, K., Wada, Y.: Remote handshaking: touch enhances video-mediated social telepresence. In: Proceedings of the SIGCHI Conference on Human Factors in Computing Systems, pp. 2143–2152 (2014)
9. Chan, A., Quek, F., Panchal, H., Howell, J., Yamauchi, T., Seo, J.H.: The effect of co-verbal remote touch on electrodermal activity and emotional response in dyadic discourse. Sensors **21**(1), 168 (2020). https://doi.org/10.3390/s21010168
10. Chan, A., Quek, F., Yamauchi, T., Seo, J.H.: Co-verbal touch: enriching video tele-communications with remote touch technology, pp. 186–194 (2021)
11. Singhal, S., Neustaedter, C., Ooi, Y.L., Antle, A.N., Matkin, B.: Flex-N-Feel: the design and evaluation of emotive gloves for couples to support touch over distance. In: Proceedings of the 2017 ACM Conference on Computer Supported Cooperative Work and Social Computing, pp. 98–110 (2017)
12. Oseni, K., Dingley, K., Hart, P.: Instant messaging and social networks: the advantages in online research methodology. Int. J. Inform. Educ. Technol. **8**(1), 56–62 (2018)
13. Ijsselsteijn, W., van Baren, J., van Lanen, F.: Staying in touch: social presence and connectedness through synchronous and asynchronous communication media. Hum.-Comput. Interact. Theor. Pract. (Part II), **2**(924), e928 (2003)
14. van Erp, J.B.F., Toet, A.: Social touch in human–computer interaction. Front. Digit. Humanit. **2**, 2 (2015)
15. Feldman, R., Singer, M., Zagoory, O.: Touch attenuates infants' physiological reactivity to stress. Dev. Sci. **13**(2), 271–278 (2010)
16. Stack, D.M.: Touch and physical contact during infancy: discovering the richness of the forgotten sense. Wiley-Blackwell Handb. Infant Dev. **1**, 532–567 (2010)
17. Holton, J.A.: "The coding process and its challenges. Sage Handb. Grounded Theor. **3**, 265–289 (2007)
18. Goldstein, P., Weissman-Fogel, I., Dumas, G., Shamay-Tsoory, S.G.: Brain-to-brain coupling during handholding is associated with pain reduction. Proc. Natl. Acad. Sci. **115**(11), E2528–E2537 (2018)

19. López-Solà, M., Geuter, S., Koban, L., Coan, J.A., Wager, T.D.: Brain mechanisms of social touch-induced analgesia in females. Pain **160**(9), 2072–2085 (2019)
20. Coan, J.A., Schaefer, H.S., Davidson, R.J.: Lending a hand: Social regulation of the neural response to threat. Psychol. Sci. **17**(12), 1032–1039 (2006)
21. Holt-Lunstad, J., Birmingham, W.A., Light, K.C.: Influence of a "warm touch" support enhancement intervention among married couples on ambulatory blood pressure, oxytocin, alpha amylase, and cortisol. Psychosom. Med. **70**(9), 976–985 (2008)
22. Price, S., et al.: The making of meaning through dyadic haptic affective touch. ACM Trans. Comput.-Hum. Interact. **29**(3), 21 (2022)
23. Zhang, Z., Héron, R., Lecolinet, E., Detienne, F., Safin, S.: "VisualTouch: enhancing affective touch communication with multi-modality stimulation. In: 2019 International Conference on Multimodal Interaction, pp. 114–123 (2019)
24. Samani, H.A., Parsani, R., Rodriguez, L.T., Saadatian, E.K., Dissanayake, H., Cheok, A.D.: Kissenger: design of a kiss transmission device. In: Proceedings of the Designing Interactive Systems Conference, pp. 48–57 (2012)
25. Wang, R., Quek, F., Tatar, D., Teh, K.S., Cheok, A.: Keep in touch: channel, expectation and experience. In: Proceedings of the SIGCHI Conference on Human Factors in Computing Systems, pp. 139–148 (2012)
26. Huisman, G., Darriba Frederiks, A.: Towards tactile expressions of emotion through mediated touch. In: CHI 2013 Extended Abstracts on Human Factors in Computing Systems, pp. 1575–1580 (2013)
27. Clynes, M.: Sentics: The Touch of Emotions. 1st edn. Anckor Press/DoubleDay, Garden City, New York (1977)
28. Watson, D., Clark, L.A.: The PANAS-X: manual for the positive and negative affect schedule-expanded form (1999)
29. Dawson, M.E., Schell, A.M., Filion, D.L.: The electrodermal system. Handb. Psychophysiol. **2**, 200–223 (2007)
30. Tsai, J.L., Chentsova-Dutton, Y., Freire-Bebeau, L., Przymus, D.E.: Emotional expression and physiology in European Americans and Hmong Americans. Emotion **2**(4), 380 (2002)
31. Kreibig, S.D.: Autonomic nervous system activity in emotion: a review. Biol. Psychol. **84**(3), 394–421 (2010)
32. Lougheed, J.P., Hollenstein, T.: Arousal transmission and attenuation in mother–daughter dyads during adolescence. Soc. Dev. **27**(1), 19–33 (2018)
33. Han, S.C., et al.: Romantic partner presence and physiological responses in daily life: attachment style as a moderator. Biol. Psychol. **161**, 108082 (2021)
34. Finset, A., Stensrud, T.L., Holt, E., Verheul, W., Bensing, J.: Electrodermal activity in response to empathic statements in clinical interviews with fibromyalgia patients. Patient Educ. Couns. **82**(3), 355–360 (2011)
35. Grosz, B., Sidner, C.L.: Attention, intentions, and the structure of discourse. Comput. Linguist. **12**, 175–204 (1986)
36. Citérin, J., Kheddar, A.: Electro-active polymer actuators for tactile displays. In: Bicchi, A., Buss, M., Ernst, M.O., Peer, A. (eds.) The Sense of Touch and its Rendering, pp. 131–154. Springer, Berlin (2008). https://doi.org/10.1007/978-3-540-79035-8_7
37. Benedek, M., Kaernbach, C.: A continuous measure of phasic electrodermal activity. J. Neurosci. Methods **190**(1), 80–91 30 June 2010
38. Critchley, H.D.: Electrodermal responses: what happens in the brain. Neuroscientist **8**(2), 132–142 (2002)
39. About FFmpeg. https://www.ffmpeg.org/about.html
40. Taigman, Y., Yang, M., Ranzato, M.A., Wolf, L.: DeepFace: closing the gap to human-level performance in face verification, pp. 1701–1708 (2014)

41. Cheok, A.D.: An instrument for remote kissing and engineering measurement of its communication effects including modified turing test. IEEE Open J. Comput. Soc. **1**, 107–120 (2020)
42. Pinar, S.E., Demirel, G.: The effect of therapeutic touch on labour pain, anxiety and childbirth attitude: a randomized controlled trial. Eur. J. Integr. Med. **41**, 101255 (2021)
43. Jackson, E., Kelley, M., McNeil, P., Meyer, E., Schlegel, L., Eaton, M.: Does therapeutic touch help reduce pain and anxiety in patients with cancer? Clin. J. Oncol. Nurs. **12**(1), 113–120 (2008)
44. Sparks, L.: Taking the "ouch" out of injections for children: using distraction to decrease pain. MCN Am. J. Matern. Child Nurs. **26**(2), 72–78 (2001)

Rapport Prediction Using Pairwise Learning in Dyadic Conversations Among Strangers and Among Friends

Takato Hayashi[1], Ryusei Kimura[1], Ryo Ishii[2], Fumio Nihei[2], Atsushi Fukayama[2], and Shogo Okada[1]([✉])

[1] Japan Advanced Institute of Science and Technology, Nomi, Ishikawa, Japan
okada-s@jaist.ac.jp
[2] Human Informatics Laboratories, NTT Corporation, Yokosuka-shi, Kanagawa, Japan

Abstract. Automatic rapport prediction is a key component in the creation of socially aware conversational agents. In our study, we aim to automatically predict a speakers' subjective rapport using their nonverbal (acoustic and facial) cues during conversations. While cues indicating rapport vary according to social relations between speakers, few studies have investigated an effective modality or combination of modalities for predicting subjective rapport. To fill this research gap, we collected both first-meeting (FM) and friend (FR) conversations from the same participants. Then, we addressed predicting subjective rapport using a common framework in both FM and FR conversations. Predicting subjective rapport is often formulated as a regression task that directly predicts rapport ratings. However, regression is not a suitable approach because it does not consider individual differences and ambiguity in subjective ratings. Thus, we adopted pairwise learning (PL). PL overcomes individual differences and ambiguity in subjective ratings because PL does not directly use rapport ratings. Our experimental results showed that PL is a more appropriate approach than regression for predicting conversations in both FM and FR conversations. We also reported an effective modality or combination of modalities for predicting subjective rapport in FM and FR conversations, respectively.

Keywords: Rapport · Pairwise Learning · Affective Computing · Emotion · Nonverbal Communication

1 Introduction

Building rapport among speakers is essential for successful relations. This study aims to automatically predict the degree of subjective rapport using a speaker's nonverbal cue in a conversation. If rapport prediction is possible, subjective rapport can be recorded in conjunction with the content of the conversation for each speaker. This recorded information provides knowledge about the preferred conversation content of a speaker. This information, therefore, is useful to personalize a conversational agent to a specific speaker.

© The Author(s), under exclusive license to Springer Nature Switzerland AG 2024
A. Coman and S. Vasilache (Eds.): HCII 2024, LNCS 14705, pp. 17–28, 2024.
https://doi.org/10.1007/978-3-031-61312-8_2

Beyond linguistic cues, rapport is conveyed through various nonverbal cues [1]. Therefore, researchers in affective computing have focused on automatically predicting rapport using verbal/nonverbal cues. Hagad et al. predicted rapport in dyadic conversations [2]. Müller et al. addressed detecting low rapport in group interactions [3]. Previous studies developed models to predict rapport in peer tutoring [4,5]. Madaio also indicated that cues for predicting rapport differ between peer tutoring among friends and among strangers [5]. Despite this finding, differences in effective cues for predicting rapport between natural conversations among friends and among strangers have not been explored.

To fill this research gap, we address predicting subjective rapport using a common framework in both natural conversations among friends and among strangers. The previous study finds that nonverbal cues indicating rapport vary according to social relations between speakers [1]. Predicting subjective rapport is often formulated as a regression task that directly predicts rapport ratings [6,7]. However, regression is not a suitable approach because it does not consider **individual differences** and **ambiguity** in subjective ratings. Thus, we adopt **Pairwise learning** (PL) to alleviate these problems.

First, subjective ratings have individual differences, which are caused by the *perceiver effect* [8] and the *response style* [9]. The *perceiver effect* is the tendency of perceivers to rate items for all targets in a particular way (e.g., positivity) [8]. For example, some perceivers often rate rapport for all targets positively, and others rate it negatively. The *response style* (RS) is a tendency of perceivers to rate items using specific categories regardless of content (e.g., extreme/midpoint RS) [10]. For example, perceivers with extreme/midpoint RS prefer the ends/center of the scale. Second, subjective affect ratings are ambiguous. When a perceiver is asked to rate the same item twice, their ratings are not necessarily the same [11]. Due to individual differences and ambiguity in subjective ratings, it is challenging for a regression model to learn the mapping from a perceiver's behavior to their rapport ratings.

PL is an attractive alternative approach. In PL, a model is trained to predict ordinal relations between two conversations based on rapport ratings reported by the same perceiver. PL overcomes individual differences and ambiguity in subjective ratings because PL does not directly use rapport ratings. Although there is enough evidence to show that PL has significant advantages over regression for emotion recognition [12,13], few studies have explored PL to predict subjective ratings in interpersonal perceptions (e.g., rapport) [7]. Hayashi et al. showed that PL is a more appropriate approach than regression for predicting subjective rapport in natural conversation among strangers [7].

Our study is composed of three main contributions. First, we collect online dyadic conversations in which the same participant communicates with multiple strangers and friends. Second, we investigate whether PL improves predictive performances of subjective rapport and whether it is superior to regression in not only first-meeting (FM) conversations but also friend (FR) conversations. We use three evaluation metrics to measure ranking performance because we address the task of ranking conversations according to the degree of subjective rapport. Third, we demonstrate an effective modality or combination of modalities for

Table 1. Dataset Summary.

First-meeting Conversation	
No. of participants (male)	69 (35)
No. of pairs of participants	96
No. of conversations	288
Friend Conversation	
No. of participants (male)	32 (16)
No. of pairs of participants	48
No. of conversations	144

predicting subjective rapport in FM and FR conversations, respectively. In our experiments, we use acoustic and facial features.

2 Data

We collected online dyadic conversations in which the same participant communicated with multiple strangers and friends.

2.1 Participants and Pairs of Participants

Participants were recruited in two ways. First, eight friend groups were recruited. Each group consisted of four participants who were friends in a school and a workplace. All participants in the four groups were male, and all participants in the other four groups were female. Therefore, the total number of participants based on this recruitment method was 32 (16 males). Second, 37 participants (19 males) who were not acquainted with participants in the friends group were recruited. All participants were Japanese speakers.

The reason for recruiting participants who were not acquainted with participants in friend groups was to collect both first-meeting (FM) and friend (FR) conversations from the same participants. First, each participant in a friend group was paired with other participants in their group. Since each participant had three friends, a total of 48 pairs of participants were obtained for FR. Then, 32 participants in friend groups were paired with three participants who were not acquainted with them. Therefore, a total of 96 pairs of participants were obtained for FM. Table 1 summarizes the statistics of this dataset.

2.2 Conversation Setting

A pair of participants communicated with each other in different rooms through a video communication system. Three conversations were recorded based on different conversation topics. Therefore, the FM dataset consisted of 288 conversations; the FR dataset consisted of 144 conversations. Each conversation lasted 20 min, and participants reported rapport ratings for their conversation partner

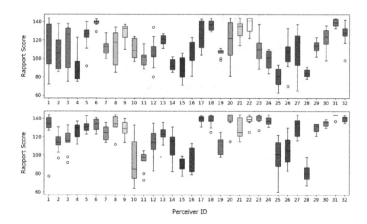

Fig. 1. A boxplot of subjective rapport ratings for each perceiver (**Upper**: first-meeting conversation, **Lower**: friend conversation).

after every conversation. The questionnaire used in our study was proposed by Bernieri et al. [14] to measure the degree of subjective rapport. They rated each item on an 8-point Likert scale. We summed the values of the 18 items after the values of the negative questions were reversed. We defined a *rapport score* as the total score.

To collect conversations with different degrees of subjective rapport from the same pair of participants, three conversations were recorded for each pair of participants based on different conversation topics: 1) self-introduction, 2) emotional episode, and 3) disclosing self-shortcomings. We selected three topics to help pairs of participants develop rapport through self-disclosure.

2.3   Conversation Topic and Rapport Score

To examine the statistical significance in the mean rapport scores between the three topics, we conducted post hoc comparisons using a t test with Bonferroni correction (the significance level was p < 0.001). We calculated the mean rapport score of the 32 perceivers common to both FM and FR.

In FM and FR, the mean rapport scores increased as the number of conversations increased. In FM, the mean values of the first (self-introduction), second (emotional episode), and third (self-shortcomings) topics were 107.08 (SD = 20.97), 113.3 (SD = 19.67), and 118.66 (SD = 18.84), respectively. The mean value of the first topic was significantly different than that of the second topic (t = 6.75, p = 0.00, df = 95); the second topic was also significantly different than the third topic (t = 4.79, p = 0.00, df = 95). In FR, the mean values of the first, second, and third topics were 118.01 (SD = 21.22), 121.61 (SD = 19.53), and 124.26 (SD = 20.72), respectively. However, a significant difference could not be found between the mean values of the first and second topics (t = 2.11, p = 0.03, df = 95) and between the second and third topics (t = 1.40, p = 0.17, df = 95).

There are two reasons for the increasing rapport in FM. First, participant comfort with their conversation partners increased as their total conversation times increased due to the exposure effect [15]. Second, rapport between participants increased because the conversation topics required more self-disclosure as the number of conversations increased. A previous study showed that self-disclosure contributes to rapport building [16].

2.4   Variability of Rapport Scores for Each Perceiver

The upper and lower boxplots in Fig. 1 demonstrate the variability of the rapport score for each perceiver on FM and FR, respectively. The figure shows individual differences in the tendency to rate subjective rapport. In both FM and FR, some perceivers rated rapport locally, while others rated it broadly. In addition, median values varied across participants. Compared to FM, perceivers rated rapport more highly and locally in FR. The mean values of mean rapport scores for each perceiver were 113.02 (SD = 11.87) and 121.46 (SD = 9.34) in FM and FR, respectively. The mean standard deviation values for each perceiver were 11.87 (SD = 5.70) and 9.34 (SD = 5.07).

3   Method

3.1   Problem Definition

The problem addressed in our study is to rank conversations according to the rapport score using perceivers' nonverbal features for each perceiver. Here, $\mathcal{C}_i = [c_{ijk} \mid j \in T_i, k \in [1, 2, 3]]$ is defined as a list containing all conversations of perceiver i, where T_i is the set containing all targets of perceiver i, and k expresses the k-th conversation topic. Each list $\mathcal{C}_i$ is associated with a list of perceiver's features $\mathcal{X}_i = [x_{ijk} \mid j \in T_i, k \in [1, 2, 3]]$ and a list of rapport scores $\mathcal{Y}_i = [y_{ijk} \mid j \in T_i, k \in [1, 2, 3]]$. Moreover, x_{ijk} provides nonverbal features of perceiver i during their k-th conversation with target j, and y_{ijk} provides the rapport score that perceiver i gives to target j in the k-th conversation. Our goal is ranking element c_{ijk} in the conversation list $\mathcal{C}_i$ according to the rapport score y_{ijk}, using the perceiver's features x_{ijk} as input. For conciseness of notation, we omit ijk in c_{ijk} in the following paragraph.

To apply PL to this problem, we developed a model f that maps the perceiver's nonverbal features x to the real value $f(x)$. In the training stage, two samples were selected from each perceiver's conversation list (e.g., c_A and c_B). The model was then trained to match ordinal relations between ground-truth rapport scores (e.g., $y_A \succ y_B$) with ordinal relations between the model's output (e.g., $f(x_A) \succ f(x_B)$). In the test stage, we obtained a predicted ranking list by ranking conversations according to the model's output.

3.2   Loss Function

We used a loss function inspired by Burges et al. [17]. Given two samples c_A and c_B, the predictive probability that c_A is higher order than c_B is given by P_{AB}:

$$P_{AB} = \frac{\exp(o_{AB})}{1 + \exp(o_{AB})}, \tag{1}$$

where $o_{AB} = f(x_A) - f(x_B)$. The true probability $\bar{P}_{AB}$ is set according to the ordinal relations between paired samples. $\bar{P}_{AB} = 1$ indicates that c_A is higher order than c_B, and vice versa. We used the cross-entropy loss function with a penalty according to the rank differences between paired samples:

$$\mathcal{L}_{AB} = \frac{\sqrt{|r_A - r_B|}}{M - 1}[-\bar{P}_{AB} \log P_{AB} - (1 - \bar{P}_{AB}) \log(1 - P_{AB})], \tag{2}$$

where r_A and r_B are the ranks of c_A and c_B in the list of conversations. M is the length of the list of conversations to which c_A and c_B belong. The loss for a paired sample with a large rank difference is higher than that for a paired sample with a small rank difference. The reason for adding a penalty was that the model emphasizes reliable paired samples. Subjective affective ratings are known to be ambiguous [11]. Paired samples with large rank differences can be considered reliable because their ordinal relationships are less likely to be reversed by variations in ratings within individuals.

3.3   Model Architecture

We developed a mapping function f inspired by Poria et al. [18]. Our mapping function was composed of unidirectional long short-term memory networks (sc-LSTM) and fully connected neural networks (FCNN).

Unimodal Mapping Function. The unimodal feature vector is given by x.

$$x = [u_1, u_2, \cdots, u_T], \tag{3}$$

where u_t is the nonverbal features extracted during the perceiver's t-th utterances, and T is the number of perceiver utterances in a conversation. Unimodal features x are input into LSTM, and the output vector corresponding to the last utterance g_T is extracted. We then map output vector g_T to real value $f_{\text{FCNN}}(g_T)$,

$$g_T = \text{LSTM}(x), \tag{4}$$

$$f_{\text{FCNN}}(g_T) = \text{FCNN}(g_T). \tag{5}$$

Multimodal Mapping Function. We use hierarchical multimodal fusion [18]. Consider the acoustic feature vector x^A and facial feature vector x^F. Each x^A and x^F are input into different unimodal LSTM networks, and output vectors g^A and g^F are connected for each utterance.

$$g^A = \text{LSTM}^A(x^A), \tag{6}$$

$$g^F = \text{LSTM}^F(x^F), \tag{7}$$

$$g^{AF} = g^A \oplus g^F = [g_1^A \oplus g_1^F, g_2^A \oplus g_2^F, \cdots, g_T^A \oplus g_T^F]. \tag{8}$$

Multimodal vector g^{AF} is input into multimodal LSTM, and the output vector corresponding to the last utterance h_T is extracted. We map the output vector h_T to the real value $f_{\text{FCNN}}(h_T)$.

$$h_T = \text{LSTM}^{AF}(g^{AF}), \tag{9}$$

$$f_{\text{FCNN}}(h_T) = \text{FCNN}(h_T). \tag{10}$$

3.4 Feature Extraction

We extracted acoustic and facial features from each conversation. We did not use linguistic features because the conversation topic was associated with the rapport score (see Sect. 2.3). If the model has access to the content of the conversation, the model may estimate the conversation topic instead of the rapport.

Acoustic Features. We used OpenSMILE software [19] to extract acoustic features from each utterance. The acoustic features corresponded to eGeMAPS [20]. Acoustic features consisted of 88 features and were standardized for each person.

Facial Features. We used OpenFace software [21] to extract the intensity of 17 action units (AUs) from each frame. Facial features were created by computing 14 statistics from the frames corresponding to each utterance. These 14 statistics are as follows: the mean, median, standard deviation, skewness, kurtosis, maximum and minimum values, mean of the first and second differences, range, slope, intercept of the linear approximation, and 25th and 75th percentile values. Facial features thus consisted of 238 features and were standardized for each person.

4 Experiment

4.1 Comparison Model

We developed regression models to compare the PL model. For regression, we standardized rapport scores (objective variable) in two different ways. First, all rapport scores were standardized (All-perceivers), so no individual differences were addressed in the subjective ratings. Second, the rapport scores were standardized for each perceiver (Single-perceiver), which may alleviate individual differences in subjective ratings when the distribution of rapport scores shifts among perceivers. The model architecture of the regression model was the same as that of the PL model. However, pointwise learning and the root mean square error (RMSE) loss were used for regression.

4.2   Experimental Procedure and Evaluation Metrics

We defined the main-perceiver participants as the 32 participants who participated in both first-meeting (FM) and friend (FR) conversations. The training and test sets consisted of the conversations of these main-perceivers. In FM conversations, the rapport ratings of 37 participants other than the main-perceiver participants were also reported. These participants were defined as sub-perceiver participants, and their conversations were included in the training sets for FM.

We evaluated the model by double cross-validation. We considered four main-perceiver participants who were friends in one group. For outer cross-validation, we applied leave-two-groups-out cross-validation. Outer cross-validation was used to evaluate the generalization performance of the model. Next, we applied inner cross-validation to train sets obtained from outer cross-validation. For inner cross-validation, we applied leave-one-group-out cross-validation. The inner cross-validation result determined the hyperparameters used in outer cross-validation. Two cross-validation tasks ensured that the same participant's conversation was not duplicated across the training, validation, and test sets. In our study, all experiments were conducted three times based on different seed values, and their average performance was reported as the experimental results.

For the learning models, the drop rate was set to 0.25, the batch size was set to 32, and the number of epochs was set to 40. The learning rate was determined by hyperparameter optimization. Three learning rates were explored: $[5e^{-6}, 1e^{-5}, 5e^{-5}]$. The number of units (unimodal/multimodal LSTM hidden- and output-layer, FCNN hidden-layer) is 128.

To evaluate the ranking performance of the models, we calculated Kendall's tau correlation coefficient (KTCC) and precision at the top 3/bottom 3 (P@3/P@-3). KTCC measures the correlation between the predicted ranking list and the ground-truth ranking list. P@3/P@-3 measures how many ground-truth top-3/bottom-3 samples are present in the predicted top-3/bottom-3 samples of a model.

5   Result

For the first-meeting (FM) and friend (FR) conversations, we show the ranking performance of the models separately. First, we compare two regression models in which the rapport scores were standardized in different ways. Second, we investigate whether PL improves ranking performance and whether it is superior to regression. Table 2 indicates the ranking performance of regression and PL. The random baseline is the average ranking performance calculated 10k times between the random and ground-truth ranking lists. Bold values represent the best performances among each modality. The asterisk denotes the best performances across modalities.

Table 2. Experimental Results

Modal	Model	Standardization	First-meeting Conv.			Friend Conv.		
			KTCC	P@3	P@-3	KTCC	P@3	P@-3
A	PL	—	**0.14***	**44.44***	**37.99**	0.00	30.21	32.99
	Regression	All-perceiver	0.06	39.43	36.92	0.00	31.60	**35.07**
		Single-perceiver	0.09	43.37	35.13	**0.05**	**35.42**	34.72
F	PL	—	**0.06**	**39.43**	**44.84***	**0.10**	**39.24**	**42.36**
	Regression	All-perceiver	0.06	36.20	44.44	0.03	36.11	36.11
		Single-perceiver	0.05	32.98	43.01	-0.04	32.29	31.94
A+F	PL	—	0.06	37.28	39.07	**0.12***	**42.36***	**42.71***
	Regression	All-perceiver	0.05	34.77	**41.58**	0.06	37.85	37.85
		Single-perceiver	**0.08**	**37.99**	**41.58**	0.07	41.68	39.24
Random			0.00	33.97	33.97	0.00	34.20	34.20

Bold values represent the best performances among each modality. The asterisk denotes the best performances across modalities.

5.1 First-Meeting Conversations

In this section, we focus on the FM experimental results. As Table 2 shows, we did not observe consistent results that the ranking performance of regression (single-perceiver) was greater than that of regression (all-perceiver) regardless of modality.

The results show that PL is more effective than regression. PL achieved the best performance across modalities for all evaluation metrics (see asterisk). In KTCC and P@3, PL (A) outperformed the regression; in P@-3, PL (F) outperformed the regression. Furthermore, for both unimodal features, the performance of PL was greater than that of regression for all evaluation metrics (see bold). Regarding multimodal features, however, the performance of PL was lower than that of regression for all evaluation metrics. Next, we can see that the model using acoustic features achieved substantially higher performance in retrieving higher-ranking conversations than lower-ranking conversations; for example, PL(A) achieved higher performance for P@3 than P@-3 (P@3 = **44.44**%/P@-3 = 37.99%). In contrast, models using facial features achieved substantially higher performance in retrieving lower-ranking conversations; for example, PL(F) achieved higher performance for P@-3 than P@3 (P@3 = 39.43%/P@-3 = **44.84**%).

5.2 Friend Conversations

In this section, we focus on the experimental results in FR. As Table 2 shows, whether regression (Single-perceiver) achieved higher ranking performance than regression (All-perceiver) depended on the modality.

The results show that PL is more effective than regression. PL (A+F) achieved the best performance across modalities for all evaluation metrics (see asterisk). Furthermore, for facial features, the performance of PL was greater than that of regression for all evaluation metrics (see bold). However, for acoustic features, the performance of PL was lower than that of regression for all evaluation metrics.

6 Discussion

6.1 Comparison of the Two Standardization Methods

In both conversations, we did not observe consistent results that the performance of regression (Single-perceiver) was greater than that of regression (All-perceiver) regardless of modality. Assuming that the distribution of rapport score shifts among perceivers, standardization (Single-perceiver) alleviates individual differences in subjective ratings. The results, therefore, imply that the distribution of rapport scores differs among perceivers. For example, the rapport score by a perceiver with a midpoint response style has an unimodal distribution, while rapport scores by a perceiver with an extreme response style have a bimodal distribution.

6.2 Comparison of Pairwise Learning and Regression

In both conversations, the PL model achieved the best performance across modalities for all evaluation metrics. The most likely explanation is that PL prevents individual differences and ambiguity in subjective ratings.

In FM conversations, PL (A) achieved higher performance than PL (F); in FR conversations, PL (F) achieved higher performance than PL (A). The result implies that differences in acoustic features between paired samples are clearer according to rapport than those in facial features in FM, and differences in facial features between paired samples are clearer according to rapport than those in acoustic features in FR.

6.3 Retrieving Higher/Lower-Ranking Rapport Conversations

In FM, models using acoustic features achieved substantially higher performance in retrieving higher-ranking conversations than lower-ranking conversations. In contrast, models using facial features achieved substantially higher performance in retrieving lower-ranking conversations. The result suggests that high rapport is encoded in acoustic features rather than facial features; low rapport is encoded in facial features rather than acoustic features. Regarding low rapport, the result is in line with a previous study finding that facial features are more indicative of low rapport than other nonverbal features (e.g., acoustic features) [3].

6.4 Limitation and Future Work

We demonstrated effective modalities for predicting subjective rapport in both FM and FR. However, we did not reveal what behavior patterns within each modality are effective for FM and FR. In future work, the next step will be to investigate how effective behavior patterns for predicting subjective rapport differ between FM and FR.

Furthermore, we can also improve models so that models can account for interspeaker influences on nonverbal behavior. We developed a model for predicting the subjective rapport based on the nonverbal behavior of one of the speakers (perceiver) in a conversation. This method has practical advantages because the system cannot always have access to the nonverbal behaviors of the conversation partner in an online conversation. However, because interspeaker influences of nonverbal behavior (e.g., synchrony) are an important cue indicating rapport [1], models may achieve higher performance when models can have access to such cues.

7 Conclusion

We addressed predicting subjective rapport using pairwise learning (PL) in both first-meeting (FM) and friend (FR) conversations. First, we collected a dataset composed of online dyadic conversations containing subjective rapport ratings. In our dataset, the same participant communicated with multiple strangers and friends. Analysis of rapport ratings provides evidence to support that subjective rapport ratings have individual differences. Second, we investigated whether PL improves predictive performances of subjective rapport and whether it is superior to regression in not only FM conversations but also FR conversations. Experimental results demonstrated that PL is a more appropriate approach than regression for predicting subjective rapport in both FM and FR conversations. Finally, we reported effective modalities for predicting subjective rapport using PL. In FM conversations, PL models using acoustic features achieved the best performance for Kendall's tau correlation coefficient (KTCC); In FR conversations, PL models using multimodal (acoustic and facial) features achieved the best performance for KTCC. Furthermore, experimental results indicated that acoustic features are effective for retrieving high rapport conversations in FM conversations. In contrast, facial features are effective for retrieving low rapport conversations in FM conversations.

References

1. Tickle-Degnen, L., Rosenthal, R.: The nature of rapport and its nonverbal correlates. Psychol. Inq. 1(4), 285–293 (1990)
2. Hagad, J.L., Legaspi, R., Numao, M., Suarez, M.: Predicting levels of rapport in dyadic interactions through automatic detection of posture and posture congruence. In: 2011 IEEE Third International Conference on Privacy, Security, Risk and Trust and 2011 IEEE Third International Conference on Social Computing (2011)
3. Müller, P., Huang, M.X., Bulling, A.: Detecting low rapport during natural interactions in small groups from Non-Verbal behaviour. In: 23rd International Conference on Intelligent User Interfaces (2018)

4. Zhao, R., Sinha, T., Black, A.W., Cassell, J.: Socially-aware virtual agents: automatically assessing dyadic rapport from temporal patterns of behavior. In: Traum, D., Swartout, W., Khooshabeh, P., Kopp, S., Scherer, S., Leuski, A. (eds.) IVA 2016. LNCS, vol. 10011, pp. 218–233. Springer, Cham (2016). https://doi.org/10.1007/978-3-319-47665-0_20

5. Madaio, M., Lasko, R., Ogan, A., Cassell, J.: Using temporal association rule mining to predict dyadic rapport in peer tutoring. In: Educational Data Mining (2017)

6. Cerekovic, A., Aran, O., Gatica-Perez, D.: Rapport with virtual agents: what do human social cues and personality explain? IEEE Trans. Affect. Comput. 8(3), 382–395 (2017)

7. Hayashi, T., et al.: A ranking model for evaluation of conversation partners based on rapport levels. IEEE Access 11, 73024–73035 (2023)

8. Kenny, D.A.: Interpersonal Perception: The Foundation of Social Relationships. Guilford Publications (2019)

9. Baumgartner, H., Steenkamp, J.-B.: Response styles in marketing research: a cross-national investigation. J. Mark. Res. 38, 143–156 (2001)

10. Kumano, S., Nomura, K.: Multitask item response models for response bias removal from affective ratings. In: 8th International Conference on Affective Computing and Intelligent Interaction (ACII) (2019)

11. Metallinou, A., Narayanan, S.: Annotation and processing of continuous emotional attributes: challenges and opportunities. In: 2013 10th IEEE International Conference and Workshops on Automatic Face and Gesture Recognition (FG) (2013)

12. Lotfian, R., Busso, C.: Practical considerations on the use of preference learning for ranking emotional speech. In: 2016 IEEE International Conference on Acoustics, Speech and Signal Processing (ICASSP), pp. 5205–5209 (2016)

13. Parthasarathy, S., Lotfian, R., Busso, C.: Ranking emotional attributes with deep neural networks. In: 2017 IEEE International Conference on Acoustics, Speech and Signal Processing (ICASSP) (2017)

14. Bernieri, F.J., Gillis, J.S., Davis, J.M., Grahe, J.E.: Dyad rapport and the accuracy of its judgment across situations: a lens model analysis. J. Pers. Soc. Psychol. 71(1), 110–129 (1996)

15. Zajonc, R.B.: Attitudinal effects of mere exposure. J. Pers. Soc. Psychol. 9(2p2), 1–27 (1968)

16. Zink, K.L., et al.: "Let me tell you about my..." provider self-disclosure in the emergency department builds patient rapport. West. J. Emerg. Med. 18(1), 43–49 (2017)

17. Burges, C., et al.: Learning to rank using gradient descent. In: Proceedings of the 22nd International Conference on Machine Learning (2005)

18. Poria, S., Cambria, E., Hazarika, D., Majumder, N., Zadeh, A., Morency, L.-P.: Context-dependent sentiment analysis in user-generated videos. In: Proceedings of the 55th Annual Meeting of the Association for Computational Linguistics (2017)

19. Eyben, F., Wöllmer, M., Schuller, B.: Opensmile: the Munich versatile and fast open-source audio feature extractor. In: Proceedings of the 18th ACM International Conference on Multimedia (2010)

20. Eyben, F., et al.: The Geneva minimalistic acoustic parameter set (GeMAPS) for voice research and affective computing. IEEE Trans. Affect. Comput. 7(2), 190–202 (2016)

21. Baltrusaitis, T., Zadeh, A., Lim, Y.C., Morency, L.-P.: Openface 2.0: facial behavior analysis toolkit. In: 13th IEEE International Conference on Automatic Face Gesture Recognition (FG 2018) (2018)

Psychological Aspects of Face-To-Face Versus Computer-Mediated Interpersonal Communication: An Integrative Review

Elina Tsigeman[1] , Larisa Mararitsa[1] , Olga Gundelah[1] , Olga Lopatina[2] ,
and Olessia Koltsova[1(✉)]

[1] Social and Cognitive Informatics Laboratory, HSE University, Saint-Petersburg, Russia
`ekoltsova@hse.ru`
[2] Social Neuroscience Laboratory, Krasnoyarsk State Medical University Named After Prof.
V.F. Voino-Yasenetsky, Krasnoyarsk, Russia

Abstract. Computer mediated (CM) communication has become pervasive in everyday lives of people in many societies, especially during and after the COVID pandemics, which has had profound effects on different aspects of human activity, including communication itself. As a response to this, empirical research comparing CM and face-to-face (FtF) communication has been steadily growing. To ensure a comprehensive understanding of the major trends in this body of literature, it is crucial to identify the main research topics emerging in this domain, and explore theoretical frameworks and methodological approaches employed in the respective studies. In this review, we examine 51 empirical studies conducted between 2010 and early 2023, that compare the effects of FtF and CM formats of communication on its psychological aspects.

We identify eight aspects of interpersonal communication, such as Synchronisation, Disclosure, and Interaction satisfaction, that are most often investigated in the existing research, while certain important aspects stay understudied. Four major theoretical frameworks prevail in the studies of these eight aspects: Social information processing theory, Hyperpersonal model of communication, Media richness theory, and Social presence theory. Further, our analysis reveals several methodological challenges, including the varying degree of measurement uniformity between subdomains devoted to different aspects. Paradoxically, we find this degree unrelated to the consistency of the results. Drawing on these findings, we suggest potential avenues for future research that can enhance our understanding of the impact of technology on human communication.

Keywords: Face-to-Face communication · Computer-mediated communication · Videoconferencing; Virtual meetings; Interpersonal communication

1 Introduction

Since the development of Web 2.0 in the early 2000s, communication has been undergoing a shift from face-to-face (FtF) to computer-mediated (CM). This became especially evident during COVID-19 pandemic, when CM communication started to prevail in both formal and informal relationships in many societies [1]. Now, CM communication is widely applied to provide medical help [2], for psychotherapy delivery [3], in education [4] and for job interviewing [5].

However, there is a lack of robust knowledge regarding the effects of communication channels on outcomes or properties of interpersonal communication [6]. Moreover, investigation of these effects and integration of the existing evidence is complicated by theoretical, conceptual and methodological heterogeneity of the respective research [7]. While similar concepts may be termed differently in different studies, concepts that have different meanings may be denoted by the same words, thus creating terminological confusion [8]. Likewise, different approaches are applied to measure the same concepts [8]. For instance, studies on the effects of communication channels on disclosure often investigate its different aspects: amount [9], intimacy [10] or breadth [11]. This diversity of terminology and measurement approaches contributes to the overall inconclusiveness of findings [8].

Existing reviews of research comparing FtF and CM formats are limited to specific aspects of communication, such as self-disclosure [12] and emotions [13]; organisational context [14]; or method – e.g. content analysis [15]. The systematic review of interpersonal outcomes of online and offline communication is limited to social media use in youth [16], thus excluding other age groups and forms of CM communication.

The present review aims to map the recent literature in the field of interpersonal communication research that compares FtF and CM channels. The review does not aim to be a systematic or to determine effect sizes. Instead, it seeks to answer three research questions: (1) "What aspects of interpersonal communication have been compared between FtF and CM communication channels?" (2) "How have these aspects been usually operationalised and measured?" and (3) "What theoretical approaches prevail in the research of these aspects?".

To answer these questions, we develop a specific strategy of article selection and of aspect identification that are described below in the Methodology section, followed by Results section. In the latter, each of the identified communication aspects is discussed in a separate subsection following the same structure: (1) elaboration on the concept definition; (2) exploration of operationalisations utilised in research; (3) examination of the prevailing theories, which offer insights into the potential differences in this aspect between FtF and CM communication; (4) discussion of the general results derived from the studies; and (5) concluding remarks summarising the key findings and implications for each aspect. The summary of our interpretations and conclusions are presented in the Discussion section.

2 Methodology

2.1 Article Search and Selection

We identified papers to be included in three steps: (1) a manual search by the co-authors through electronic databases (Google Scholar, Scopus) using a list of relevant keywords (e.g. 'face-to-face communication'; 'computer-mediated communication'; 'videoconferencing'; 'virtual meetings'; 'online communication'); (2) examination of the reference lists from the papers found at step (1); and (3) search expansion to papers linked to those detected on the previous two steps via Connected papers visual tool [17].

Being aware of the dynamic nature of CM communication habits and attitudes, we limited our selection to papers published between 2010 and 2023. Studies were included if they analysed aspects of interpersonal communication, notwithstanding the specific channel or application used. In total, 179 papers published between 2010 and 2023 were identified. We excluded studies assessing group communication or social monitoring (e.g. passive consumption of social news); or studies that assessed exclusively the volume of communication, channel preferences or well-being of participants in FtF and CM communication that do not characterise psychological aspects of communication. Lastly, we considered FtF interaction as a 'baseline' or control condition against which all other communication channels should be compared. Fifty-one papers met these criteria and have been included in the analysis. For a comprehensive list of these papers, refer to Supplementary materials Table S1 (see https://osf.io/j9amx/). This table provides the references and information on the theoretical foundations of these studies, the aspects of interpersonal communication examined, the instruments utilised, the measures employed to assess these aspects, and the brief summaries of the results.

2.2 Identification of Interpersonal Communication Aspects

Two experts analysed publications, focusing on psychological outcomes of interpersonal communication. They aggregated these outcomes into broader aspects based on similarity of assessed constructs rather than terminology, resolving disagreements through discussions until reaching a consensus. This categorisation does not serve as a definitive classification of communication aspects; rather, it endeavours to propose a structure for a discussion of concepts, hypotheses, methods and results in the new field of research comparing FtF and CM communication.

The process yielded eight psychological aspects of interpersonal communication assessed in online and offline settings. Figure 1 (created with the help of Miro online whiteboard) displays these aspects in an octagon, with line width representing the frequency of aspect co-occurrence in the studies. Figure 2 shows the number of studies in our sample exploring each of the identified aspects.

Additionally, we identified the following popular research topics: "emotions and affect", "channel preferences", "social wellbeing", "volume of communication", "social network composition" and "productivity". These topics do not represent psychological aspects of directed interpersonal communication per se and, therefore, are not analysed in detail.

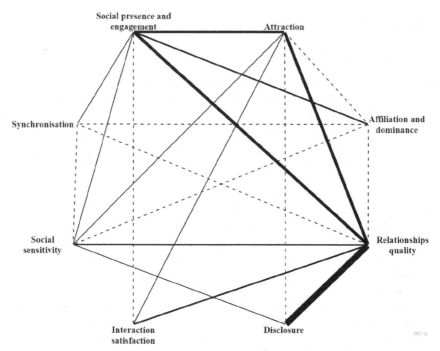

Fig. 1. Psychological aspects of directed communication assessed in empirical research (2010–2023.) Line: co-occurrence of two aspects in the same paper; width of solid lines: co-occurrence frequency (2–6); dotted line: single co-occurrence.

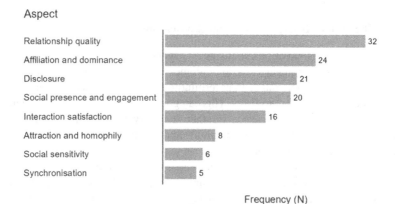

Fig. 2. Frequencies of assessment of each psychological aspects of interpersonal communication aspect in 2010–2023 research.

3 Results

3.1 Social Presence and Engagement

Social presence is the feeling that the other person is present in CM interaction as a 'real' person [18]. This feeling is linked to social engagement, which entails involvement in conversation and paying attention to communication partner [19]. Further, it links to compliance (or conformity) – an individual's willingness to cooperate, or obey the requests of another person [20]. Thus, we united social presence, social engagement and compliance as the dimensions of this aspect.

Recent studies, e.g. [21], have primarily used constructs from the Network Minds social presence Inventory [22] and author-developed items measuring feelings of 'being in sync' and 'on the same page' with the communication partner [6]. Behavioural cues such as gaze were also utilized to evaluate social engagement [23]. Compliance was assessed through experimental procedures to estimate predicted and actual compliance with requests made to both friends and strangers [20, 24]. The dimensions of social presence and engagement, along with their assessment instruments, are presented on Figure S1 in Supplementary materials (see https://osf.io/j9amx/).

Theory most commonly used to study this aspect is the Social presence theory [18]. In accordance with it, mediated channels transmit reduced feeling of social presence. Decreased feeling of social presence, in turn, reduces pressure of the social norms and respective expectations [25, 26] and affects social engagement [21] and compliance [20]. These processes might be attributed to reduced social cues available in CM communication as suggested by the Cues filtered-out theory [27].

In accordance with the above theories, comparative studies have consistently found higher social presence in FtF conditions compared to CM [21, 28]. At the same time, research on social engagement has been less consistent, reporting either reduced perceived engagement in CM [29], or no difference between channels [6]. These conflicting findings may be attributed to the specific CM channels used. Text-based instant messaging used by Sprecher [29] may convey lower social presence compared to video communication used by Brucks and Levav [6]. Additionally, participants might have experienced greater engagement after a collaborative task [6] compared to a brief self-disclosure task [29]. Further, FtF contacts showed higher engagement compared to VC contacts, although the latest proposed to convey the richest social cues in comparison to other CM channels [30]. A closer eye contact and mutual gazing typical for FtF interactions, likely contribute to this difference [21]. In an experimental study children playing a collaborative video game were exposed to a VC condition that allowed for mutual gaze; in this mode, they displayed levels of engagement with a partner comparable to that in FtF condition, but lower engagement in the VC no-gaze condition [21].

Lastly, two studies on compliance are in agreement with the above theories: they find higher compliance with requests in FtF rather than in CM communication [20, 24].

Overall, recent studies support the Social presence theory and the Cues filtered-out theory, showing FtF advantages in social presence and related outcomes. However, VC seems to result in the outcomes comparable to FtF condition, except for eye-contact and mutual gazing.

3.2 Synchronisation

Synchronisation refers to the unconscious alignment of behaviours, actions, emotions, or physiological responses between communication partners [31]. We found three dimensions of recently researched synchrony. Interpersonal behavioural synchrony involves coordinated non-verbal behaviours (e.g. gestures or facial expressions) and speech (e.g. turn-taking synchronisation or prosodic matching) [32]. Mimicry is the tendency to unconsciously mimic others during conversation [6]. Inter-brain synchrony involves physiological alignment [33].

Recent articles evaluated synchronisation through speech and video analysis using the distance between partners' linguistic semantic categories and the distance between their mean intensity of facial expressions as markers of mimicry [6]. Further, they applied brain signal analysis using electroencephalography (EEG) [30]. The dimensions of synchronisation and respective assessment instruments are summarised in Figure S2 in Supplementary materials (see https://osf.io/j9amx/).

The Theory of media synchronicity [34] suggests that media vary in synchronicity, with low synchronicity media like texting being less effective for real-time communication compared to high synchronicity channels like FtF and VC. Previous findings indicate that interpersonal synchronisation relies on the alignment of physiological processes, such as heart rhythms, hormonal release, and neural oscillations [35].

On this basis, a recent study with mother-child dyads compared inter-brain synchrony in CM and FtF interactions. The findings highlighted the role of brain-to-brain synchrony in the communication and confirmed disrupted synchronisation in VC, showing more synchronous brain activations in FtF than in VC condition [30]. This data shows that even rich media like VC impose synchronisation disruptions [36].

Further, recent literature demonstrates that disrupted synchronisation is due to delays in signal transmission and network latencies [36]. An experimental study showed that delay in the transmission of a verbal signal can reach 300 ms in VC compared to FtF communication [36], and leads to disrupted behavioural synchronisation in a conversation.

Unlike other forms of synchronization, mimicry was found equal in VC and FtF communication [6].

Overall, reviewed studies showed inhibited inter-brain and behavioural synchronisation in VC in comparison to FtF interactions, while there is lack of research on mimicry.

3.3 Disclosure

Disclosure refers to statements about the one's own personality, thoughts, feelings, and experiences [37]. Previous literature examined dimensions of factual and perceived disclosure, tendency to self-disclose via different channels, and information seeking behaviour.

Identified studies measured factual disclosure via the number of self-disclosure statements or questions asked [9, 38], self-reported general tendency to self-disclose via different channels [39, 40] and perceived disclosure in an interaction [41]. The dimensions of disclosure and respective assessment instruments are presented on Figure S3 in Supplementary materials3.

On the basis of the Social presence theory [18], researchers suggested that the lack of social cues in CM interactions inhibits disclosure, while FtF communication creates an environment for spontaneous and intimate disclosure [38]. Walther suggested two theories, predicting the opposite results: the Social information processing theory (SIP; [42]) and the Hyperpersonal model of communication [43]. These theories suggest that strangers use intensive self-disclosure as a strategy to overcome CM communication difficulties and lack of personal information. The Internet-enhanced self-disclosure hypothesis [44] agrees that CM communication stimulates disclosure and help to develop stronger social ties. The Perception-behaviour intensification mechanism [10] explains, that perceptions of disclosures' intimacy are intensified in CM channels and interlocutors are forced to reciprocate with intimate disclosures.

In agreement with Walther's theories, strangers did more self-disclosures with greater intimacy and showed more information seeking in CM rather than in FtF [9, 10]. Subjective estimates of disclosure were also higher after CM than FtF contacts [10, 45].

However, in closer relationship, disclosure tends to be more intimate in FtF contacts rather than in CM. Studies demonstrated greater self-disclosure to friends in FtF rather than online context [39, 46, 47]. One study showed greater disclosure breath in less developed romantic relationships in FtF than in CM, while partners in more developed relationships preferred FtF contacts for intimate self-disclosures. The other study used relationship duration as a proxy to relationship development stage and demonstrated no effect of relationship stage on self-disclosure in CM and FtF channels [40]. Thus, Walther's theories may apply exclusively to early relationship development stages.

Contradictory results on disclosure may be partially explained by variability in assessment methods. For example, Baccon and collaborators [38] showed greater factual disclosure in FtF than in CM, but no difference in perceived disclosure. Further, mixed findings may occur due to uncontrolled moderators such as stage of relationship development. Further exploration of factors affecting the switch from intensive (but possibly more selective and less authentic) online disclosure to preferably FtF self-disclosure in closer relationships is required.

3.4 Affiliation and Dominance

The Interpersonal Theory [48] describes interpersonal social behaviour along two interrelated dimensions: dominance/submissiveness and warmth/coldness or affiliation and dominance [49]. Expression of affiliation and dominance includes displays of liking, interest, eagerness to communicate, willingness to help or collaborate, warmth, as well as expressions of influence, and power. In reviewed research, we found affiliation, collaboration and power and dominance as dimensions of this aspect.

Affiliative cues measured in previous studies include amount of gestures, laughing, smiling, and head nods registered via video annotation and coding [21, 50, 51]. The digital affiliative cues include excessive punctuation, typed laughter and emoticons [51]. Less explored markers of affiliation include a level of urinary oxytocin [52], a hormone presumably involved in human attachment [53]. For dominance assessment, authors used either perceived dominance in relationships [54] or markers of dominance found in speech [55]. See Figure S4 in Supplementary materials (see https://osf.io/j9amx/) for the dimensions of affiliation and dominance and respective assessment instruments.

According to the Social presence theory [18] and the Theory of media synchronicity [34], the channels conveying greater social presence and providing a greater sense of immediacy require more socioemotional interaction, leading to higher expressed and perceived affiliation and dominance, while leaner and asynchronous channels impair perceptions of affiliation and dominance [55, 56]. On the basis of the Cues filtered-out theory [27], the Media richness theory [57] and the Modality and information richness theory [58] researchers predicted decrease in expressed and perceived affiliation and dominance in CM communication due to reduced social and non-verbal cues [50, 58].

The empirical research has shown mixed results. Some studies find no difference in affiliative behaviours between the channels [6]. However, certain indicators of affiliation displayed variances across communication channels, such as slight distinctions in the frequency of smiles, vocal intensity, pitch variation, and face touches [50]. Further, higher oxytocin level after FtF contact in comparison to interaction via IM was reported [52]. Moreover, affiliative cue perception accuracy was found to be greater in FtF interactions than in phone calls [56].

Feaster [54] tested the hypothesis that individuals selectively use channels for face-threatening situations, depending on power relations between individuals and found overall preference for FtF contacts notwithstanding power distribution in the relationship. The other study used a number of words said by the interlocutor as a marker of dominance in the interaction and the number of role changes in a conversation as the degree of collaboration [55]. This study revealed more words spoken in FtF interactions than in VC, but a higher frequency of role changes in VC compared to FtF. These findings might be also attributed to disrupted synchronisation due to network latencies [6].

Reported small to negligible differences in affiliation and dominance indirectly support the Media compensation theory [59] that proposes individuals adapt their communication behaviours to meet their communication goals in restricted CM contacts. Presumably, individuals use strategies that allow for conveying affiliation and dominance even with reduced non-verbal cues, social presence and synchronicity.

However, the results are inconclusive. The above papers explored communication in different settings such as collaborative work [6, 55], communication between cohabitating romantic partners [56] or child-parent dyads [52]. These settings potentially vary in the level of affiliation demonstrated by the conversing parties. The lack of research on dominance in CM interactions is unfortunate, as CM channels have the potential to reduce the impact of power and social status on dominance in communication. The switch to CM contacts in formal settings thus may have profound effects on team work and productivity.

3.5 Attraction and Homophily

Attraction is an affective positive evaluation of the other person [60]. It includes such dimensions as interpersonal, romantic, physical, and social attraction. Additional dimension, perceived homophily, correlates with the desire to continue communication similarly to attraction [61, 62].

Recent studies predominately rely on the same assessment instrument – the Measurement of Interpersonal Attraction [63] or its variants. See Figure S5 in the Supplementary materials (see https://osf.io/j9amx/) for the dimensions of attraction and perceived homophily and respective assessment instruments.

The Social presence theory [18] and the Media richness theory [57] state that richer channels provide a greater sense of social presence and allow to convey and receive more social cues. Researchers suggest that cues of attraction and homophily, such as gestures and eye contact, are also affected, thus modifying a sense of intimacy, closeness and similarity [28]. On the basis of the Social identity model of deindividuation effects [64], researchers expected poorer social outcomes (including lower attraction and lower perceived similarity) in CM communication due to lower sense of identifiability and self-awareness in CM contacts [28].

Walther's theories predict the opposite results. The SIP theory hypothesises that individuals adapt to the lack of social information and non-verbal cues in CM contacts and can still form strong social relations in CM, although this process is slower. A similar proposition was made recently in the Media compensation theory, that states individuals adapt to restrictions of CM channels by changing their communicative behaviour [59]. Further, in the Hyperpersonal model of communication [43] Walther proposed that CM communication provide even better social outcomes (including attraction), because a sender in CM has a greater ability for self-presentation and impression management compared to FtF.

Empirical studies supported benefits of FtF interaction for attraction. One study showed that physical co-presence enhances interpersonal attraction in comparison to VC interaction [28]. Similarly, both interviewers and applicants reported lower interpersonal attraction after a VC job selection interviews in comparison to FtF [65]. Communication via IM also was not more intimate and did not result in higher liking than FtF as was predicted by Walther [29]. In close relationship, the highest social attraction was found between offline friends and significantly lower attraction in mixed-mode friendships and online friendships [66]. However, homophily appeared equal in mixed-mode and offline friendships, but lower in online friendships [66].

On the other hand, Walther's predictions were also empirically supported by the separate stream of research, exploring modality switching [67]. This paradigm explores how relationships change when individuals, who initially communicated via one channel (e.g. were acquainted on an online dating site) start using the other channel (e.g. meet FtF). These studies showed higher attraction after interaction via leaner channels (e.g. text-based vs VC) and decrease in attraction after a FtF contact [68, 69]. One study also emphasised the role of homophily for the attraction formation, showing the linear association between the similarity expressed in emails and the desire to continue FtF communication [69].

Overall, FtF and CM communication seem to have distinct effects on attraction and homophily and other factors such as context, and relationship goals may moderate these effects. Future longitudinal studies might gain deeper insights into attraction dynamics in different channel over time.

3.6 Social Sensitivity

Social (or interpersonal) sensitivity refers to an individual's ability to perceive and understand others' emotions, thoughts, feelings and traits in social situations [70]. It involves recognition of verbal and non-verbal cues, such as body language, facial expressions, tone of voice, and interpretation of others' emotional states and intentions. This aspect also includes dimensions of self-expression and impression management as concepts, that heavily rely on social sensitivity [71].

In the reviewed papers social sensitivity was assessed using questionnaires or interview performance [5, 65]. One study also measured social sensitivity by comparing the congruency in personality traits estimated by a person and their communication partner [6]. We present identified dimensions of social sensitivity and respective assessment instruments on Figure S6 in Supplementary materials (see https://osf.io/j9amx/).

On the basis of the Social presence theory [18] and the Media richness theory [57], researchers assumed that FtF communication allows for both better "mind reading" and impression management due to more social cues available than in CM contact [5]. In opposite, the SIP theory [42] suggests that individuals adapt to CM limitations relying on compensatory cues. For example, in VC interactions individuals intensify voice and facial expression [72].

Empirical evidence supports the advantages of FtF over CM communication for social sensitivity. Research found limited use of self-presentation in CM communication: applicants reported that they used more impression management tactics in FtF than VC interviews [5]. Similarly, participants also perceived that they self-expressed more in FtF rather than in CM contact with friends [47]. These differences in self-presentation might explain differences in social sensitivity. In one study, both interviewers and applicants estimated each other's competence and trustworthiness higher in FtF than in VC interviews [65].

However, an experimental study by Brucks & Levav [6] found no difference in congruency between one's own and partners' estimates of personality traits between channels. However, null differences found in this study may signal that a short interaction between strangers is equally ineffective for personality traits recognition in both FtF and VC channels.

To sum up, comparative research regarding the effect of channel on social sensitivity and impression management is scarce and requires further investigation.

3.7 Interaction Satisfaction

Summarising operationalisations of psychological outcomes of communication from several studies, we broadly defined some of them as Interactions satisfaction – individuals' feelings and subjective perceptions of success regarding a single communication event. This aspect includes dimensions of interaction pleasantness, perceived support in interaction and interaction success.

It must be noted that there was no reliable and validated instrument to assess interaction satisfaction in recent research. The reviewed papers assessed participants' satisfaction using 1 to 5 author-developed items. These items either directly ask participants to estimate their satisfaction with an interaction with someone ("How satisfied were you with the interaction overall?"; [73]) or asked to evaluate satisfaction within specific dimensions such as support, enjoyment or pleasantness [29, 74, 75]. The dimensions of interactions satisfaction and respective assessment instruments are presented on Figure S7 in Supplementary materials (see https://osf.io/j9amx/).

The Communicative Media Affordances perspective posits that each communication channel possesses objective and subjective (as perceived by users) characteristics that either enable or constrain communication potentials [76]. Consequently, individuals may subjectively consider certain channels to be more enjoyable, fulfilling, and better at meeting their communication needs compared to others. In addition, the Media Naturalness Theory (or the Psychobiological model; [77]) proposes that people are more evolutionary adapted to FtF rather than to CM interactions. CM channels that deviate from FtF interaction thus are perceived as less pleasant and satisfying.

Despite large variability in assessment methods and largely unknown psychometric properties of measures, results regarding the differences on interaction satisfaction between the channels are more consensual than on any other psychological aspect of interpersonal communication. Studies show that FtF communication is subjectively more pleasant, result in higher satisfaction and provide overall more positive emotions [40, 73, 75, 78–81].

The only aspect that showed equal satisfaction in CM and FtF channels was perceived support. A study on supportive interactions found no differences in satisfaction with support between FtF and IM channels [79]. However, gender can moderate the difference between the channels: support from males was perceived as more sensitive in IM than FtF, while female support was perceived as less sensitive and of lower quality in IM than FtF [82].

In light of these findings, future research on interaction satisfaction could strive towards developing a standardised assessment method that draws upon the methods presented in recent literature. This will enable researchers to compare and apply study findings more broadly.

3.8 Relationship Quality

Relationship quality is a broad concept that describes multiple dimensions of interpersonal attitudes and behaviours, including trust, closeness, support, and overall relational satisfaction. Recent literature examined dimensions of relational satisfaction, quality of relationship among friends, dating partners or children and parents, trust and predicted outcome value. We also distinguished closeness as a separate dimension, as multiple authors focused on this specific dimension of relationship quality.

Mostly, studies used self-reported one-item [80] or multidimensional measures such as the Friendship Qualities Scale [83]. Refer to Figure S8 in Supplementary materials (see https://osf.io/j9amx/) for dimensions and assessment tools.

According to the SIP theory [42], CM and FtF contacts result in equal relationship quality. As suggested by the Channel complementarity theory [84] and the Media multiplexity theory [85], use of multiple communication channels can even enhance relational satisfaction and tie strength by combining the benefits of immediacy and non-verbal cues with convenience and eliminated time and space constrains. Related to this, the Electronic propinquity theory [86] suggests that CM communication contributes to greater feeling of closeness and bonding, and improved relationship quality due to reduced physical barriers and elevated communication frequency. In opposite, the Social displacement hypothesis [87] suggests that online communication can devastates interpersonal relationships if CM channels replace FtF interaction.

Empirical findings are mixed. One study showed lower quality of online-only friendships than FtF [88] and the other reported no significant differences in quality between online and offline friendships [89], although both these studies were based on the McGill Friendship Questionnaires.

Findings regarding the combination of FtF and CM channels are more consensual. Authors reported higher relationship quality between friends [83] and romantic partners [90] who integrated channels. Both FtF and CM contacts also contribute to teens' relationships with parents and peers [91]. However, contradictory evidence was found in a study by Antheunis and collaborators [66] where FtF friendships were estimated higher than mixed. In romantic relationship, FtF contacts were also estimated as contributing to higher intimacy and relationship quality [40] and higher relationship satisfaction [80] than CM contacts. Further, the context of communication (e.g. physical distance) moderate the impact of communication channel on relationship quality. Long-distance strong ties with romantic partners, friends, and family rely heavily on CM contacts [92].

Relationship quality between strangers after a single interaction is rarely studied in recent research. One study reported null differences in trust in economic game played by strangers after a FtF or CM collaborative task [6]. Closeness between strangers especially suffer in case of the leanest interaction via text in comparison to all other channels (voice call, VC and FtF) [29].

Modality switching paradigm serves as an intermediate between close relationship (e.g. friendship) and complete strangers. Three studies explored the change in relationship quality after modality switching. Overall, individuals reported growth in partners' perceptions and closeness after FtF meeting [69, 93, 94]. However, the link between relational satisfaction and modality switching was moderated by time. Too long online communication resulted in hyperpersonal attraction, leading to disillusionment after a FtF contact [69, 93, 94].

Overall, empirical research shows that individuals can form and maintain relationships online, but the best relational outcomes occur when channels are combined.

4   Discussion

This review analysed the recent comparative literature on psychological aspects of FtF and CM interpersonal communication. While the review does not claim to be systematic or comprehensive, it summarises recent research methodologies, tendencies and limitations, as well as highlights future research directions.

We identified eight aspects of interpersonal communication that have been most often compared between communication channels in recent studies. Although our distinction of concepts was based rather on expert opinion than on strict criteria, we assume it generally reflects main research areas in this field.

According to Figs. 1 and 2, Relationship quality of most interest to researchers. Many aspects are studied along with it, apparently, because they are considered as factors, moderators or mechanisms. Two other important "centres of interest" are social presence and engagement, and attraction.

Methodology development in the field follows several trends. First, surveys and questionnaires remain widely used to gather data on various aspects of interpersonal communication due to subjective nature of measured concepts, such as attraction. Researchers either develop study-specific items (as in case of interaction satisfaction) or use well validated instruments (as in case of attraction). Large-scale online surveys have gained popularity in recent years, e.g. as in the study by Antheunis and collaborators [66] involving data of 2,188 SNS users.

Second, researchers employ behavioural markers to operationalise affiliation, including such subtle indicators as head nod frequency. Most commonly, the analysis of video recordings is either based on experts' estimates [51] or conducted automatically using machine learning algorithms [95]. Further, most resent studies apply content analysis to extract various communication markers from texts (written messages or speech transcripts) or audio(-visual) data in order to measure e.g. the amount of expressed similarity or the depth of self-disclosure. In the context of digital communication, researchers also employ digital markers such as emoji use. Advances in natural language processing and machine learning algorithms have contributed to behavioural markers advances and accessibility in recent years.

Finally, advances in equipment and analytical tools allow researchers to benefit from such markers of communication outcomes as EEG [23] or hormones [52]. Specifically, these methods have been applied for synchronisation and affiliation assessment.

Two challenges must be mentioned in relation to methodological approaches. First, the same behavioural markers are being employed for analysis of different phenomena (e.g. number of words as a marker of both collaboration and dominance in a conversation). Secondly, simultaneous use of both self-reported and objective methods sometimes leads to a confusion of concepts, as in the case of factual and perceived disclosure. These challenges complicate obtaining conclusive and/or interpretable results.

Based on our analysis, we observe varying degrees of methodological convergence across different research subdomains. For instance, attraction research relies on the Measurement of Interpersonal Attraction [63]. Conversely, when it comes to research on interaction satisfaction, we have found a lack of methodological convergence, as there is currently no widely recognised or validated assessment method utilised uniformly in this field. This variability presumably threatens the credibility of research and findings in the field [8]. However, methodological convergence does not necessarily align with consensus in results. Thus, despite the scarcity of reliable instruments, research on interaction satisfaction shows a remarkable agreement among findings across studies. In contrast, research on attraction, despite employing a consistent methodology, so far has been yielding diverging conclusions.

We identify several influential theories guiding the recent research in the area: the Hyperpersonal model of communication [43] and the Social information processing theory, or SIP [42]; the Social presence theory [18]; the Cues filtered-out theory [27]; the Social displacement [87] and the Social enhancement [96] hypotheses; the Media richness theory [57]; the Channel complementarity theory [84] and the Social compensation theory [97]. Some of them (Hyperpersonal model of communication, SIP, Social presence theory, Media richness theory, and Cues filtered-out theory) serve as "domain-general" theories and are used to generate and test hypotheses about multiple aspects of communication, including attraction, relationship quality, and social presence, using a wide range of methodologies [9, 29, 40, 66, 89]. In most of these theories, channels that mediate communication are described in terms of disadvantages they have in comparison with FtF communication, which is recognised as the gold standard. This approach might lead to biased research results, where CM communication always turns out to be inferior to FtF. Other theories that describe positive sides of CM communication, such as Media multiplexity theory [85] or Perception-behaviour intensification mechanism [10] are rarely used but seem to be promising for explaining differentiated effects of specific channels on psychological aspects of communication in real-life communication settings.

Overall, the reviewed studies generally support the advantages of FtF communication, particularly in such areas as Attraction, Interaction satisfaction, Social sensitivity, social presence, Engagement, and Synchronisation. Results related to affiliation, dominance, relationship quality, and disclosure appear to be more nuanced, often contingent on moderators, such as relationship strength, goals and duration.

In conclusion, it is important for future research to use theoretical frameworks that emphasise the positive aspects of CM communication, as this will greatly enhance our comprehension of the subject. Exploration of the positive effects of CM communication will also facilitate the development of technologies and enable us to provide guidance for its appropriate use. Ultimately, this will contribute to the improvement of communication channels and their impact on society.

References

1. Barrero, J.M., Bloom, N., Davis, S.J.: Why working from home will stick. National Bureau of Economic Research (2021). https://doi.org/10.3386/w28731
2. Ignatowicz, A., Atherton, H., Bernstein, C.J., Bryce, C., Court, R., Sturt, J., et al.: Internet videoconferencing for patient–clinician consultations in long-term conditions: a review of reviews and applications in line with guidelines and recommendations. Digital Health **5**, 2055207619845831 (2019). https://doi.org/10.1177/2055207619845831
3. Thomas, N., McDonald, C., de Boer, K., Brand, R.M., Nedeljkovic, M., Seabrook, L.: Review of the current empirical literature on using videoconferencing to deliver individual psychotherapies to adults with mental health problems. Psychol. Psychother. Theory Res. Pract. **94**, 854–883 (2021). https://doi.org/10.1111/papt.12332
4. Adipat, S.: Why web-conferencing matters: rescuing education in the time of COVID-19 pandemic crisis. Front. Educ. **6** (2021). https://www.frontiersin.org/articles/10.3389/feduc.2021.752522
5. Basch, J.M., Melchers, K.G., Kurz, A., Krieger, M., Miller, L.: It Takes more than a good camera: which factors contribute to differences between face-to-face interviews and video-conference interviews regarding performance ratings and interviewee perceptions? J. Bus. Psychol. **36**, 921–940 (2021). https://doi.org/10.1007/s10869-020-09714-3
6. Brucks, M.S., Levav, J.: Virtual communication curbs creative idea generation. Nature **605**, 108–112 (2022). https://doi.org/10.1038/s41586-022-04643-y
7. Linden, A.H., Hönekopp, J.: Heterogeneity of research results: a new perspective from which to assess and promote progress in psychological science. Perspect. Psychol. Sci. **16**, 358–376 (2021). https://doi.org/10.1177/1745691620964193

8. Elson, M., Hussey, I., Alsalti, T., Arslan, R.C.: Psychological measures aren't toothbrushes. Commun Psychol. **1**, 25 (2023). https://doi.org/10.1038/s44271-023-00026-9

9. Antheunis, M.L., Schouten, A.P., Valkenburg, P.M., Peter, J.: Interactive uncertainty reduction strategies and verbal affection in computer-mediated communication. Commun. Res. **39**, 757–780 (2012). https://doi.org/10.1177/0093650211410420

10. Jiang, L.C., Bazarova, N.N., Hancock, J.T.: From perception to behavior: disclosure reciprocity and the intensification of intimacy in computer-mediated communication. Commun. Res. **40**, 125–143 (2013). https://doi.org/10.1177/0093650211405313

11. Wang, J.-L., Jackson, L.A., Zhang, D.-J.: The mediator role of self-disclosure and moderator roles of gender and social anxiety in the relationship between Chinese adolescents' online communication and their real-world social relationships. Comput. Hum. Behav. **27**, 2161–2168 (2011). https://doi.org/10.1016/j.chb.2011.06.010

12. Nguyen, M., Bin, Y.S., Campbell, A.: Comparing online and offline self-disclosure: a systematic review. Cyberpsychol. Behav. Soc. Netw. **15**, 103–111 (2012). https://doi.org/10.1089/cyber.2011.0277

13. Derks, D., Fischer, A.H., Bos, A.E.R.: The role of emotion in computer-mediated communication: a review. Comput. Hum. Behav. **24**, 766–785 (2008). https://doi.org/10.1016/j.chb.2007.04.004

14. Rhoads, M.: Face-to-face and computer-mediated communication: what does theory tell us and what have we learned so far? J. Plan. Lit. **25**, 111–122 (2010). https://doi.org/10.1177/0885412210382984

15. Rains, S.A., Peterson, E.B., Wright, K.B.: Communicating social support in computer-mediated contexts: a meta-analytic review of content analyses examining support messages shared online among individuals coping with illness. Commun. Monogr. **82**, 403–430 (2015). https://doi.org/10.1080/03637751.2015.1019530

16. Dredge, R., Schreurs, L.: Social media use and offline interpersonal outcomes during youth: a systematic literature review. Mass Commun. Soc. **23**, 885–911 (2020). https://doi.org/10.1080/15205436.2020.1810277

17. Tarnavsky Eitan, A., Smolyansky, E., Harpaz, I.K., Perets, S.: Connected Papers (2022). https://www.connectedpapers.com/

18. Short, J., Williams, E., Christie, B.: The Social Psychology of Telecommunications. Wiley, New York (1976)

19. Croes, E.A.J., Antheunis, M.L.: Perceived intimacy differences of daily online and offline interactions in people's social network. Societies **11**, 13 (2021). https://doi.org/10.3390/soc11010013

20. Roghanizad, M.M., Bohns, V.K.: Should i ask over zoom, phone, email, or in-person? communication channel and predicted versus actual compliance. Soc. Psychol. Pers. Sci. **13**, 1163–1172 (2022). https://doi.org/10.1177/19485506211063259

21. Shahid, S., Krahmer, E., Swerts, M.: Video-mediated and co-present gameplay: effects of mutual gaze on game experience, expressiveness and perceived social presence. Interact. Comput. **24**, 292–305 (2012). https://doi.org/10.1016/j.intcom.2012.04.006

22. Harms, C., Biocca, F.: Internal consistency and reliability of the networked minds measure of social presence. In: Seventh annual international workshop: Presence. Universidad Politecnica de Valencia Valencia, Spain (2004)

23. Schwartz, L., Levy, J., Endevelt-Shapira, Y., Djalovski, A., Hayut, O., Dumas, G., et al.: Technologically-assisted communication attenuates inter-brain synchrony. Neuroimage **264**, 119677 (2022). https://doi.org/10.1016/j.neuroimage.2022.119677

24. Roghanizad, M.M., Bohns, V.K.: Ask in person: you're less persuasive than you think over email. J. Exp. Soc. Psychol. **69**, 223–226 (2017). https://doi.org/10.1016/j.jesp.2016.10.002

25. Wilson, J.M., Straus, S.G., McEvily, B.: All in due time: the development of trust in computer-mediated and face-to-face teams. Organ. Behav. Hum. Decis. Process. **99**, 16–33 (2006). https://doi.org/10.1016/j.obhdp.2005.08.001
26. Lieberman, A., Schroeder, J.: Two social lives: how differences between online and offline interaction influence social outcomes. Curr. Opin. Psychol. **31**, 16–21 (2020). https://doi.org/10.1016/j.copsyc.2019.06.022
27. Culnan, M.J., Markus, M.L.: Information technologies. In: Handbook of Organizational Communication, pp. 420–444. Sage, Newbury Park, CA (1987)
28. Croes, E.A.J., Antheunis, M.L., Schouten, A.P., Krahmer, E.J.: Teasing apart the effect of visibility and physical co-presence to examine the effect of CMC on interpersonal attraction. Comput. Hum. Behav. **55**, 468–476 (2016). https://doi.org/10.1016/j.chb.2015.09.037
29. Sprecher, S.: Initial interactions online-text, online-audio, online-video, or face-to-face: effects of modality on liking, closeness, and other interpersonal outcomes. Comput. Hum. Behav. **31**, 190–197 (2014). https://doi.org/10.1016/j.chb.2013.10.029
30. Schwartz, L., Levy, J., Endevelt-Shapira, Y., Djalovski, A., Hayut, O., Dumas, G., et al. Technologically-assisted communication attenuates inter-brain synchrony. bioRxiv, p. 2022.06.06.494185 (2022). https://doi.org/10.1101/2022.06.06.494185
31. Rennung, M., Göritz, A.S.: Prosocial consequences of interpersonal synchrony. Zeitschrift für Psychologie. **224**, 168–189 (2016). https://doi.org/10.1027/2151-2604/a000252
32. Cirelli, L.K.: How interpersonal synchrony facilitates early prosocial behavior. Curr. Opin. Psychol. **20**, 35–39 (2018). https://doi.org/10.1016/j.copsyc.2017.08.009
33. Hu, Y., Cheng, X., Pan, Y., Hu, Y.: The intrapersonal and interpersonal consequences of interpersonal synchrony. Acta Physiol (Oxf.) **224**, 103513 (2022). https://doi.org/10.1016/j.actpsy.2022.103513
34. Dennis, A.R., Valacich, J.S.: Rethinking media richness: towards a theory of media synchronicity. In: Proceedings of the 32nd Annual Hawaii International Conference on Systems Sciences 1999 HICSS-32 Abstracts and CD-ROM of Full Papers. Maui, HI, USA: IEEE Computing Social, p. 10 (1999). https://doi.org/10.1109/HICSS.1999.772701
35. Koban, L., Ramamoorthy, A., Konvalinka, I.: Why do we fall into sync with others? Interpersonal synchronization and the brain's optimization principle. Soc. Neurosci. **14**, 1–9 (2019). https://doi.org/10.1080/17470919.2017.1400463
36. Boland, J.E., Fonseca, P., Mermelstein, I., Williamson, M.: Zoom disrupts the rhythm of conversation. J. Exp. Psychol. Gen. **151**, 1272–1282 (2022). https://doi.org/10.1037/xge0001150
37. Altman, I., Taylor, D.A.: Social Penetration: The Development of Interpersonal Relationships, pp. viii, 212. Holt, Rinehart & Winston, Oxford, England (1973)
38. Baccon, L.A., Chiarovano, E., MacDougall, H.G.: Virtual Reality for teletherapy: avatars may combine the benefits of face-to-face communication with the anonymity of online text-based communication. Cyberpsychol. Behav. Soc. Netw. **22**, 158–165 (2019). https://doi.org/10.1089/cyber.2018.0247
39. Valkenburg, P.M., Sumter, S.R., Peter, J.: Gender differences in online and offline self-disclosure in pre-adolescence and adolescence. Br. J. Dev. Psychol. **29**, 253–269 (2011). https://doi.org/10.1348/2044-835X.002001
40. Boyle, A.M., O'Sullivan, L.F.: Staying connected: computer-mediated and face-to-face communication in college students' dating relationships. Cyberpsychol. Behav. Soc. Netw. **19**, 299–307 (2016). https://doi.org/10.1089/cyber.2015.0293
41. Ruppel, E.K.: Use of communication technologies in romantic relationships: self-disclosure and the role of relationship development. J. Soc. Pers. Relat. **32**, 667–686 (2015). https://doi.org/10.1177/0265407514541075
42. Walther, J.B.: Interpersonal effects in computer-mediated interaction: a relational perspective. Commun. Res. **19**, 52–90 (1992). https://doi.org/10.1177/009365092019001003

43. Walther, J.B.: Computer-mediated communication: impersonal, interpersonal, and hyperpersonal interaction. Commun. Res. **23**, 3–43 (1996). https://doi.org/10.1177/009365096023 001001
44. Valkenburg, P.M., Peter, J.: Social consequences of the internet for adolescents: a decade of research. Curr. Dir. Psychol. Sci. **18**, 1–5 (2009). https://doi.org/10.1111/j.1467-8721.2009. 01595.x
45. Bruss, O.E., Hill, J.M.: Tell me more: online versus face-to-face communication and self-disclosure. PsiChi J. 3–7 (2010).https://doi.org/10.24839/1089-4136.JN15.1.3
46. Desjarlais, M., Joseph, J.J.: Socially interactive and passive technologies enhance friendship quality: an investigation of the mediating roles of online and offline self-disclosure. Cyberpsychol. Behav. Soc. Netw. **20**, 286–291 (2017). https://doi.org/10.1089/cyber.2016. 0363
47. Ranney, J.D., Troop-Gordon, W.: Problem-focused discussions in digital contexts: the impact of information and communication technologies on conversational processes and experiences. Comput. Hum. Behav. **51**, 64–74 (2015). https://doi.org/10.1016/j.chb.2015.04.038
48. Moskowitz, D.S., Zuroff, D.C.: Assessing interpersonal perceptions using the interpersonal grid. Psychol. Assess. **17**, 218–230 (2005). https://doi.org/10.1037/1040-3590.17.2.218
49. Stevanovic, M., Henttonen, P., Kahri, M., Koski, S.: Affiliation and dominance in female and male dyads: when discoordination makes happy. Gend. Issues **36**, 201–235 (2019). https://doi.org/10.1007/s12147-018-9218-0
50. Croes, E.A.J., Antheunis, M.L., Schouten, A.P., Krahmer, E.J.: Social attraction in video-mediated communication: the role of nonverbal affiliative behavior. J. Soc. Pers. Relat. **36**, 1210–1232 (2019). https://doi.org/10.1177/0265407518757382
51. Sherman, L.E., Michikyan, M., Greenfield, P.M.: The effects of text, audio, video, and in-person communication on bonding between friends. Cyberpsychology. 72013).https://doi.org/10.5817/CP2013-2-3
52. Seltzer, L.J., Prososki, A.R., Ziegler, T.E., Pollak, S.D.: Instant messages vs. speech: hormones and why we still need to hear each other. Evol. Hum. Behav. **33**(1), 42–45 (2012). https://doi.org/10.1016/j.evolhumbehav.2011.05.004
53. Feldman, R.: Oxytocin and social affiliation in humans. Horm. Behav. **61**, 380–391 (2012). https://doi.org/10.1016/j.yhbeh.2012.01.008
54. Feaster, J.C.: Expanding the Impression management model of communication channels: an information control scale. J. Comput.-Mediat. Commun. **16**, 115–138 (2010). https://doi.org/10.1111/j.1083-6101.2010.01535.x
55. Hatem, W.A., Kwan, A., Miles, J.: Comparing the effectiveness of face to face and computer mediated collaboration. Adv. Eng. Inform. **26**, 383–395 (2012). https://doi.org/10.1016/j.aei.2012.01.001
56. Sadikaj, G., Moskowitz, D.S.: I hear but I don't see you: interacting over phone reduces the accuracy of perceiving affiliation in the other. Comput. Hum. Behav. **89**, 140–147 (2018). https://doi.org/10.1016/j.chb.2018.08.004
57. Daft, R.L., Lengel, R.H.: Organizational information requirements, media richness and structural design. Manage. Sci. **32**, 554–571 (1986). https://doi.org/10.1287/mnsc.32.5.554
58. Ramirez, A., Burgoon, J.K.: The effect of interactivity on initial interactions: the influence of information valence and modality and information richness on computer-mediated interaction. Commun. Monogr. **71**, 422–447 (2004). https://doi.org/10.1080/0363452042000307461
59. Hantula, D.A., Kock, N., D'Arcy, J.P., DeRosa, D.M.: Media compensation theory: a Darwinian perspective on adaptation to electronic communication and collaboration. In: Saad, G. (ed.) Evolutionary Psychology in the Business Sciences, pp. 339–363. Springer, Berlin (2011). https://doi.org/10.1007/978-3-540-92784-6_13
60. Byrne, D., Griffitt, W.: Interpersonal attraction. Annu. Rev. Psychol. **24**, 317–336 (1973). https://doi.org/10.1146/annurev.ps.24.020173.001533

61. Byrne, D.: An overview (and underview) of research and theory within the attraction paradigm. J. Soc. Pers. Relat. **14**, 417–431 (1997). https://doi.org/10.1177/0265407597143008
62. Montoya, R.M., Horton, R.S.: A meta-analytic investigation of the processes underlying the similarity-attraction effect. J. Soc. Pers. Relat. **30**, 64–94 (2013). https://doi.org/10.1177/0265407512452989
63. McCroskey, J.C., McCain, T.A.: The measurement of interpersonal attraction. Speech Monographs **41**, 261–266 (1974). https://doi.org/10.1080/03637757409375845
64. Reicher, S.D., Spears, R., Postmes, T.: A social identity model of deindividuation phenomena. Eur. Rev. Soc. Psychol. **6**, 161–198 (1995). https://doi.org/10.1080/14792779443000049
65. Sears, G.J., Zhang, H., Wiesner, W.H., Hackett, R.D., Yuan, Y.: A comparative assessment of videoconference and face-to-face employment interviews. Manag. Decis. **51**(8), 1733–1752 (2013). https://doi.org/10.1108/MD-09-2012-0642
66. Antheunis, M.L., Valkenburg, P.M, Peter, J.: The quality of online, offline, and mixed-mode friendships among users of a social networking site. Cyberpsychol. J. Psychosoc. Res. Cyberspace **6** (2012)
67. Ramirez, A., Zhang, S.: When online meets offline: the effect of modality switching on relational communication. Commun. Monographs. **74**, 287–3102007). https://doi.org/10.1080/03637750701543493
68. Antheunis, M.L., Schouten, A.P., Joseph, B., Walther: The hyperpersonal effect in online dating: effects of text-based CMC vs. videoconferencing before meeting face-to-face. Media Psychol. **23**(6), 820–839 (2020). https://doi.org/10.1080/15213269.2019.1648217
69. Sharabi, L., Caughlin, J.: What predicts first date success? A longitudinal study of modality switching in online dating. Pers. Relat. **24**(2), 370–391 (2017). https://doi.org/10.1111/pere.12188
70. Hall, J.A., Bernieri, F.J. (eds.): Interpersonal Sensitivity: Theory and Measurement. Psychology Press (2001). https://doi.org/10.4324/9781410600424
71. Leary, M.R., Allen, A.B.: Personality and persona: personality processes in self-presentation. J. Pers. **79**, 1191–1218 (2011). https://doi.org/10.1111/j.1467-6494.2010.00704.x
72. Trujillo, J.P., Levinson, S.C., Holler, J.: A multi-scale investigation of the human communication system's response to visual disruption. Royal Soc. Open Sci. **9**, 211489 (2022). https://doi.org/10.1098/rsos.211489
73. Kafetsios, K., Chatzakou, D., Tsigilis, N., Vakali, A.: Experience of emotion in face to face and computer-mediated social interactions: an event sampling study. Comput. Hum. Behav. **76**, 287–293 (2017). https://doi.org/10.1016/j.chb.2017.07.033
74. Achterhof, R., Kirtley, O.J., Schneider, M., Hagemann, N., Hermans, K.S.F.M., Hiekkaranta, A.P., et al.: Adolescents' real-time social and affective experiences of online and face-to-face interactions. Comput. Hum. Behav. **129**, 107159 (2022). https://doi.org/10.1016/j.chb.2021.107159
75. Sacco, D.F., Ismail, M.M.: Social belongingness satisfaction as a function of interaction medium: face-to-face interactions facilitate greater social belonging and interaction enjoyment compared to instant messaging. Comput. Hum. Behav. **36**, 359–364 (2014). https://doi.org/10.1016/j.chb.2014.04.004
76. Hutchby, I.: Technologies, texts and affordances. Sociology **35**, 441–456 (2001). https://doi.org/10.1177/S0038038501000219
77. Kock, N.: The psychobiological model: towards a new theory of computer-mediated communication based on Darwinian evolution. Organ. Sci. **15**, 327–348 (2004). https://doi.org/10.1287/orsc.1040.0071
78. Bayer, J.B., Ellison, N.B., Schoenebeck, S.Y., Falk, E.B.: Sharing the small moments: ephemeral social interaction on Snapchat. Inf. Commun. Soc. **19**, 956–977 (2016). https://doi.org/10.1080/1369118X.2015.1084349

79. Holtzman, S., DeClerck, D., Turcotte, K., Lisi, D., Woodworth, M.: Emotional support during times of stress: can text messaging compete with in-person interactions? Comput. Hum. Behav. **71**, 130–139 (2017). https://doi.org/10.1016/j.chb.2017.01.043

80. Pollmann, M.M.H., Norman, T.J., Crockett, E.E.: A daily-diary study on the effects of face-to-face communication, texting, and their interplay on understanding and relationship satisfaction. Comput. Hum. Behav. Rep. **3**, 100088 (2021). https://doi.org/10.1016/j.chbr.2021.100088

81. Subrahmanyam, K., Frison, E., Michikyan, M.: The relation between face-to-face and digital interactions and self-esteem: a daily diary study. Hum. Behav. Emerg. Tech. **2**, 116–127 (2020). https://doi.org/10.1002/hbe2.187

82. High, A.C., Solomon, D.H.: Communication channel, sex, and the immediate and longitudinal outcomes of verbal person-centered support. Commun. Monogr. **81**, 439–468 (2014). https://doi.org/10.1080/03637751.2014.933245

83. Baiocco, R., Laghi, F., Schneider, B., Dalessio, M., Amichai-Hamburger, Y., Coplan, R., et al.: Daily patterns of communication and contact between Italian early adolescents and their friends. Cyberpsychol. Behav. Soc. Netw. **14**, 467–471 (2011). https://doi.org/10.1089/cyber.2010.0208

84. Dutta-Bergman, M.J.: Interpersonal communication after 9/11 via telephone and internet: a theory of channel complementarity. New Media Soc. **6**, 659–673 (2004). https://doi.org/10.1177/146144804047086

85. Haythornthwaite, C.: Social networks and Internet connectivity effects. Inf. Commun. Soc. **8**, 125–147 (2005). https://doi.org/10.1080/13691180500146185

86. Korzenny, F.: A theory of electronic propinquity: mediated communication in organizations. Commun. Res. **5**, 3–24 (1978). https://doi.org/10.1177/009365027800500101

87. Kraut, R., Patterson, M., Lundmark, V., Kiesler, S., Mukophadhyay, T., Scherlis, W.: Internet paradox: a social technology that reduces social involvement and psychological well-being? Am. Psychol. **53**, 1017–1031 (1998). https://doi.org/10.1037/0003-066X.53.9.1017

88. Glüer, M., Lohaus, A.: Participation in social network sites: associations with the quality of offline and online friendships in German preadolescents and adolescents. Cyberpsychol. **10** 2016).https://doi.org/10.5817/CP2016-2-2

89. Scott, R.A., Stuart, J., Barber, B.L.: Contemporary friendships and social vulnerability among youth: understanding the role of online and offline contexts of interaction in friendship quality. J. Soc. Pers. Relat. **38**(12), 3451–3471 (2021). https://doi.org/10.1177/02654075211029384

90. Caughlin, J.P., Sharabi, L.L.: A communicative interdependence perspective of close relationships: the connections between mediated and unmediated interactions matter. J. Commun. **63**, 873–893 (2013). https://doi.org/10.1111/jcom.12046

91. Manago, A.M., Brown, G., Lawley, K.A., Anderson, G.: Adolescents' daily face-to-face and computer-mediated communication: associations with autonomy and closeness to parents and friends. Dev. Psychol. **56**, 153–164 (2020). https://doi.org/10.1037/dev0000851

92. Tillema, T., Dijst, M., Schwanen, T.: Face-to-face and electronic communications in maintaining social networks: the influence of geographical and relational distance and of information content. New Media Soc. **12**, 965–983 (2010). https://doi.org/10.1177/1461444809353011

93. McEwan, B., Zanolla, D.: When online meets offline: a field investigation of modality switching. Comput. Hum. Behav. **29**, 1565–1571 (2013). https://doi.org/10.1016/j.chb.2013.01.020

94. Ramirez, A., Bryant, E.M., Sumner, C.F., Cole, M.: When online dating partners meet offline: the effect of modality switching on relational communication between online daters. J. Comput.-Mediated Commun. **20**(1), 99–114 (2015). https://doi.org/10.1111/jcc4.12101

95. Poria, S., Majumder, N., Mihalcea, R., Hovy, E.: Emotion recognition in conversation: research challenges, datasets, and recent advances. IEEE Access. **7**, 100943–100953 (2019). https://doi.org/10.1109/ACCESS.2019.2929050

96. Kraut, R., Kiesler, S., Boneva, B., Cummings, J., Helgeson, V., Crawford, A.: Internet Paradox Revisited. J. Soc. Isssues **58**, 49–74 (2002). https://doi.org/10.1111/1540-4560.00248
97. Peter, J., Valkenburg, P.M., Schouten, A.P.: Developing a model of adolescent friendship formation on the internet. Cyberpsychol. Behav. **8**, 423–430 (2005). https://doi.org/10.1089/cpb.2005.8.423

Supporting Hybrid Interaction: A Design Approach for Mitigating the "Barrier" Encountered by Remote Participants in Hybrid Working Environments

Ichiro Umata[1]([envelope]), Takumi Ishikawa[2], Sumaru Niida[1], and Tsuneo Kato[2]

[1] KDDI Research, Inc., The Okura Prestige Tower, 2-10-4 Toranomon, Minato-Ku, Tokyo 105-0001, Japan
{xih-umata,su-niida}@kddi.com
[2] Department of Information Systems Design, Doshisha University, Kyotanabe-Shi, Kyoto 610-0321, Japan
cguf0027@mail4.doshisha.ac.jp, tsukato@mail.doshisha.ac.jp

Abstract. The design and evaluation process of a remote communication system that supports hybrid work is presented. Based on the previous psychological, HCI and CSCW studies, we design and evaluate hybrid collaboration support systems that allow viewpoint control of remote office images for remote workers. The aim of the design phases was to ascertain the system specifications and the potential application domain, and the evaluation phase tested the effectiveness of the system using objective and quantitative metrics. Although the evaluation phase was still in the preliminary stage with a small data set, the results suggest that the system and the design method have promising possibilities.

Keywords: Computer Mediated Communication · Design and Evaluation Methodologies for Social Computing and Social Media · Multicultural Environments in Social Computing and Social Media

1 Introduction

The number of remote workers increased extremely rapidly in the situation created by the COVID-19 pandemic whereby working from home became a realistic workstyle option for many people. This change brought about both benefits and disadvantages to society: remote working can eliminate or reduce the time spent commuting and enable more effective use of time, whereas it has negative effects in terms of communication with colleagues [1, 2].

Previous human-computer interaction and psychological studies also have shown that video communication has different characteristics from those of face-to-face communication. Strickland reported that the emergence of leadership is less prominent in video communication than in face-to-face interactions [3]. Heath and Luff pointed out that video technology transforms nonverbal and verbal conduct, introducing certain asymmetries into the social interaction between users [4]. Bos et al. reported that video and audio conferences show some evidence of what they termed delayed trust (slower progress toward full cooperation) and fragile trust (vulnerability to opportunistic behavior) [5]. Ruppel et al. showed that self-disclosure was higher in face-to-face communication than in computer-mediated communication [6].

In this study, we report our design process for a remote communication system that supports hybrid work by providing remote workers with a higher degree of freedom in controlling the viewpoints of the video images of their remote office. First, we held several ideation sessions to examine the possibilities of a telecommunication system that provides a higher degree of freedom in image setting utilizing 360-degree camera images. Second, we observed the behavior of users in an actual collaboration task using the system, and improved the system based on the observation. Third, we held another series of evaluation sessions to test the resulting systems with different interface design features.

2   Phase 1: Design Sessions

We examined the effects of a telecommunication system that provides a higher degree of freedom in controlling image and audio perspective settings compared to conventional systems. We did this by holding expert-led workshops where the systems were implemented in a remote office collaboration setting (see Figs. 1, 2, and 3) [7]. The system allowed remote users to select the viewpoint of the remote office where a group of several peoples were collaborating face-to-face. The experts consisted of corporate researchers, university professors, and university students from the fields of sociology, cognitive science, and human-computer interaction.

In the workshops, two or three people joined in a meeting by accessing a remote office where four people were interacting face-to-face. We had two one-hour sessions with different participants. During these sessions they discussed the benefits and disadvantages of the system, and the situations where it could be effectively applied. They pointed out that the freedom of viewpoint helped remote participants to understand the flow of the conversation and aided their collaboration, and that taking speech turn was easier compared to conventional video conference systems with a fixed viewpoint. On the other hand, they raised a concern regarding privacy in some situation; ex. in interactions involving participants who are not familiar with each other.

Fig. 1. Remote workspaces set up Nishi-shinjuku area

Fig. 2. Inside the remote workspaces

Fig. 3. Setting of the office workspace

3 Phase 2: Evaluation Sessions Observing User Behaviors

We set an application domain to support creative and collaborative discussion among familiar to each other and people with similar social status to reduce potential concerns over privacy. We held a series of evaluation sessions with six university students majoring in sociology. They had two one-hour sessions to discuss how to integrate the various online systems of the university. Five participants interacted face-to-face, and a remote participant accessed the group interaction using the system (see Fig. 4) [7].

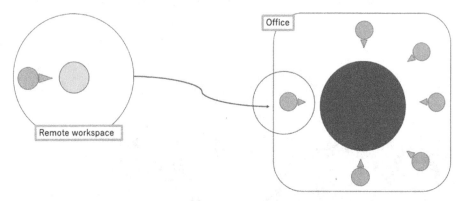

Fig. 4. Concept of the phase 2 sessions.

Although the remote participants engaged in some viewpoint controlling behaviors (see Figs. 5, 6 and 7) and pointed out the advantages of the freedom to change the view settings in the post session interview, those behaviors were not observed as often as expected: they were limited to situations where they were not engaged in searching or note-taking tasks. They reported that operating the mouse to control the viewpoints was not particularly easy. Based on their comments, we improved the viewpoint control interface, developing a touch panel interface and a gesture recognition interface.

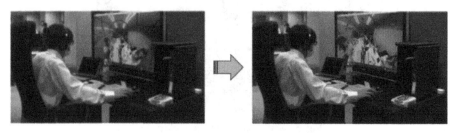

Fig. 5. Zooming up the speaker.

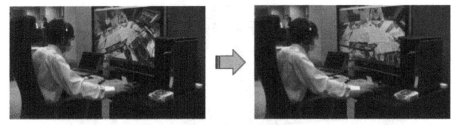

Fig. 6. Rotating the image and zooming up the speakers note.

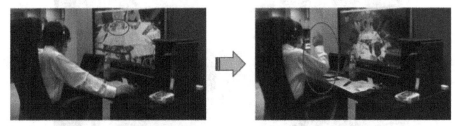

Fig. 7. Adjusting the viewpoint and observing the speaker's gestures. Then showing an OK gesture to the remote participants (without speaking).

4   Phase 3: Sessions to Evaluate the Improved Systems

In the system evaluation phase, we introduced two more conditions with different view angle control interfaces. We expected this would lighten the load on users and help overcome the difficulties with the mouse interface observed in phase two. We compared four system variations: (1) fixed viewpoint system (almost equivalent to the conventional remote conference systems such as Zoom), (2) viewpoint control with a mouse (like the phase two version), (3) viewpoint control with a touchpad (newly developed), and (4) viewpoint control with hand gesture recognition (newly developed). Examples of hand gestures are shown in Fig. 8

Currently, we have finished recording sessions with six collaborating groups in which a remote person joined a collocated pair. The participants were students of Doshisha University (aged 20 to 25), and all the participants in each group were familiar to each other. All the groups engaged in the task under all four conditions in randomized orders. They collaboratively worked on the picture completion task from the Torrance Tests of Creative Thinking [8], where they are given several incomplete pictures or cues, and they are asked to complete these in the most imaginative way possible. Their utterances were recorded with an utterance recording tool developed by Hylable Inc. [9]. The experimental settings are shown in Figs. 9 and 10.

In the following, we present the results of our preliminary analyses. Three indices of utterance behavior were analyzed quantitatively to examine the interactive activity under the four experimental conditions.

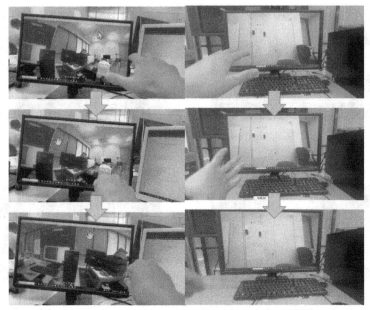

Grip and drag for angle control   Turn the palm outside for zooming

Fig. 8. Examples of the hand gestures

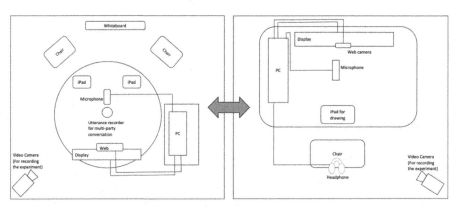

Fig. 9. Setup of condition (1) fixed viewpoint system.

4.1 Total Utterance Durations by the Group Participants

Based on the assumption that the total utterance duration would serve as an index of interactive activity, we performed the Friedman rank sum test for the total utterance duration under the four experimental conditions. The result showed a significant difference among the conditions ($X^2_{(3)} = 8.2, p < .043$). However, pairwise comparisons using the Wilcoxon signed rank test with p value adjustment by the Bonferroni method showed no significant differences.

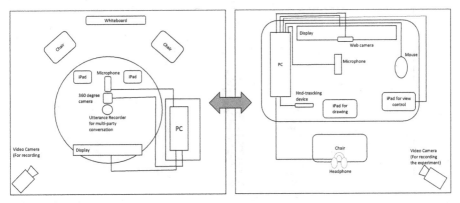

Fig. 10. Setup of condition (2) viewpoint control with a mouse, (3) viewpoint control with a touchpad, and (4) viewpoint control with hand gesture recognition.

Table 1. Total durations of utterances for each group

Group	(1) fixed viewpoint	(2) viewpoint control with a mouse	(3) viewpoint control with a touchpad	(4) viewpoint control with hand gesture
1	352875	359375	265500	316000
2	552250	570250	730750	546500
3	451625	654750	753750	486500
4	497625	559375	578375	575250
5	511750	558625	554625	396750
6	127125	502875	675375	74000
Average	415541.6667	534208.3333	593062.5	399166.6667
SD	156905.1797	98597.46658	179189.2985	186008.3107

Table 1 shows the total durations of utterances for each group, and Fig. 11 shows the average duration of total utterances under each experimental condition.

4.2 Utterance Duration Rates of the Remote Participant

Based on the assumption that the utterance duration rate of the remote participants would serve as an index of the difficulty experienced by the remote participants in joining in the task with the collocated pairs, we performed a Friedman rank sum test for the utterance duration rate of the remote participants under the four experimental conditions. However, there was no significant difference among the four experimental conditions ($X^2_{(3)} = 6.2$, $p < .102$).

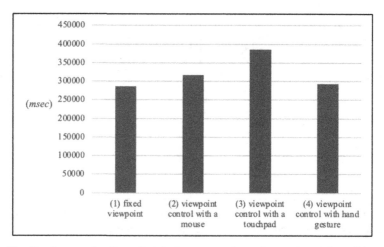

Fig. 11. Average duration of total utterances under each experimental condition

Table 2. Utterance duration rates of the remote participant

Group	(1) fixed viewpoint	(2) viewpoint control with a mouse	(3) viewpoint control with a touchpad	(4) viewpoint control with hand gesture
1	0.450584485	0.565913043	0.56826742	0.642405063
2	0.505205976	0.497150373	0.568080739	0.509149131
3	0.275947966	0.380488736	0.597014925	0.234326824
4	0.345892992	0.406703911	0.337583748	0.280312907
5	0.380801172	0.426717386	0.466982195	0.27347196
6	0.353982301	0.455630127	0.478437905	0.222972973
Average	0.385402482	0.455433929	0.502727822	0.36043981
SD	0.081426361	0.067471433	0.096536849	0.173438295

Table 2 shows utterance duration rate of the remote participant, and Fig. 12 shows the average utterance duration rate of the remote participant under each experimental condition.

4.3 Utterance Overlaps Between the Remote Participants and Each of the Pair

As another index reflecting interactive activity, we performed a Friedman rank sum test for the amounts of utterance overlaps between the remote participants and the collocated pairs. We calculated utterance overlaps between each remote participant and each of the pair for each groups; thus, we have two overlap values for each group. The amounts of

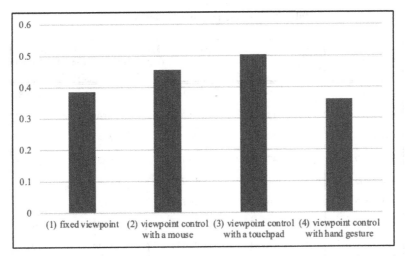

Fig. 12. Average utterance duration rate of the remote participant under each experimental condition

overlaps $O_{(g, r, p)}$ of all l utterances of each remote participant r and one of the collocated pair p for each group g were calculated as follows (u_x is xth utterance of the remote participant r, and o_x is the utterance overlap of r and p during u_x):

$$O_{(g,r,p)} = \sum_{x=1}^{l} o_x/u_x$$

This index represents the amount of overlapping occurrences between two speakers, covering not only utterance collisions in conflictive interactions such as in tough negotiating situations but also backchannels and agreement responses in active and collaborative interaction.

The Friedman rank sum test showed a significant difference among the conditions ($X^2_{(3)} = 19.134, p < .001$).

Pairwise comparisons using the Wilcoxon signed rank test with p value adjustment by the Bonferroni method showed significant differences between (1) fixed viewpoint system and (3) viewpoint control with a touchpad ($p < .021$), between (3) viewpoint control with a touchpad and (4) viewpoint control with hand gesture recognition ($p < 0.01$), and between (2) viewpoint control with a mouse and (4) viewpoint control with hand gesture recognition ($p < .006$). There was also a marginally significant difference between (1) fixed viewpoint system and (2) viewpoint control with a mouse ($p < .074$).

Table 3 shows the utterance overlap index values, and Fig. 13 shows the average overlap index value under each experimental condition.

4.4 Discussion of the Analyses

Although the preliminary results presented above are not sufficiently robust due to the small amount of data, they suggest that a remote collaboration system that provides a higher degree of freedom in viewpoint setting is a promising development. The analysis

Table 3. The utterance overlap index values

Overlap Index	(1) fixed viewpoint	(2) viewpoint control with a mouse	(3) viewpoint control with a touchpad	(4) viewpoint control with hand gesture
O(g1, r, p1)	10.371	12.42	5	10.682
O(g1, r, p2)	15.883	21.354	21.808	15.813
O(g2, r, p1)	16.295	20.331	27.284	13.338
O(g2, r, p2)	42.748	34.109	63.137	35.606
O(g3, r, p1)	11.383	15.707	61.501	10.595
O(g3, r, p2)	10.833	16.811	47.173	12.033
O(g4, r, p1)	17.113	25.839	25.143	14.107
O(g4, r, p2)	14.144	28.871	23.814	19.944
O(g5, r, p1)	14.917	21.411	19.636	5.716
O(g5, r, p2)	29.741	32.204	28.516	8.617
O(g6, r, p1)	0	29.079	50.591	0
O(g6, r, p2)	2.707	22.827	38.632	0.673
Average	15.51125	23.41358333	34.35291667	12.26033333
SD	11.36087882	6.75122469	17.90725886	9.37720769

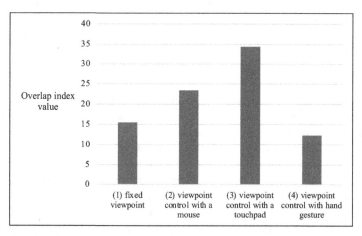

Fig. 13. Average overlap index value under each experimental condition

of the total utterance duration in Sect. 4.1 showed significant differences among the four conditions. Although the results of the pairwise comparisons were not significant, Fig. 10 shows the average duration of total utterances is largest under condition (3) "viewpoint control with a touchpad", suggesting the system helped to promote active engagement among participants. Viewpoint control using a mouse and hand gestures was associated with shorter total utterance durations, suggesting that those interfaces were not particularly helpful.

In the interview after experiment sessions, the remote participants commented that the touch panel interface was the easiest to use, and the hand gesture interface was the most difficult.

Contrary to our expectation, the analysis of the utterance duration rate of the remote participants did not show a significant difference among conditions. Although the graph shown in Fig. 12 suggests a similar tendency to that shown in Fig. 11, our assumption was not confirmed based on our preliminary investigations with a small data set.

The analysis of the utterance overlaps between the remote participants and the collocated pairs showed clear and interesting results. Use of the touchpad interface resulted in a significantly higher overlap index value than that of (1) fixed viewpoint system and (4) viewpoint control with hand gesture recognition. Use of the mouse control interface resulted in a significantly higher overlap index value than that of (4) viewpoint control with hand gesture recognition. The experiment participants were familiar to each other, and the task setting experiment there was little potential for conflict: they were not required to narrow down their list of outcomes; thus, their interaction showed few negotiating utterances indicative of conflict. Rather, agreement responses and backchannels were frequently observed, showing the active and friendly nature of their collaboration. It is likely that (3) viewpoint control with a touchpad will contribute to the realization of a friendly collaborative environment for performing creative tasks, as demonstrated in our experiment.

However, as the sample size was very small, we are now recording new sessions to obtain more reliable results.

5 Summary

We presented the design and evaluation process for several hybrid collaboration support systems that provides a greater degree of freedom in selecting or controlling the viewpoints setting of remote office images. Based on the previous psychological, HCI, and CSCW studies, we designed a trial system that was examined in expert-led workshops using the systems in a remote office collaboration setting as a first step. Then we held a series of evaluation sessions in a more concrete and detailed application setting in which participants engaged in creative collaborative discussion. As the third step, we evaluated several versions of our systems in a creative collaboration setting and subjected the data obtained to objective and quantitative analysis. Although the objective evaluation process in the third step was still in a preliminary stage, the results showed a promising direction for the interaction support systems with viewpoint control using quantitative indices, and suggested the effectiveness of such design and evaluation processes.

Acknowledgments. The work presented in Sect. 2 was supported by "The Demonstration Project for Smart City Services Using 5G and Other Advanced Technologies (5G and Other Services) in the Nishi-Shinjuku Area in FY2021" of the Tokyo Metropolitan Government. The work presented in Sect. 4 was supported by the Council for Science, Technology and Innovation(CSTI), Cross-ministerial Strategic Innovation Promotion Program (SIP), the 3rd period of SIP "Creation of new ways of learning and working in a post-COVID-19 era" Grant Number JPJ012347 (Funding agency: JST).

Disclosure of Interests. The authors have no competing interests to declare that are relevant to the content of this article.

References

1. Ipsen, C., van Veldhoven, M., Kirchner, K., Hansen, J.P.: Six key advantages and disadvantages of working from home in Europe during COVID-19. Int. J. Environ. Res. Public Health **18**(4), 1826 (2021). https://doi.org/10.3390/ijerph18041826
2. Battisti, E., Alfiero, S., Leonidou, E.: Remote working and digital transformation during the COVID-19 pandemic: economic-financial impacts and psychological drivers for employees. J. Bus. Res. **150**, 38–50 (2022). https://doi.org/10.1016/j.jbusres.2022.06.010
3. Strickland, L.H., Guild, P.D., Barefoot, J.C., Paterson, S.A.: Teleconferencing and leadership emergence. Hum. Relat. **31**(7), 583–596 (1978)
4. Heath, C., Luff, P.: Disembodied conduct: communication through video in a multi-media office environment. In: Proceedings of the SIGCHI Conference on Human Factors in Computing Systems (CHI 1991). Association for Computing Machinery, pp. 99–103, New York, NY, USA (1991). https://doi.org/10.1145/108844.108859
5. Bos, N., Olson, J., Gergle, D., Olson, G., Wright, Z.: Effects of four computer-mediated communications channels on trust development. In: Proceedings of the SIGCHI Conference on Human Factors in Computing Systems (CHI 2002), pp. 135–140 (2002). https://doi.org/10.1145/503376.503401
6. Ruppel, E.K., Gross, C., Stoll, A., Peck, B.S., Allen, M., Kim, S.Y.: Reflecting on connecting: meta-analysis of differences between computer-mediated and face-to-face self-disclosure. J. Comput.-Mediat. Comm. **22**, 18–34 (2017). https://doi.org/10.1111/jcc4.1217
7. Umata, I., Niida, S.: Perspective settings in online interaction: user behavior observation of online interaction support system with perspective selection function. In: Human Communication Group Symposium 2022 HCG2022 C-3-3 (2022). (In Japanese)
8. Torrance, E.P.: The Manifest: A Guide to developing a creative career. Library of Congress Cataloging-in-Publication Data, USA (2002)
9. Mayuko Matsuoka, M., Mizumoto, T.: Toward a better discussion in English: a quantitative perspective of feedback. In: Proceedings of the 26th Korea TESOL International Conference (KOTESOL), pp. 175–180 (2018). https://koreatesol.org/sites/default/files/pdf_publications/KOTESOL.2018--Extended.Summaries...pdf

Physiologically Expressive Robotic Hand as a Lifelike Presence

Tomoko Yonezawa[1,2,3](✉), Xiaoshun Meng[1], and Xin Wan[1]

[1] Kansai University, 2-1-1, Ryozenji-Cho, Takatsuki, Osaka 569-1095, Japan
[2] ATR Interaction Science Laboratories, 2-2-2, Hikaridai, Soraku-gun, Kyoto 619-0288, Japan
[3] Keio University, 5322, Endo, Fujisawa, Kanagawa 252-0882, Japan
yone@kansai-u.ac.jp

Abstract. In this study, we propose a robot hand that demonstrates a combination of various voluntary grips and involuntary physiological expressions on the skin as a tactile expression representing emotions. The robot hand is implemented using skin expressions such as variable gripping strength and speed, goosebumps, perspiration, and temperature, which can be tactually perceived by the user. The focus is on how human impressions of the robot change in human–robot touch communication, and we evaluated the combination of various conditions. By combining involuntary physiological expressions on the skin (goosebumps, sweating, and body temperature) with the grip of a hand robot as a tactile voluntary expression, we investigated the influence of the difference in expression between the robot's fear–stress context and the normal context on the impression of the robot. We particularly focused on how the robot's tangible expressions affect the user's emotions, such as fears corresponding to the experimental context, and we analyzed whether this would lead to a sense of empathy, discomfort, etc. We confirmed that the user's empathy, which could not be elicited by involuntary expressions alone, tended to be elicited by a combination of voluntary and involuntary expressions and that this tendency differed depending on the type of involuntary expressions.

Keywords: Physiological expressions · Robotic hand · Gripping motions · Crossmodal expressions · Emotion and empathy

1 Introduction

Humans possess intelligence and sociability that manifest in gestures, facial expressions, and speech. Consequently, they sometimes make gestures and statements contrary to their instinctive emotions, such as lying or behaving in a manner different from their true feelings, as expressed through a combination of complex modalities. In other words, humans sometimes hide their true feelings, going against their biological mechanisms. However, they cannot completely conceal them due to various physiological responses, inadvertently revealing more about themselves than intended. This study is intended to incorporate such involuntary physiological responses into a robot, creating a communication robot that effectively conveys underlying truths.

A handshake is a greeting and form of contact among people meeting for the first time in many cultures and is widely used to promote mutual understanding and communication. Additionally, when humans hold hands in various situations, slight changes in the gripping power and the surface state reveal the other's feelings. The human hand is hyper-sensory and expressive, making it an effective tool for conveying emotions and intentions. Subtle movements and pressure of the hand powerfully transmit nonverbal information, especially about emotions and moods.

Human-robot interaction has been developed to make realistic human-like robots, such as androids, and animal-like robots. On the other hand, such robots are not considered to have the presence of a living being. To achieve really affective social touch [1], we proposed and investigated the combination of involuntary physiological expressions on the skin (goosebumps, sweating, and body temperature) with the grip of a hand robot as a tactile voluntary expression to show a real feeling as a bodily emotion.

2   Related Research

Tactile communication is one of the most primitive channels known as mother-child or mother-fetus communication before verbal communication [2, etc.]. There has been much research on tactile communication robots [3, etc.] in recent years.

Nakanishi et al. [4] focused on how human emotions are conveyed through different types of touch to a robot and how the robot responds to these emotions, and their findings demonstrated that robots can understand human touch and exhibit emotional responses, indicating an advancement in the robot's ability to interact emotionally with humans. The study combining tactile and vocal speech by a robot [5] showed that tactile interaction alone could elicit positive emotional responses and that their combination caused positive emotions stronger than every single expression. The results were evidenced by higher physiological responses measured through facial muscle activity (zygomaticus major EMG) and skin conductance levels (SCL). This implies that tactile interaction is an effective means of emotional communication, and its combination with vocal interaction can amplify this effect from physiological aspects.

Human skin is one of the primary interfaces between our internal and external environments [6]. Exposure to external factors, such as not only air temperature and toxins but also internal psychological factors and emotional states, results in various symptomatic expressions on the skin. As 30% of dermatology patients exhibit signs of psychological issues [7], there are complex and deep interactions between skin and mental states.

Hence, we advocate that physiological expressions on robots' skin should be essential in touch communication, which conveys internal states and brings about a deep mutual understanding. Focusing on the involuntary physiological reactions like goosebumps, sweating, and trembling displayed on the robot's skin, our aim was to develop a system that could convey the instinctual emotions of a robotic hand by regulating both involuntary and voluntary expressions. We explore how these elements can elicit a feeling of lifelikeness and evoke empathetic emotions in human-robot communication.

3   Robotic Hand System with a Sense of Life

3.1   System Overview

For this paper, we investigated a mechanism that allows users to tactually perceive a robot's emotional expression through the voluntary grip manner of the robotic hand's fingers on the user's hand and the involuntary physiological phenomena on the robot's skin in hand-in-hand communication.

First, we proposed emotional expressions of a robotic hand, combining voluntary expressions such as the gripping of the robot hand with three types of involuntary physiological expressions embedded in the skin on the back of the hand. The system combines a gripping actuation unit of the robotic hand [11], a goosebumps actuation unit [9,10, etc.], a sweat actuation unit [9,10, etc.], and a temperature actuation unit. The robot hand was created by modifying a commercially available toy, the Monster Magic Hand from Kawada [13]. A PC running Windows 10 OS connects to an AVR controller (Arduino UNO) to control the hand grip and physiological expressions on its surface. A speaker is connected to the PC to make the robot's voice. All implemented units, as follows, are placed together as an integrated system.

3.2   Gripping Actuation Unit [11]

Figure 1 illustrates the simple configuration of the robotic hand. Each of the four fingers of the robotic hand, excluding the thumb, has two joints, allowing simultaneous inward bending from the index finger to the little finger. The four fingers bend by pulling the finger base plate toward the arm. The servomotor (GWS servo, S03T, 2bbMG, JR type, speed: 0.33 s/60 °C) installed on the arm of the robotic hand pulls the nylon string (HW 507, bobbin wire tegus) tied to the base plate of the four fingers to control the bending motion of the fingers in a gripping action. The extent of the bending based on the pulling angle of the servomotor becomes the grip strength. The timing for gripping and releasing actions determines the hand-holding duration.

The strength varies according to the servomotor's operation, ranging in from 0 to intensity 90 (MAX), which corresponds to the degrees of the servomotor. The torque applied to the back of the user's hand is ranges from 1.57 [N] to 3.73 [N] based on the conversion formula 0.0102 kgf (kilogram-force) = 1 [N]). The grip duration is defined as the time from the completion of the grip action to the beginning of the release action, ranging from 0.5 s to 10 s. Specifically, the arousal and pleasure of the robot in Russell's emotional circumplex [14] change the strength and duration of the grip manner for each in the tentative design.

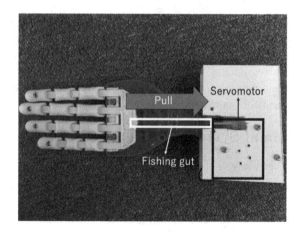

Fig. 1. Configuration of the Robotic Hand

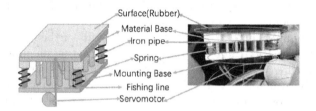

Fig. 2. Structure of the Goosebump Unit

3.3 Physiologically Expressive Units

Goosebumps Actuation Unit [9,10, etc.] The structure of the developed goosebump unit is shown in Fig. 2, and the appearance of the goosebump protrusions is shown in Fig. 3. To generate tactile stimuli perceived as independent protrusions, the intervals between each protrusion were set to 4.5 mm based on the tactile resolution [8]. The goosebumps unit is embedded in the robotic hand. The 50×36 [mm] surface of the unit is covered with silicone material and processed rubber, which allows 36 same-height protrusions, arranged in six vertical and six horizontal rows, to rise simultaneously. The protrusions are created by pushing up multiple iron pipes (outer diameter: 2.1 mm) from inside the unit. The iron pipes are fixed to a mounting base, and a servomotor placed beneath the mounting base operates the material base up and down. When the servomotor pulls the fishing line attached to the material base downward, the iron pipes press against and protrude through the rubber surface to express the goosebumps. When the traction of the servo motor stops, the rebound force of springs installed at the four corners of the unit pushes the material base up, causing the goosebumps to disappear.

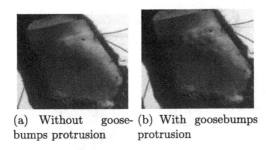

(a) Without goose-
bumps protrusion

(b) With goosebumps
protrusion

Fig. 3. Generating Goosebumps Covered with a Silicone Robber Sheet

Sweat Actuation Unit [9,10, etc.] To achieve various sweating levels on the skin, from slightly moistened to sweat drops or flow, we prepared multiple sweat glands based on previous research [12]. Figure 4 shows the sweating system structure. The sweat glands were placed in the goosebumps pipe. Figure 5 shows an actual view of the system. The pump section, which increases the air pressure inside a container and pushes out water, is installed outside the stuffed toy robot, and a soft silicone tube with an inner diameter of 0.5 mm and an outer diameter of 1mm is passed through the iron pipes inside the goosebump unit. To give it the strength to be fixed to the surface material while maintaining a size comparable to human eccrine sweat glands, a harder silicone tube with an inner diameter of 0.4 mm and an outer diameter of 0.6 mm was embedded into the surface material. The harder silicone tube was connected to the silicone tubes inside the iron pipes with a diameter of 0.5 mm. The average speed of sweat is 0.0625 ml/s, and the amount of sweating changes depending on the duration of water release. The pump output needs to be sufficient to be distributed across numerous sweat glands; therefore, in this implementation, the number of sweat glands was limited to five, and they were set in dispersed positions. To represent the robot's sweating, the pump should operate for at least 1.6 s.

Temperature Actuation Unit. To represent body temperature, a Peltier device (30×30 mm, TES1-12705) was placed on the palm of the robot hand to conduct heat to a heat dissipation film (Fig. 7).

4 Evaluation

We investigated whether users could perceive the emotions of a robot by combining the gripping action of the robot hand with involuntary expressions of goosebumps, sweating, and temperature. We conducted three experiments combining the gripping expression and each involuntary expression. The common factors in the experiments were 1) the gripping manner (strong-quick, middle, weak-slow) and 2) the scenario contexts (with or without stress). The evaluation items for all experiments were scared, cold, tense, discomfort, and empathetic

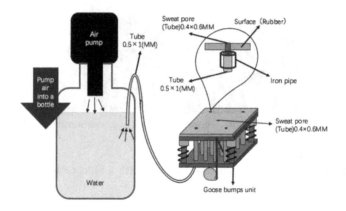

Fig. 4. Structure of Sweating Unit

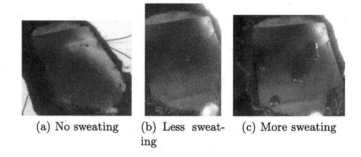

(a) No sweating   (b) Less sweat-   (c) More sweating
                    ing

Fig. 5. Manifestation of Sweating (on five locations of the black surface material)

feelings of the participants; scared and cold feelings of the robot; and the robot's expression change.

Experimental Hypotheses: **Hypothesis 1:** If the voluntary and involuntary expressions of the robot do not align, users will feel a sense of discomfort toward the robot's expressions. **Hypothesis 2:** If the voluntary and involuntary expressions of the robot are aligned, the robot will be perceived as more human-like, consequently evoking a sense of empathy. **Hypothesis 3:** The participants' emotions will change (aligning more closely to the robot's tendencies) based on the robot's expressions.

The participants were informed about the experiment, which used a plush robot, under informed consent, including the provision that they could stop the experiment at any time for any reason. To prevent preconceived notions, detailed functions of the robot were not disclosed in this explanation. No participants wished to withdraw before or during the experiment.

Common Factors in Three Experimental Conditions: We prepared the factors of A) the context in two levels: with (Co1) or without stress (Co2), and B) the expressive strength in the grip in three levels: strong and quick (Gr1), normal (Gr2), and weak and slow (Gr3).

Fig. 6. Appearance of the Sweating on the Robot Hand's Skin

Fig. 7. Structure of Temperature Unit

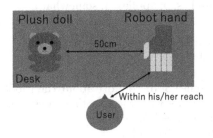

Fig. 8. Experimental Environment Settings

Here, strong (Gr1), normal (Gr2), and weak (Gr3) mean the grip with 1.57 [N] (40 [deg.]), 3.73 [N] (60 [deg.]), and 5.40 [N] (80 [deg.]) strengths, respectively. Quick (Gr1), normal (Gr2), and slow (Gr3) reflect a change of strength in 0.6, 1.2, and 1.8 s, respectively.

The context factor was set by two dialogues. The scripts began as follows:

– Plush Toy: "Hey, can you see Mr. A?"
– Experimental Robot Hand: "What?"

The script with stress (Co1) continued:

– Plush Toy: "Behind you, there's a demon."

The script without stress (Co2) continued:

– Plush Toy: "Today is a nice day, isn't it?"

Experimental Environment: In the experimental room, the air conditioning was set to 26 °C. Figure 6 shows the placement settings of the robotic hand and a plush bear toy as the other presence.

Experimental Procedure: Participants were instructed to sit 10 cm from the experimental desk, which held the plush toy and the robot hand, and were asked not to move or lift them. Before the experiment, they were instructed to grip the robot hand without exerting force, ensuring that their thumb touched the back of the robot hand. They were also instructed to keep gripping the robotic hand and to stroke the back of the robotic hand with their thumb continuously from the start to the end signal of the experimental session. The conversational scripts were output in a voice corresponding to the context, and the robot's involuntary and voluntary grip expressions were presented based on the experimental conditions after the conversation.

To facilitate the perception of a large amount of sweating and high temperature, the robot hand was programmed to grip the user's hand for 5 s initially, according to the operation duration of the goosebumps for 5 s and the sweating and temperature for 8 s.

Evaluation Items: The evaluation used a 5-point Likert scale (degrees to which each evaluation item applies, 5: applies, 4: somewhat applies, 3: neutral, 2: somewhat does not apply, 1: does not apply) for each evaluation item as below:

Qa: The user felt scared.
Qb: The user felt cold.
Qc: The user felt tense.
Qd: The user felt a sense of discomfort about the robot's expression.
Qe: The user felt empathy with the robot's expression.
Qf: The robot seemed to feel scared.
Qg: The robot seemed to feel cold.
Qh: The user sensed a change in the robot's expression.

4.1   Goosebumps Expression Experiment

Experimental Conditions: There are three factors, as follows. Factor A is the robot's gripping expression factor assigned as A1: Gr1, A2: Gr2, and A3: Gr3. Factor B is the goosebumps expression factor: the height of the goosebumps at B1: 2 mm (protrusions elevate) or B2: 0 mm (disappear) from the initial state of 1 mm protrusions. Factor C is the stressed context: C1: Co1, with stress and C2: Co2, without stress. The 12 conditions involving the three factors were investigated in a within-subjects experimental design.

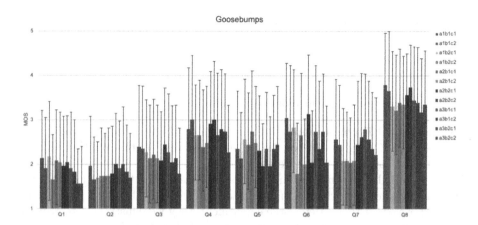

Fig. 9. Averages of MOS Values: Goosebumps

Table 1. Analysis of MOS Values: Goosebumps

		Self Frightened		Self Cold		Self Tense		Robot Frightened	
		f	p	f	p	f	p	f	p
Main Effects	A	3.969	**<0.026**	0.203	0.817	0.541	0.469	0.296	0.745
	B	3.535	0.073	0.117	0.735	0.843	0.368	0.885	0.357
	C	1.325	0.262	0.013	0.908	0.541	0.496	18.864	**<0.003**
1st-order	AB	0.290	0.749	1.342	0.271	0.435	0.650	3.283	**<0.046**
Interaction	AC	1.517	0.230	0.489	0.661	0.830	0.442	0.541	0.586
	BC	0.023	0.881	0.657	0.426	0.129	0.723	3.714	0.067
2nd-order Interaction	ABC	0.572	0.568	1.056	0.356	0.704	0.499	0.388	0.6805

		Robot Cold		Robot Empathy		Robot Expression Change		Robot Discomfort	
		f	p	f	p	f	p	f	p
Main Effects	A	1.136	0.330	0.211	0.810	0.779	0.465	0.305	0.738
	B	0.468	0.500	0.006	0.939	1.019	0.323	0.029	0.865
	C	4.294	**0.020**	3.027	0.059	1.924	0.159	2.797	0.072
1st-order	AB	3.676	**0.033**	4.969	**0.011**	4.366	**0.018**	4.412	**0.017**
Interaction	AC	0.285	0.753	0.168	0.846	0.274	0.761	0.704	0.499
	BC	0.375	0.546	0.920	0.347	0.467	0.501	0.994	0.329
2nd-order Interaction	ABC	0.002	0.997	0.710	0.497	0.054	0.947	0.588	0.559

Display in bold for p<.05

Results: The results of the repeated-measures three-factor ANOVA for the counterbalanced experiment results are shown in Fig. 9 and Table 1. Here, we tested the potential for emotion transmission and empathy through the combination of the proposed robot hand's goosebumps expression changes and its voluntary gripping actions.

Effectiveness in Conveying Fear: For the evaluation item "Qa: The user felt scared," significant differences were found related to Factor A (the robot hand's gripping condition). Furthermore, multiple comparisons using Ryan's method (for main effects) indicated A2>A3.

For the evaluation item "Qf: The robot seemed to feel scared," significant differences were found related to Factor C (the robot's state), suggesting that the fear emotion conveyed by the robot's conversation content was effective. Additionally, in the simple main effects of the AB interaction, multiple comparisons showed B1>B2 when the gripping action was A1.

For the evaluation item "Qg: The robot seemed to feel cold," no significant main effects were found. However, in the simple main effects of the AB interaction, multiple comparisons showed A3>A2 when the goosebumps expression was B1.

Effectiveness in Provoking Empathy: For the evaluation item "Qe: The user felt empathy with the robot's expression," no significant main effects were found. However, in the simple main effects of the AB interaction, multiple comparisons showed B1>B2 when the gripping action was A2.

For the evaluation item "Qh: The user sensed a change in the robot's expression", no significant main effects were found. However, in the simple main effects of the AB interaction, multiple comparisons showed B1>B2 when the gripping action was A2.

Effectiveness in Feeling Discomfort: For the evaluation item "Qd: The user felt a sense of discomfort with the robot's expression," no significant main effects were found. However, in the simple main effects of the AB interaction, multiple comparisons showed B2>B1 when the gripping action was A2.

Discussions Concerning the Grip and Goosebumps Expressions: Results showed that changes in the robot hand's gripping action affected participants' perception of fear. However, no significant difference was found in conveying the robot's fear, suggesting that the change in gripping action alone might be insufficient for expressing fear, similar to the change in goosebumps.

However, the combination of gripping action and goosebumps was recognized to transmit and changing emotions. In condition A2, B1 compared to B2 showed the robot's expression to be more empathetic. This supports Hypothesis 2. Additionally, participants felt a sense of discomfort toward the robot's expression. Multiple comparisons revealed this specifically in condition A2, in which B2>B1. This suggests that the participants might have perceived the combined expressions as inconsistent, leading to discomfort, confirming Hypothesis 1.

However, the combination of expressions did not affect the participants' emotional changes. This might be due to the experimental environment making it difficult for participants to understand the robot's varied expressions of fear. Therefore, it is considered necessary to examine the experimental environment in future studies.

Summary: In this experiment, we investigated whether combining a robot hand's gripping action, goosebump expression changes, and the robot's situation would help users understand the robot's emotions and feel empathy toward its expressions.

The results showed that while the voluntary expression of the robot hand's gripping action and the involuntary affective expression of goosebumps alone might be insufficient to transmit the robot's emotions or elicit user empathy, the combination of voluntary and involuntary expressions (particularly in condition A2, in which B1 was compared to B2) successfully induced empathy in users. Additionally, when users perceived these expressions as inconsistent, they felt a sense of discomfort toward the robot.

The extent to which participants empathized with the robot's expressions likely depended heavily on individual differences in the robot's movements and expressions, as well as the participants' personal perceptions. The effectiveness of the gripping action in conveying fear appears limited, suggesting that fear, like other emotions, is complex and difficult to fully convey through a single action.

Future studies should reconsider the experimental environment and aspects such as the control range of goosebump protrusions in the system.

4.2   Evaluation of Robot's Skin Perspiration Expression

Experimental Conditions: There are three factors, as follows. Factor A is the stressed context: A1: Co1, with stress and A2: Co2, without stress. Factor B is the perspiration expression factor. The amount of perspiration was set to B1:

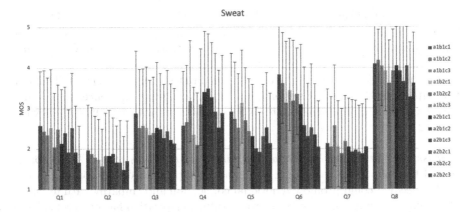

Fig. 10. Averages of MOS Values: Sweat

low, 0.0625 (ml/s), in 1.6 s, and B2: high, 0.0625 (ml/s), in 8 s. Factor C is the robot's gripping expression factor, assigned as C1: `Gr1`, C2: `Gr2`, and C3: `Gr3`. The 12 conditions involving the three factors were investigated in a within-subjects experimental design.

Results: The results of the repeated-measures three-factor ANOVA for the counterbalanced experiment results are shown in Fig. 10 and Table 2. We tested the potential for emotion transmission and empathy through the combination of the proposed robot hand's perspiration amount and voluntary gripping action.

Table 2. Analysis of MOS Values: Sweat

		Self Frightened		Self Cold		Self Tense		Robot Frightened	
		f	p	f	p	f	p	f	p
Main Effects	A	2.868	0.104	0.364	0.552	1.221	0.281	24.012	**<0.001**
	B	1.102	0.305	4.685	**<0.041**	2.055	0.167	3.955	0.059
	C	2.160	0.127	0.339	0.714	1.088	0.345	2.144	0.129
1st-order	AB	0.010	0.921	0.006	0.938	0.164	0.689	0.328	0.572
Interaction	AC	1.918	0.158	0.067	0.935	0.257	0.774	0.261	0.771
	BC	2.122	0.131	1.157	0.323	0.047	0.954	1.171	0.319
2nd-order Interaction	ABC	1.000	0.376	0.031	0.969	0.222	0.802	0.801	0.455

		Robot Cold		Robot Empathy		Robot Expression Change		Robot Discomfort	
		f	p	f	p	f	p	f	p
Main Effects	A	2.452	0.137	8.049	**0.009**	2.389	0.136	3.551	0.073
	B	1.116	0.302	1.116	0.302	3.693	0.067	9.940	**0.004**
	C	1.908	0.160	1.908	0.160	1.695	0.195	1.934	0.156
1st-order	AB	0.613	0.442	1.175	0.290	0.117	0.736	1.099	0.3059
Interaction	AC	0.743	0.481	0.545	0.583	0.952	0.393	2.730	0.076
	BC	0.016	0.984	0.253	0.777	2.769	0.073	1.302	0.282
2nd-order Interaction	ABC	0.454	0.638	0.927	0.403	0.125	0.883	0.170	0.844

Display in bold for p<.05

For all evaluation items, no significant differences were found in the robot hand's gripping expressions or any interactions.

Regarding main effects: For the evaluation items "The user felt cold" (Qb) and "The user felt a sense of discomfort with the robot's expression" (Qd), significant differences were found only for the perspiration factor, with Qb and Qd showing B1>B2.

For the evaluation items "The robot seemed to feel scared" (Qf) and "The user felt empathy with the robot's expression" (Qe), significant differences were found only for the robot's internal state expression factor, with Qf and Qe showing A1>A2.

Discussions Concerning the Grip and Perspiration Expressions: The combination of the robot hand's gripping action and perspiration expression was evaluated to see if it could promote emotional connection and empathy with humans. Generally, and in previous experimental results, perspiration has been considered indicative of heat or fear.

However, in this experiment, the change in the amount of perspiration did not influence any aspect other than "the feeling of discomfort in the robot's expression." Additionally, the change in the gripping action did not show significant differences in any of the evaluation items. This suggests that the expression of perspiration, unrelated to the robot's perceived fear, caused confusion and discomfort among the experiment participants.

One reason for this could be that the set amount of perspiration was insufficient to convey varying levels of fear clearly. In this context, empathy refers to understanding the fear expressed by the robot's state expressions. The effectiveness of internal state expressions was shown in the empathy items, suggesting that while participants understood the robot's emotional expressions, these expressions did not significantly impact their emotions.

Summary: In this experiment, we investigated whether the combination of a robot hand's perspiration amount and its voluntary gripping action could transmit emotions and elicit empathy for the robot's expressions.

The results revealed that it was not the gripping action of the robot hand itself but the perspiration and the robot's state expression that influenced specific evaluation items. The fact that expressing perspiration under all conditions caused discomfort among participants suggests a mismatch between the environment and physiological expressions. Further investigation is needed to determine whether the expression of fear was not accurately conveyed through changes in perspiration amount or if the use of the robot's perspiration to express fear was intuitively difficult to understand.

4.3   Experiment on Perspiration Expression Related to Temperature

Experimental Conditions: There are three factors, as follows. Factor A is the stressed context: A1: Co1, with stress and A2: Co2, without stress. Factor B is the temperature expression factor: B1: The temperature rises to 35 °C, B2: temperature maintains 30 °C, and B3: temperature drops to 25 °C, from the initial temperature of 30 °C. Factor C is the robot's gripping expression factor, assigned as C1: Gr1, C2: Gr2, and C3: Gr3. The 12 conditions involving the three factors were investigated in a within-subjects experimental design.

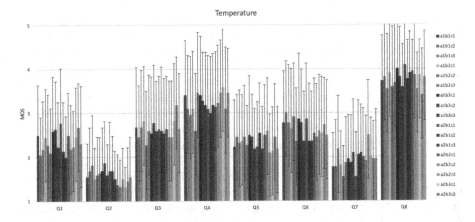

Fig. 11. Averages of MOS Values: Temperature

Table 3. Analysis of MOS Values: Temperature

		Self Frightened		Self Cold		Self Tense		Robot Frightened	
		f	p	f	p	f	p	f	p
Main Effects	A	0.095	0.761	4.686	**<0.042**	0.279	0.603	0.909	0.351
	B	1.932	0.158	1.030	0.366	1.493	0.236	0.409	0.667
	C	5.621	**<0.007**	0.935	0.401	0.337	0.716	1.121	0.335
1st-order	AB	0.030	0.971	0.656	0.524	0.784	0.463	0.405	0.670
Interaction	AC	0.025	0.975	0.225	0.800	0.838	0.440	0.927	0.404
	BC	1.323	0.268	0.223	0.925	1.21	0.313	0.180	0.948
2nd-order Interaction	ABC	0.589	0.672	0.745	0.564	0.062	0.993	0.838	0.505
		Robot Cold		Robot Empathy		Robot Expression Change		Robot Discomfort	
		f	p	f	p	f	p	f	p
Main Effects	A	0.823	0.374	0.049	0.827	0.191	0.667	0.192	0.666
	B	0.152	0.859	0.192	0.826	0.198	0.821	1.837	0.172
	C	4.294	**0.020**	3.027	0.059	1.924	0.159	2.797	0.072
1st-order	AB	1.991	0.149	0.227	0.798	1.127	0.334	0.520	0.598
Interaction	AC	0.507	0.606	0.402	0.671	0.283	0.755	0.291	0.749
	BC	1.125	0.350	0.211	0.932	0.235	0.918	0.883	0.478
2nd-order Interaction	ABC	0.586	0.673	0.394	0.813	0.774	0.564	0.954	0.437

Display in bold for p<.05

Results: The results of the repeated-measures three-factor ANOVA for the counterbalanced experiment results are shown in Fig. 11 and Table 3.

Regarding the main effects: For the evaluation item "The user felt scared" (Qa), significant differences were found due to changes in the robot hand's gripping expression. Moreover, multiple comparisons using Ryan's method (for main effects) indicated C1>C3.

For the evaluation item "The user felt cold" (Qb), significant differences were found only due to the robot's state expression.

For the evaluation item "The robot seemed to feel cold" (Qg), significant differences were found only due to changes in the robot hand's gripping action. Ryan's method of multiple comparisons (for main effects) showed C3>C2.

Discussions for the Grip and Temperature Expressions: The experiment showed that a strong, fast movement of the robot hand might be a factor in inducing fear in participants. Furthermore, changes in the robot's displayed state of fear suggest that it was not the robot's internal feeling of fear that affected the participants, but rather the robot's quick movements that caused surprise or fear.

Finally, changes in the robot's skin temperature did not influence empathy toward or sensory transmission from the robot. This could be due to the temperature range of 25, 30, and 35 °C being relatively comfortable or indistinguishable for humans. Therefore, it may be necessary to incorporate a more distinct sensation of hot and cold in future experiments.

5   Discussions

5.1   Possibilities of Proposed Method

In this experiment, we conducted three tests to examine the impact of the combination of a robot's gripping action and physiological expressions on human emotions and empathy.

Firstly, by combining goosebumps expression with the gripping action, we found that the changes in the robot hand's gripping action influenced participants' emotions, eliciting empathy and discomfort. However, no significant difference was observed in conveying the robot's fear, suggesting that changes in gripping action alone, similar to goosebumps changes, might be insufficient for expressing fear. Nonetheless, the combination of gripping action and goosebumps was recognized in terms of transmitting and changing emotions, with some combinations eliciting empathy toward the robot's expressions. Therefore, it is believed that complex, combined expressions are more effective at eliciting human empathy than singular expressions.

Moreover, the combination of gripping action and perspiration showed that changes in the amount of perspiration caused confusion and discomfort in participants, unrelated to the robot's perceived fear. Additionally, changes in the robot's skin temperature did not significantly affect empathy or sensory transmission, possibly due to the temperature range being relatively comfortable or indistinguishable for humans.

These results indicate the potential for users to empathize with a robot's emotional transmission and expressions through the combination of physiological expressions and gripping action. However, when users perceive a mismatch between the robot's voluntary and involuntary expressions, it can diminish the persuasiveness of the robot's emotional expressions and cause confusion or discomfort. Therefore, it is important to consider how the combination of a robot's voluntary and involuntary expressions align or conflict from a human perspective.

5.2 Limitations and Prospects

On the other hand, the outcomes can be explored more deeply by improving robots' skin expressions for further enhancement and accuracy. In particular, it is important to explore methods of capturing the nuances of human emotions influenced by various cultural and social backgrounds and expressing them as robot skin reactions.

Regarding the physiological expressions on the robot's skin in the experimental environment, future experiments need to investigate whether some variations in these expressions failed to accurately convey the robot's emotions or whether the nuances of emotions that the robot aimed to convey could not be sufficiently or adequately expressed in the set experimental environment.

The outcomes are based on the limited design of the proposed robot, especially in the designed range of the expressions for each involuntary and voluntary modality. Changing the temperature range in the experiment may also change the effectiveness. Moreover, the shape and communication context in the experiments were in a limited design. If we replace the robotic hand with other shapes such as plush toys, we should carefully examine experiments in different tactile communication contexts.

It is necessary to build a guideline for representing emotions through involuntary physiological expressions on the skin based on the robot's honest mind while maintaining an artificial emotion as a public stance. This approach allows the barely concealed true feelings to become subtly apparent. Moreover, considering the trade-off between intuitiveness and eeriness that can coexist, it is essential to design guidelines regarding the degree of application and the design itself.

Furthermore, by adding the functionality to read skin data of the object the robot touches, it becomes possible to infer the emotions of the other party. This will allow for a more accurate understanding of human emotions and their reflection on the robot's skin, potentially making interactions between humans and robots more dynamic and emotionally rich.

5.3 Safety and Security Concerns and Countermeasure Guidelines

Research into the ethical and social aspects of emotional expression robots is important. It is essential to explore how the emotional expressions of robots influence human emotions and behaviors and to establish guidelines for the appropriate use of these technologies. For example, touch between humans and robots was discussed in [15].

New technologies such as the proposed system should be constantly involved and updated in agreement with such guidelines. Partner robots with enhanced authenticity via strong empathetic interaction may be abused at the same time that empathy is secured. Similarly, robots that express physiology may be more intuitive and more prone to elicit disgust. To determine the optimal values of these trade-offs, it will be necessary to further clarify the influence of robots with physiological representations on human society. Therefore, it is necessary to carry out detailed, long-term examinations as a continuation of this research.

We should consider the uncanny valley [16,17], which is known as a problem in human-like robots. If robots express physiological expressions that mimic those of living beings, it may cause highly unpleasant and disgusting feelings. Such feelings may damage the user's trust in the robot. On the other hand, this physiological expression also suggests a system expressing excessive intimacy of interaction with the other party. For instance, there is a risk that people may feel sexually uncomfortable with the system. To avoid the feeling, the system design should emphasize the genderless nature of the robot, assuming an animal-like or toddler-like presence.

Next, fake-empathetic expressions with fake-physiological phenomena may elevate the reliability of the robot's emotion. If the robot shows fake emotions that deceive the user, there is a concern that robots may become tools for fraud. From the viewpoint of security, features that enhance authenticity are important for building relationships with users through expressions of attachment, but they must be sufficiently secure and protected so as not to be edited by a third party.

6 Conclusion

In this study, we implemented emotional expressions by combining various voluntary gripping actions (grip strength and speed) of a robot hand with involuntary physiological expressions on the skin (goosebumps, perspiration, temperature changes).

We also examined the impact of the robot hand's gripping actions and physiological expressions on participants' emotions and empathy. The results showed that when each skin expression or gripping action was presented alone, it did not significantly influence the participants' emotions or empathy. However, certain combinations of gripping action and goosebumps elicited empathy toward the robot's expressions.

Therefore, we suggested that complex, combined methods evoke human empathy more effectively than singular expressions. Additionally, when participants felt that the robot's internal emotional state of did not align with its expressions, the persuasiveness of the robot's emotional expressions could diminish and cause confusion or discomfort. This indicates the importance of consistency between voluntary and involuntary expressions in affecting participants' empathy and understanding of emotions.

In the future, we need to evaluate by combining multiple involuntary expressions for further enriched expressions of robots' physical emotion.

Acknowledgement. This research was supported in part by JST Moonshot R&D Program (Grant Number JPMJMS2215), JST CREST Grant Number JPMJCR18A1 Japan, and JSPS KAKENHI 23K11202, 23K11278, 21K11968. JPMJMS2215 supported investigating the proposed system's safety and security, and the others supported the system implementation and the experiment.

References

1. Cooney, M., Nishio, K., Ishiguro, H.: Affectionate interaction with a small humanoid robot capable of recognizing social touch behavior. ACM Trans. Interact. Intell. Syst. **4**(4), 1–32 (2014)
2. Hertenstein, M.J.: Touch: its communicative functions in infancy. Hum. Dev. **45**(2), 70–94 (2002)
3. Argall, B.D., Billard, A.G.: A survey of tactile human-robot interactions. Robot. Auton. Syst. **58**(10), 1159–1176 (2010)
4. Andreasson, R., Alenljung, B., Billing, E., Lowe, R.: Affective touch in human-robot interaction: conveying emotion to the Nao robot. Int. J. Soc. Robot. **10**, 473–491 (2018)
5. Sawabe, T., et al.: Robot touch with speech boosts positive emotions. Sci. Rep. **12**(1), 6884 (2022)
6. Osman, O.T.: The skin as a mode of communication. Expert Rev. Dermatol. **5**(5), 493–496 (2010)
7. Beltraminelli, H., Itin, P.: Skin and psyche-from the surface to the depth of the inner world. J. Deutschen Dermatol. Gesellschaft **6**(1), 8–14 (2008)
8. Vallbo, A.B., Johansson, R.S.: The tactile sensory innervation of the glabrous skin of the human hand. Active touch **2954**, 29–54 (1978)
9. Meng, X., Yoshida, N., Yonezawa, T.: Evaluations of involuntary cross-modal expressions on the skin of a communication robot. In: 2015 12th International Conference on Ubiquitous Robots and Ambient Intelligence (URAI), pp. 347–352. IEEE (2015)
10. Meng, X., Yoshida, N., Wan, X., Yonezawa, T.: Quantitative effects on multiple involuntary physiologic expressions that convey the fear of robots. J. Japan Soc. Fuzzy Theory Intell. Inf. **33**(4), 501–515 (2021). (In Japanese)
11. Meng, X., Yoshida, N., Wan, X., Yonezawa, T.: Emotional gripping expression of a robotic hand as physical contact. In: Proceedings of the 7th International Conference on Human-Agent Interaction, pp. 37–42 (2019)
12. Meng, X., Yoshida, N., Wan, X., Yonezawa, T.: Instinctive expressions through involuntary representation on robot's haptic skin. Hum. Interface Soc. J. **22**(3), 235–250 (2020). (In Japanese)
13. KAWADA. Monster Magic Hand. https://www.jancode.xyz/4972825204474/
14. Russell, J.: A circumplex model of affect. J. Pers. Soc. Psychol. **39**, 1161–1178 (1980)
15. Van Erp, J.B.F., Toet, A.: How to touch humans: guidelines for social agents and robots that can touch. In: Proceedings of the 2013 Humaine Association Conference on Affective Computing and Intelligent Interaction (2018). https://doi.org/10.1109/ACII.2013.145
16. Mori, M.: The uncanny valley: the original essay by Masahiro Mori. IEEE Spectrum **6**, 1–6 (1970)
17. Mori, M., MacDorman, K.F., Kageki, N.: The uncanny valley [from the field]. IEEE Robot. Autom. Mag. **19**(2), 98–100 (2012)

Social Media for Community, Society and Democracy

Opinion Types on Social Media: A Review of Approaches to What Opinions Are in Social vs. Computational Science

Svetlana S. Bodrunova[(✉)] [iD]

Saint Petersburg State University, Saint Petersburg 199004, Russia
s.bodrunova@spbu.ru

Abstract. Today's public opinion research has rapidly transformed to include opinions expressed within new forms of mediatized communication, including those on social networks and messengers. Computational communication studies have provided for new approaches in opinion mining and detection, and many new approaches to how 'opinions' are seen in research have emerged. The growth of the academic field that (re)conceptualizes opinion as a term, including for automated and AI-based opinion detection, has gradually turned from a spurring advantage to an inhibitory obstacle for further public opinion studies. The diversity of this field, being a problem itself, also produces scientific sub-problems that we try to address. The three of them are: (1) the widening differences between the 'traditional' (pre-computational) opinion studies, already highly diverse, and computational opinion mining; (2) the shared methodological basis of the computational communication studies that mostly reduce 'opinion' to the lexical-semantic levels of speech, largely ignoring social-group, political, cultural, temporal, and narrative aspects of opinion formation; (3) our unawareness of whether the gap between human and AI-created human-like representation of opinions can ever be overcome, and, if not, how the machine sees opinions and why they cannot reach the logic of human judgment on opinionated content. In this paper, we review the three periods of formation of opinion studies, which have brought on the 'traditional' (very diverse), computational, and human-like computational views on how opinions look like in academic representation. Our main focus is on how the pre-computational and computational methods of opinion detection could enrich each other and whether full similarity between opinion formulation and/or representation by artificial intelligence and human beings could ever be reached. In the conclusion, we hint on the future directions of conceptual research on the nature and essence of human and human-like opinion.

Keywords: public opinion · opinion types · opinion mining · social media · AI-based research · computational social science

1 Introduction

Public opinion research in the 21st century has rapidly expanded to include opinions expressed within new forms of mediatized communication. Computational communication studies [1] have provided for new approaches in opinion mining and detection, and many new forms of how 'opinions' are seen in research have emerged.

This growth of the conceptual field of opinion studies has not yet been properly described, reviewed, and discussed in terms of conceptual gaps and shared understandings of what opinions actually are, both in people's minds and as textual expressions. This conceptual diversity, to our viewpoint, is gradually turning from a plausible advantage into a conceptual obstacle that prevents proper meta-studies, as well as detection and recognition of both research gaps and conceptual/methodological overlappings. It also prevents formation of more general lines in opinion mining and development of opinion detection methods based on clear understanding of what opinions are (or should be). Thus, the scholarly community needs to pay attention to the diversity of the field of opinion studies, embrace it, and organize a discussion on how we (re)conceptualize opinion as a term for today's social science, including the computational communication and public opinion research.

This problem has three sub-issues that we would like to focus upon in the review below. To our viewpoint, they constitute the core of the diversity problem.

First, there is a gap between 'traditional' studies of public opinion, including polling, journalism studies of opinionated content, argumentation theories, or socio-political studies of public choice such as the 'opinion leaders' [2], 'two-step communication flows' [3], or 'spiral of silence' [4] research, and computational detection of opinions.

Second, conceptual diversity in automated opinion mining may, paradoxically, be an illusion, as multiple methods of clustering and classification of texts, as diverse as sentiment analysis, topic modeling, and summarization, all employ the lexical-semantic level of where opinion resides in the 'oral-written' [5] talk on social networks. Focusing on words/word combinations, such methods naturally disregard the complicated discursive structure of opinions; there are attempts to integrate larger language structures into automated opinion detection, but they anyway still largely ignore the temporal, narrative, cultural, and political aspects of opinion formation in publics and social groups. This methodological ignorance creates a gap between traditional and computational opinion studies yet insurmountable.

Third, there is another question of growing importance. It is the one on how opinions are seen (perceived and represented) by artificial intelligence vs. the human understanding of opinion. Today's research on AI-based opinion detection largely follows the idea that the neural-network models of opinion detection eventually detect and produce opinions undistinguishable from the human ones, coming close to human judgment and human imagination on opinion as to the obvious ideal, – be it via abstractive summarization as the method that comes the closest to human speech production or responses by versions of GPT bots. However, a question remains whether there is a tiny but ever-reproduced chink between the human and the machine's overall patterns of discourse (and opinion) formation, and, if it is, indeed, reproduced, what it exactly is and why it is always there.

These questions, posed widely enough, cannot, of course, be answered via one review paper; however, by it, we call for the scholarly discussion on the aforestated issues. Below, we (perhaps, superficially enough) review the most widespread approaches to what opinion is in traditional social sciences and humanities; after that, we try to show how many methods of the current computational communication studies reduce opinion in text to the lexemes that bear certain semantics and how scarce is the theoretical discussion on opinion-related terminology in computational and AI-based opinion detection. The new stage of opinion detection we link to the appearance of the methods of human-like representation of opinion, and it is exactly where the question of the human/machine chink in opinion representation rises in full scale. In the conclusion, we discuss future directions for theoretical development of the opinion-related conceptual field.

2 'Traditional' Public Opinion Studies in Relation to Today's Computational Opinion Detection

The study of opinions in several sub-fields of pre-computational social science has naturally had a crucial impact on the computational search for opinions in datasets collected online. The sub-fields that have produced meaningful contributions are, first of all, classical linguistics and sociolinguistics, media studies, argumentation theory, discourse theory, and works in the field of sociology and political studies of public opinion. We will now briefly review them, although, of course, such an overview is far from being enough to understand the influence of different branches of social science upon today's understanding of opinion, including in computational and machine-learning-based works.

2.1 Linguistics: Opinion as a Manifestation of Subjectivity

An important role in the design of computational studies of textual data is played by the understanding of opinion as one of the types of subjectivity; this understanding has come from linguistics [6, 7]. Subjectivity can take not only personal, but also extrapersonal and strategic forms [8], which are found, among other things, in the deliberative and the decision-making process [9]. The post-Cartesian discussion of the types of subjectivity and intersubjectivity, however, has not yet found a clear connection with the understanding of opinion as a collective attitude detectable through polling, due to the rootedness of subjectivity in speech, in the form of specific statements, including the narrative.

Yet, computational linguistics quickly built a bridge from subjectivity to sentiment analysis [10], bypassing more complex classifications of opinions. Some researchers, however, have proposed to see a psychological phenomenon behind the linguistic expression of opinion. This phenomenon is called by them a 'private state', which becomes public via speaking in public, including through its expression on social networks [11, 12]. Thus, opinions in opinion mining may be viewed as mirrors of 'private states' of individuals with attitudinal components.

2.2   Argumentation Theory: Opinion as Argument and Deliberation Core

From the philosophers of public discussion (from de Tocqueville to Habermas) to the theorists of argumentation stretches the thread of interpretation of opinion as an argument in a dispute. Arguments as a part of public opinion probably have the least capacity for simple accumulation in amounting user utterances online and, at the same time, the greatest deliberative potential. The structure of an argument is usually difficult to identify automatically, but it is argumentation that determines the general deliberative quality of judgment. This comes from the conviction, as in the works by Habermas, that consensus (and the arguments that lead to or from it) is rooted not in the positions of individual citizens but in the language itself, in the linguistic structures that express logic and the discursive shape that allows for eliminating emotions, private motivations, and logical errors from the consensus-oriented discussion. This allows for establishing agreement as a natural outcome of optimal causal reasoning (including arguments) [13, 14].

Interestingly, the deep language rootedness of agreement, consensus, and balance of opinions, on one hand, opposes critical discourse analysis, as it denies the deliberative actors the importance of their personal traits. However, at the same time, it echoes the basic premise of critical discourse analysis where the language 'accounts for the interrelations between the social functions, the cognitive structures and the discursive expressions of ideologies' [15: 1], thus integrating, not eliminating, social and cognitive features of interlocutors into the argumentation via complex relations of those with the discursive shape of their speech. Thus, the difference between the Habermassian view on the nature of consensus and the view on the nature of argumentation in the critical discourse may lie, to the most part, in what is normatively allowed into the argument – that is, what part of the argument in terms of its rationality and individuality, may be legitimately considered a part of politically and/or socially relevant public opinion.

In computational opinion research, this has so far manifested in the form of identifying opinions in a structural relationship with the carrier of opinion [16] and its addressee [17]. However, one should pay more attention to the fact that discourses themselves may turn out to be the largest possible structures that are carriers of (networked) opinions. In particular, we have shown that macro-narrative structures can take shape in online discussions and capture not only social attitudes, but also the configurations of actors around them [18]. The scholars are well aware [19] that analysing the networked opinion structure demands linking detection of semantics to the network theory [20], including research on modularity [21], but so far it is rare that the *changing* opinion of users on a given issue is seen as a cumulatively developing narrative of arguments and emotions within a dynamic network, as we have proposed in [18].

2.3   Political Studies of Public Opinion: Opinion as a Marker of Social Inclusion and a Political Statement

Another branch of social theory clearly opposes the discourse-based approaches to opinion, as it roots public opinion in the publics – that is, in the structure of social relations, political standing of individuals, and the interplay between them. Starting from the foundational books by Walter Lippmann, 'public opinion' as a term [22] was instated in its quality of a separate political phenomenon capable of political influence upon decision-making and change of political behaviors, however elusive the notion of the 'public' could be [23].

However, in the political studies of public opinion, there is an ever-reproducing duality of whether political public opinions are simple aggregations of the majority/minority political attitudes (with complex relations of impact lying at the level of formation of *individual* opinions later aggregated via voting, polling, etc.) or a complex that interlinks individual opinions with certain social structures that shape public opinion on the macro-level of its public representation. The first-wave empirical studies of formation of the voting choices [2], opinion spreading between media, opinion leaders, and other citizens [3, 24], personal influence [25], or drug utilization acceptance [26] all placed the *formation* of opinion at the level of an influenced individual, while aggregation of opinion was made on the level of publics.

Later, however, the similarly influential models of opinion aggregation took into consideration the dynamics of communication and visual impact [4]. The formation of opinions was still seen as rooted in the individual traits of people, but the 'social radar' that each individual has allowed for integrating the social and communicative structure of the surrounding society into the process of opinion formation and opinion expression. Of the works in the field of social psychology of choice and formation of the majority /minority as dynamic structures influenced by social relations and pre-existing opinion cues, the most famous still belong to Elizabeth Noelle-Neumann and her followers. Based on the work of Alexis de Tocqueville, she defined public opinion as an opinion whose expression would not lead to social exclusion [2, 27]. It is in the works of Noelle-Neumann and her followers and critics, as well as in the works on the 'silent majority' [28, 29], that for the first time precisely cumulative patterns of opinion with their points of growth and breakdown, as well as cumulative effects in public opinion, were clearly described.

Our later studies [30, 31] that follow this thinking suggest putting an even bigger accent upon the cumulative nature of opinion formation on the Internet, due to the nature of user expression in the online realms. While opinions studied by Lazersfeld, Katz, Noelle-Neumann, or Lassiter were structured and similar in their cognitive and linguistic shape, online, we deal with opinions of various forms quite unpredictable in terms of timing of their appearance, from long well-grounded statements to single-word exclamations to liking, all mixed in one short time period. This is why single user utterances or 'tiny acts of political participation' [32] can only *potentially* be considered opinion bearers, as they may not bear one, may bear its elements, or may change within one user's speech within minutes. Thus, opinion formation, if we want to know it with all possible precision, needs to be principally studied and detected on the level of a public, with the help of machine learning capable of quick enough detection of user positions from various forms of statements and deeds. We also need to integrally take into account user relations and power structures in the texts, thus making opinions at least partly or distortedly (with allowances thoroughly considered) relevant to the social group structure and the structure of political publics offline, opening the road to hybrid deliberation thinking [31]. In this, we need to remember that cumulative opinions are ever-changing, they are today's Protea that partly form by discussion, partly by single expression, and partly via commented sharing where the message changes from repost to repost, thus residing *both* in individual interpretations and the dynamics of differences between them.

2.4 Media Studies: Opinion as a Genre and Non-Fact

Approaches to understanding what an opinion is and how it looks, of course, have developed in classical communication studies, including media theory; here, without distinguishing between opinion and non-opinion, it would not be possible to build an industrial understanding of the profession, train journalists, and study public discussion from the organizational perspective. We will not review here the history of the study of (public) opinion in social communication studies, as we will leave this task for the near future; for now, we will only point out the provisions from the media theory that are directly related to the cumulative nature of opinions in online discussions and the formats of agreement in them.

Thus, first of all, it should be noted that the term 'public opinion' is used less and less in media studies, as it was impossible to identify public opinions it using traditional methods of media science, and the identification of opinions at the level of the whole society went into polling sociology, leaving media studies with the analysis of media content, which, alas, was too often passed off as the study of public opinion (and not the opinions of institutional actors and the media themselves). Secondly, media researchers drew a watershed between fact and non-factual text (including opinion as a 'non-fact' and commentary as a genre), which led to the understanding of opinion as a detailed, multilevel author's statement (unlike a set of lexemes in computational linguistics or short statements in claims analysis). Opinion as a 'long text' is also found in the study of consumer reviews [33]; one should also not forget that the most extensive genre form expressing opinion remains a critical article (and criticism in general).

2.5 Deliberation Studies: Opinions as Institutionalized Means of Consensus

We cannot help mentioning a separate area of communication studies, in which public opinion was studied specifically as a communicative and deliberative phenomenon. Thus, the academic discourse on the nature of opinions and the forms of discussion in which they nest [34] took place in journals dedicated to public opinion studies (*Public Opinion Quarterly, International Journal of Public Opinion Research, Javnost – The Public, Deliberation*, and several others). The research in these journals was clearly democratizing in nature and linked the nature of opinions to the structure of public discussion and the nature of institutions that ensure democratic development, which divided the study of opinion as a concept in these journals and in media theory. But both media theory and the deliberative theory of opinion had less influence than we would like on computational communication studies, which, in turn, largely relied not on sociopolitical understanding of the nature of opinion in the public sphere or on the social functions of opinions, but on the structure of speech and the possibilities of its automated analysis. So far, attempts to classify opinions based on the position of media or deliberation studies are rare in computational research (an example of an early work sees in [35]; a later successful attempt is [36]).

3 A Critical Reduction: Opinion Mining with Social Media Data

The research field of opinion mining from texts of mass media, social networks, and messengers utilizes a wide range of computational (including neural-network) methods of analyzing text data. The scholars who work in this field know well that, unlike many other areas of social and interdisciplinary science, it is segmented according to the methods employed, not to the theories that would define its guiding principles. Thus, it includes vast zones dedicated to sentiment analysis [37–39], topic modeling [40, 41], and other methods of clustering and classification of text data, automated content analysis, etc.

Each of these methods, however, does not deal directly with opinion as described by sociology, political science, or linguistics. For instance, sentiment analysis reduces 'opinion' to a negative/positive tone of utterance in relation to the studied object or its so-called aspects (individual features that are of interest for the researcher). Topic modeling and other methods of strict and non-strict (fuzzy) clustering and classification [42] cluster texts into groups based on topical proximity, and 'real' opinions are extracted from there using qualitative methods (most often through interpretative reading). Content analysis shows the degree of salience of a particular vocabulary, which is attributed to the carrier of an opinion (again, positive/negative, too often not complex and nuanced); etc. From most findings made using the main opinion mining methods today, only indirect conclusions can be drawn about the real opinions of users, as, in most computational methods, 'opinions' are reduced to the sets of tokens grouped 'around' an object, presumably expressing a positive or negative attitude to it.

Of course, we are aware of attempts of much more complex sentiment analysis that take into account stable expressions, evaluative [43, 44] and object-oriented [45] statements, but the principle of identifying opinions does not change due to this: This principle is still 'an object + groups of tokens around it.' More complex models of topic-optional text classification also have already been developed: Thus, Davan and colleagues [46] created a multidimensional detector of content containing opinions using 54 text categories, thereby approaching the reflection of 'real' user opinions and their fragmentation on three platforms. In general, multi-word (multi-dictionary) and multi-vector (multi-feature) opinion detection also allows for determining the strength of opinions [47] and their polarity [48], as well as for increasing the number of discovered 'units of opinion'; but neither the common approaches to what is an opinion unit exist yet – and such a question is not even being raised.

At the same time, some works, most often based on simpler methods such as qualitative and quantitative coding (e.g., following the Krippendorff's advice [49]) and automated and/or computational methods without fine-tuning, describe user opinions closer to a sociological understanding of opinion. For example, opinions in online discussions look in research like attitudes towards an object (but most often in the form of 'good/bad', which is still very close to the 'yes/no' sentiment analysis [50]), elements of peer review and appraisal [51], elements of argumentation [52], enthymemes ('collapsed' syllogisms [53]), etc., but mostly without separation into formal linguistic structures and structures of meaning, which prevents efficient opinion tracing. Some researchers create categories of opinions for the tasks in specific case studies (e.g., even use the so-called Kellert categories from the social psychology of human-animal relations [54]). Also, a number of researchers ([55]; an overview of early works can be found in [10]) proposed to distinguish between 'comparable' and 'incomparable' opinions on the subject.

Computational methods mainly demonstrate that, in the works employing them, 'opinion' is understood primarily in a 'consumer' way – as an opinion on some object, product, service, event, etc., which can be drastically simplified to the binary opposition of good vs. bad. However, as is known from political science and communication studies, deliberative opinions can be constructed differently, as statements of a values-based nature, calls to action, rhetorical speech figures, and many more. Much before the advent of social networks, such purposeful statements were studied, for example, in the claims analysis. So far, to our great pity, claims analysis has not taken its proper place in opinion mining, being overshadowed by lexicon-oriented approaches, although its application in the field of analysis of policing documents has been extremely effective (the use of the method for studying emergent opinions on the European Union is shown in [56, 57]). Back in the 2000s, there was an important attempt (although described extremely briefly, within two pages only) to combine the search for types of opinions, their polarization, dynamics, and discursive effects within the framework of claims analysis of Internet texts [58], much anticipating our studies of cumulative deliberation.

Computational communication researchers can also find useful the 'issue stance' term ('statement on the issue of the agenda' [59]), which is close by meaning to 'claim.' In computational research, the study of claims and issue stances as such is gradually gaining weight [51, 60], but much more attention is needed to opinion as a complex value- or demands-based statement and the possibility of their detection and modeling.

4 The 'Summarization Turn' and the (Nonextant) 'Thinking Gap' Between Human and AI-Sensed Opinions

A new stage in the study of online opinions came when, in the mid-2010s, the methods of multivariate analysis and conditional random fields [17] were replaced by neural network methods and technologies [61]. It seemed that a new generation of methods would immediately bring the possibilities of integrating the above-described diversity of understanding opinions into the practice of opinion mining. So far, however, the connection between the latest methods and classical views on the nature of opinion is weak and requires much deeper study.

The most promising method of identifying opinions at the moment is textual summarization. Of the four originally developed types of summarizations, extractive and abstractive ones are widely used today. The first briefly conveys the meaning of a text or group of texts through the isolation and assembly of the most significant fragments. Abstractive summarization creates its own text based on a long text or a group of texts, summarizing the meaning of the original/originals, as if a person briefly conveyed their meaning in his/her own words. Summarization is beginning to be applied today in the study of the structure and dynamics of opinions in online discussions, including the dynamics of opinion formation.

Experiments in the late 2010s combined extractive summarization with the methods of topic evolution studies, 'attaching' the most characteristic fragments of user speech to the 'growing' topical 'branches.' With the development of neural-network models for text analysis, abstractive summarization has become a priority, as such models are capable of creating textual representations based on longer user texts with a certain degree of acceptability and, via this, track opinions not in a fragmentary or indicative but in a coherent human-like way. This, in effect, may allow for representing large-scale online discussions in a readable way useful for scholars who would see the opinion development from the birds-eye view.

In 2023, our working group proposed a method for representation of topics and opinions in online discussion that we have called the 'opinion tree.' It combines three neural-network and one iterative method to represent topic-opinion structure of a text collection, working well with user text of varying length (Reddit datasets). The neural-network methods are the 'smart' topic modeling (a BERTopic model with the HDBSCAN algorithm of defining the topics and gathering them in super-topics), word embeddings for text standardization, and abstractive summarization (a Pegasus model) for each 'branch'; the 'branch bifurcation points' are defined via iterative topic remodeling of pre-defined topics [62]. So far, the method is being fine-tuned for the data in non-English languages.

The most important result of this method for opinion mining is, however, our conclusion on the nature and types of opinions discovered if one applies summarization of various fixed length within the model. As our experiments with different summarization length have shown, two conclusions may be made. First, it is quite possible to find the optimal way to represent content in which both the variety of forms of opinionated user expression may be observed and the convenience of quickly evaluating the content of a discussion, including the opinions in it, is preserved. Second, we have observed three distinct types of opinion representation that may hint to various sub-areas of pre-computational public opinion studies. In particular, these are: (1) 'collapsed' opinions that resemble enthymemes and only indicate the presence of opinionated statements; (2) opinions in the form of statements containing assessment, but not in the 'good/bad' form but in more complex forms of human-like statements; (3) polar opinions clearly marking users' sided positioning on a given issue. Thus, the machine was capable of capturing the essence and polarity of opinions; the latter, captured in the form of polar attitudes and an explicit, detailed evaluative attitudes, could significantly advance today's automated research of political polarization.

Moreover, the model captured disagreement on issues at the 'branch ends', expressing it in the form of rhetoric questions absent in the original texts, thus showing the elements of 'machine thinking.' This clearly points out to the aforementioned chink between the original (human) and machine-represented form of opinion, posing new questions on how the machine 'thinks' and how one can rely upon and trust this 'thinking' and the machines' choice of forms for user opinion representation [63].

This diversity of opinion representation within the framework of one test discussion and only one method of its representation leads to an important new methodological premise in the field of opinion research on the Internet. Thus, almost all computational methods before the neural-network era assumed that the desired form of opinion that a scholar would wish to detect (e.g., attitudes, arguments, or statements) was set by the researcher. Today's methods, in particular the summarization approach, make it possible to identify a range of types of user opinions post-factum, without squeezing them into the Procrustean bed of a predetermined vision upon the nature of public opinion. This can radically change the design of research in the field of opinion mining and create the ground for new classifications of opinion that are closer to user texts.

5 Conclusion

The paper has discussed the conceptual approaches to public opinion influential today in automated (big-data, computational, and AI-based) opinion mining. We have shown that the pre-computational diversity of approaches to what (human and public) opinion is has been both amplified by computational approaches and – simultaneously – reduced by the orientation of many computational methods to detecting simplified opinions suitable for consumer studies on the level of lexicons. This made computational communication studies for some time period largely disregard the social-structural, narrational, genre, cultural, and temporal aspects of opinion formation on social media and messengers. However, today's neural-network methods allow for coming much closer to the human-like opinion representations, and new questions of integrating the aforementioned aspects gain the growing importance.

Moreover, we have shown that, due to the linguistic shape of user commenting and micro-acting online, opinion formation moves to the level which earlier was regarded as the level of simple aggregation and summing up of opinions. Thus, even-changing in time, current user opinions may only be detected as cumulative entities via machine-learning methods. Summarization suits this goal, especially if it can be used both post-factum and in real time.

Opinions detected by the machines come closer and closer to human-like forms; however, machines, as we have found, may choose unexpected forms of opinion representation absent in the original data. This poses a range of questions for further research.

First, the question is: What is an accumulated opinion? What is a cumulative expression of opinion? And what can be accepted politically as cumulative view/attitude statement by a deliberative (micro-) public? Second, as cumulative opinions can *only* be captured via (semi-)automated research methods, we need to ask: What does the machine recognize as cumulative opinion? Does the latter differ from its human interpretation? Third, we need to explore the variety of opinion representation forms employed by the machines and understand what defines and shapes their choice of particular forms in formation of final opinion representations. Fourth, we need to define the grounds for trust to opinion detection by machine, as we do not know yet whether the gap between human and human-like opinion detection will be growing. How and why do we trust machines to detect online opinions, and how do we trust the machine-detected cumulative opinions? These questions need to guide our today's studies of cumulative opinion formation and hybrid deliberation.

Acknowledgments. This research has been conducted on behalf of the Center for International Media Research of St. Petersburg State University, Russia.

Disclosure of Interests. The authors have no competing interests to declare that are relevant to the content of this article.

References

1. Van Atteveldt, W., Peng, T.Q.: When communication meets computation: opportunities, challenges, and pitfalls in computational communication science. Commun. Methods Meas. **12**(2–3), 81–92 (2018)
2. Lazarsfeld, P.F.: The People's Choice. Columbia University Press, New York (1944)
3. Katz, E.: The two-step flow of communication: an up-to-date report on an hypothesis. Public Opin. Q. **21**(1), 61–78 (1957)
4. Noelle-Neumann, E.: The spiral of silence a theory of public opinion. J. Commun. **24**(2), 43–51 (1974)
5. Lutovinova, O.V.: Internet as a new 'oral-written' communication system. News RSPU: AI Herzen **71**, 58–65 (2008)
6. Kennedy, C.: Two kinds of subjectivity. In: Meier, C., van Wijnbergen-Huitink, V. (eds.) Subjective Meaning: Alternatives to Relativism, pp. 105–126. De Gruyter, Berlin – Boston (2016)
7. Narrog, H.: Three types of subjectivity, three types of intersubjectivity, their dynamicization and a synthesis. In: Olmen, D., Cuyckens, H., Ghesquière, L. (eds.) Aspects of grammaticalization: (Inter)subjectification and directionality, pp. 19–46. De Gruyter Mouton, Berlin – Boston (2016)
8. De Cock, B.: Subjectivity, intersubjectivity and non-subjectivity across spoken language genres. Span. Context **12**(1), 10–34 (2015)
9. Buchanan, J.T., Henig, E.J., Henig, M.I.: Objectivity and subjectivity in the decision-making process. Ann. Oper. Res. **80**, 333–345 (1998)
10. Liu, B.: Sentiment analysis and subjectivity. In: Indurkhya, N., Damerau, F.J. (eds.) Handbook of natural language processing, 2nd edn., pp. 627–666. Routledge, London (2010)
11. Wiebe, J., Wilson, T., Cardie, C.: Annotating expressions of opinions and emotions in language. Lang. Resour. Eval. **39**, 165–210 (2005)
12. Katiyar, A., Cardie, C.: Investigating LSTMs for joint extraction of opinion entities and relations. In: Proceedings of the 54th Annual Meeting of the Association for Computational Linguistics. vol. 1, pp. 919–929. Long Papers (2016)
13. Habermas, J.: Political communication in media society: does democracy still enjoy an epistemic dimension? The impact of normative theory on empirical research. Commun. Theory **16**(4), 411–426 (2006)
14. Jezierska, K.: With Habermas against Habermas: Deliberation without consensus. J. Deliberative Democracy **15**(1), 13 (2019). https://delibdemjournal.org/article/id/598/
15. Van Dijk, T.A.: Opinions and ideologies in the press. In: Bell, A., Garrett, P. (eds.) Approaches to Media Discourse, pp. 21–63. Blackwell, Oxford (1998)
16. Choi, Y., Breck, E., Cardie, C.: Joint extraction of entities and relations for opinion recognition. In: Proceedings of the 2006 Conference on Empirical Methods in Natural Language Processing, pp. 431–439 (2006)
17. Yang, B., Cardie, C.: Joint inference for fine-grained opinion extraction. In: Proceedings of the 51st Annual Meeting of the Association for Computational Linguistics, vol. 1, pp. 1640–1649. Long Papers (2013)
18. Nigmatullina, K., Bodrunova, S.S., Polyakov, A., Kasymov, R.: Narrative communities on social networks and the roles of legacy media in them: the case of user complaints in Russian regions. In: Proceedings of the International Conference on Human-Computer Interaction, pp. 271–286. Springer Nature Switzerland, Cham (2023)
19. Bastos, M.T., Raimundo, R.L.G., Travitzki, R.: Gatekeeping Twitter: message diffusion in political hashtags. Media Cult. Soc. **35**(2), 260–270 (2013)

20. Castells, M.: Communication, power and counter-power in the network society. Int. J. Commun. **1**(1), 238–266 (2007)
21. Newman, M.E.: Modularity and community structure in networks. Proc. Natl. Acad. Sci. **103**(23), 8577–8582 (2006)
22. Lippmann, W.: Public Opinion. Routledge, London (1922/2017)
23. Lippmann, W.: The Phantom Public. Routledge, London (1925/2017)
24. Katz, E., Lazarsfeld, P.F.: Personal Influence: The Part Played by People in the Flow of Mass Communications. The Free Press, Glencoe (IL) (1955)
25. Merton, R.K.: Patterns of Influence: a study of interpersonal influence and communications behavior in a local community. In: Lazarsfeld, P.F., Stanton, F.N. (eds.) Communications Research, 1948–9, pp. 180–219. Harper and Brothers, New York (1949)
26. Menzel, H., Katz, E.: Social relations and Innovation in the medical profession. Public Opin. Q. **19**, 337–352 (1955)
27. Noelle-Neumann, E., Petersen, T.: The spiral of silence and the social nature of man. In: Kaid, L.L. (ed.) Handbook of Political Communication Research, pp. 339–356. Routledge, London (2004)
28. Lassiter, M.D.: The Silent Majority. Princeton University Press (2013)
29. Mustafaraj, E., Finn, S., Whitlock, C., Metaxas, P.T.: Vocal minority versus silent majority: discovering the opinions of the long tail. In: Proceedings of the 2011 IEEE Third International Conference on Privacy, Security, Risk and Trust and 2011 IEEE Third International Conference on Social Computing, pp. 103–110. IEEE (2011)
30. Bodrunova, S.S.: Cumulative deliberation: new normativity in studying public spheres online [Kumulyativnaya deliberatsiya: nobaya normativnost' v izuchenii publichnyh sfer onlain], Vestnik Moskovskogo universiteta, Seriya 10: Zhurnalistika **1**(48), 87–122 (2023)
31. Bodrunova, S.S.: The concept of cumulative deliberation: linking systemic approaches to healthier normativity in assessing opinion formation in online discussions. J. Assoc. Inform. Sci. Technol. 1–13 (2023). https://doi.org/10.1002/asi.24850
32. Margetts, H., John, P., Hale, S., Yasseri, T.: Political Turbulence: How Social Media Shape Collective Action. Princeton University Press (2015)
33. Qazi, A., Raj, R.G., Hardaker, G., Standing, C.: A systematic literature review on opinion types and sentiment analysis techniques: tasks and challenges. Internet Res. **27**(3), 608–630 (2017)
34. Scheufele, D.A.: Deliberation or dispute? An exploratory study examining dimensions of public opinion expression. Int. J. Public Opin. Res. **11**(1), 25–58 (1999)
35. Murakami, K., et al.: Automatic classification of semantic relations between facts and opinions. In: Proceedings of the Second Workshop on NLP Challenges in the Information Explosion Era (NLPIX 2010), pp. 21–30 (2010)
36. Carrillo-de-Albornoz, J., Aker, A., Kurtic, E., Plaza, L.: Beyond opinion classification: extracting facts, opinions and experiences from health forums. PLoS ONE **14**(1), e0209961 (2019)
37. Liang, P.W., Dai, B.R.: Opinion mining on social media data. In: 2013 IEEE 14th International Conference on Mobile Data Management, vol. 2, pp. 91–96. IEEE (2013)
38. Păvăloaia, V.D., Teodor, E.M., Fotache, D., Danileţ, M.: Opinion mining on social media data: sentiment analysis of user preferences. Sustainability **11**(16), 4459 (2019)
39. Qiu, J., Lin, Z., Shuai, Q.: Investigating the opinions distribution in the controversy on social media. Inf. Sci. **489**, 274–288 (2019)
40. Blei, D.M., Lafferty, J.D.: Topic models. In: Text Mining, pp. 101–124. Chapman and Hall/CRC (2009)
41. Stoyanov, V., Cardie, C.: Topic identification for fine-grained opinion analysis. In: Proceedings of the 22nd International Conference on Computational Linguistics (CoLing-2008), pp. 817–824 (2008)

42. Najadat, H.M., Alzu'bi, A.A., Shatnawi, F., Rawashdeh, S., Eyadat, W.: Analyzing social media opinions using data analytics. In: Proceedings of the 2020 11th International Conference on Information and Communication Systems (ICICS), pp. 266–271. IEEE (2020)

43. Kobayashi, N., Inui, K., Matsumoto, Y., Tateishi, K., Fukushima, T.: Collecting evaluative expressions for opinion extraction. In: Keh-Yih, Su., Jun'ichi Tsujii, Jong-Hyeok Lee, Oi Yee Kwong, (eds.) IJCNLP 2004. LNCS (LNAI), vol. 3248, pp. 596–605. Springer, Heidelberg (2005). https://doi.org/10.1007/978-3-540-30211-7_63

44. Toprak, C., Jakob, N., Gurevych, I.: Sentence and expression level annotation of opinions in user-generated discourse. In: Proceedings of the 48th Annual Meeting of the Association for Computational Linguistics, pp. 575–584 (2010)

45. Maynard, D., Gossen, G., Funk, A., Fisichella, M.: Should I care about your opinion? Detection of opinion interestingness and dynamics in social media. Future Internet 6(3), 457–481 (2014)

46. Dhawan, P., Bhardwaj, G., Kaushal, R.: Analysis and Classification of Multi-opinionated Content in the Era of Cyber Activism. In: Alexandrov, D.A., Boukhanovsky, A.V., Chugunov, A.V., Kabanov, Y., Koltsova, O. (eds.) DTGS 2017. CCIS, vol. 745, pp. 31–44. Springer, Cham (2017). https://doi.org/10.1007/978-3-319-69784-0_3

47. Wilson, T., Wiebe, J., Hwa, R.: Just how mad are you? Finding strong and weak opinion clauses. In AAAI 4, 761–769 (2004)

48. Mikula, M., Machová, K.: Classification of opinions in conversational content. In: Proceedings of the 2015 IEEE 13th International Symposium on Applied Machine Intelligence and Informatics (SAMI), pp. 227–231. IEEE (2015)

49. Krippendorff, K.: Content Analysis: An Introduction to its Methodology. Sage Publications, London (2018)

50. Lee, M.J., Chun, J.W.: Reading others' comments and public opinion poll results on social media: social judgment and spiral of empowerment. Comput. Hum. Behav. 65, 479–487 (2016)

51. Ishida, T., Seki, Y., Kashino, W., Kando, N.: Extracting citizen feedback from social media by appraisal opinion type viewpoint. J. Nat. Lang. Process. 29(2), 416–442 (2022)

52. Somasundaran, S., Wilson, T., Wiebe, J., Stoyanov, V.: QA with attitude: Exploiting opinion type analysis for improving question answering in on-line discussions and the news. In: Proceedings of ICWSM (2007)

53. Rajendran, P., Bollegala, D., Parsons, S.: Contextual stance classification of opinions: a step towards enthymeme reconstruction in online reviews. In: Proceedings of the Third Workshop on Argument Mining (ArgMining 2016), pp. 31–39 (2016)

54. Fidino, M., Herr, S.W., Magle, S.B.: Assessing online opinions of wildlife through social media. Hum. Dimens. Wildl. 23(5), 482–490 (2018)

55. Alharbi, F.R., Khan, M.B.: Identifying comparative opinions in Arabic text in social media using machine learning techniques. SN Appl. Sci. 1(3), 213 (2019)

56. Koopmans, R., Muis, J.: The rise of right-wing populist Pim Fortuyn in the Netherlands: a discursive opportunity approach. Eur J Polit Res 48(5), 642–664 (2009)

57. Statham, P., Koopmans, R.: Political party contestation over Europe in the mass media: who criticizes Europe, how, and why? Eur. Polit. Sci. Rev. 1(3), 435–463 (2009)

58. Fang, Wu., Huberman, B.A.: How public opinion forms. In: Papadimitriou, C., Zhang, S. (eds.) WINE 2008. LNCS, vol. 5385, pp. 334–341. Springer, Heidelberg (2008). https://doi.org/10.1007/978-3-540-92185-1_39

59. Scheufele, D.A., Eveland, W.P.: Perceptions of 'public opinion' and 'public' opinion expression. Int. J. Public Opin. Res. 13(1), 25–44 (2001)

60. Alkhalifa, R., Kochkina, E., Zubiaga, A.: Opinions are made to be changed: Temporally adaptive stance classification. In: Proceedings of the 2021 Workshop on Open Challenges in Online Social Networks, pp. 27–32 (2021)

61. Liu, P., Joty, S., Meng, H.: Fine-grained opinion mining with recurrent neural networks and word embeddings. In: Proceedings of the 2015 Conference on Empirical Methods in Natural Language Processing, pp. 1433–1443 (2015)

62. Blekanov, I.S., Tarasov, N., Bodrunova, S.S., Sergeev, S.L.: Mapping opinion cumulation: topic modeling-based dynamic summarization of user discussions on social networks. In: Proceedings of the International Conference on Human-Computer Interaction, pp. 25–40. Springer Nature Switzerland, Cham (2023). https://doi.org/10.1007/978-3-031-35915-6_3

63. Bodrunova, S.S., Blekanov, I.S., Tarasov, N.: 'Opinion tree': A method for mapping online discussions based on neural-network topic modeling and abstractive summarization ['Derevo mneniy': metod dinamicheskogo meppinga onlain-diskussiy na osnove neyrosetevogo tematicheskogo modelirovaniya i abstraktivnoy summarizatsii]. Accepted for publication in Monitoring Obshchestvennogo Mneniya: Ekonomicheskie i Sotsial'nye Peremeny for 2024.

Emotional Dynamic and Opinion Cumulation on Social Networks in Kazakhstan

Galiya Ibrayeva$^{(\boxtimes)}$ ⓘ and Aliya Nurshaikhova ⓘ

Al-Farabi Kazakh National University, 71 Al-Farabi Prospect, Almaty 050040, Kazakhstan
galiya.ibrayeva@gmail.com

Abstract. Social networks manifest themselves as educational and information resources as well as a discussion milieu that casts strong influence upon public opinion. Finding themselves in the social media environment, users with lower levels of critical thinking and/or media literacy may become more susceptible to transformation of his/her position on the issue discussed, often due to emotional, not rational effects. Thus, polarization of views in user talk is multi-reasoned, emerging on both rational-choice and emotional grounds, while the latter may also vary significantly in the intensity and polarity of sentiment (from, e.g., mild empathy to strong hatred). Recent studies demonstrate that not only emotional content but more complicated attitudes, such as openly expressed trust and distrust, affect patterns of opinion formation online. It is crucial not only to detect emotions via lexicon analysis but also map the public distrust via discovering the actors to whom distrust and negativity, as well as open trust, as directed. This allows for getting a bigger picture on how the emotional stance and emotion-based attitudes work in deliberative online milieus. The results of the study show that public sentiment reveals the distrust that has formed in the legal branch of government and the lack of confidence in the positive adoption of new laws that protect human rights. We reveal the inertia of government institutions in responding to public crises with cumulative emotional outbursts in user talk; the lack of official response to them gave rise to new emotional waves, no less disturbing to the public. At this background, though, a positive factor was the involvement of the Mazhilis of Parliament in public discussion of acute crisis events.

Keywords: Kazakhstan · opinion · social network · emotion

1 Introduction

Social networks manifest themselves as educational and information resources as well as a discussion milieu that casts strong influence upon public opinion. Finding themselves in the social media environment, users with lower levels of critical thinking and/or media literacy may become more susceptible to transformation of his/her position on the issue discussed, often due to emotional, not rational effects. Thus, polarization of views in user talk is multi-reasoned, emerging on both rational-choice and emotional grounds, while the latter may also vary significantly in the intensity and polarity of sentiment (from, e.g., mild empathy to strong hatred).

© The Author(s), under exclusive license to Springer Nature Switzerland AG 2024
A. Coman and S. Vasilache (Eds.): HCII 2024, LNCS 14705, pp. 95–106, 2024.
https://doi.org/10.1007/978-3-031-61312-8_7

As the cumulative deliberation theory suggests [1], another important exogenous factor that affects polarization of views in online discussions is platform affordances and the historic context of platform use (e.g., habitual presence of certain political groups) in a given culture [2]. Thus, 'openspace' platforms like Facebook, Twitter, or Instagram are expected to create more 'opinion crossroads' [3] and, thus, allow for higher inclusion and publicity (which hints to higher deliberative quality of dialogue on single-user level), while messenger-like platforms [4], including Telegram, may create closed-up echo-chamber communities of biased and destructive views [5, 6]. However, on the platform level, Facebook and Twitter are also known for an opposite effect of fostering homophily of views, including in Russia [3] and Kazakhstan, keeping users within their filter bubbles. On the contrary, Instagram and Telegram may allow for consuming more diverse views, depending on how they work in a given national culture. In Kazakhstan [7] where the social networks market is rich due to popularity of both American (Facebook, Instagram, YouTube) and Russian/Russian-originated platforms (VK.com, Telegram), emotional patterns of opinion formation and cumulation may also very significantly on various platforms, as well as thanks to the use of either Kazakh or Russian language for networked communication.

Recent studies demonstrate that not only emotional content but more complicated attitudes, such as openly expressed trust and distrust, affect patterns of opinion formation online [6, 8]. It is crucial not only to detect emotions via lexicon analysis but also map the public distrust via discovering the actors to whom distrust and negativity, as well as open trust, as directed. This allows for getting a bigger picture on how the emotional stance and emotion-based attitudes work in deliberative online milieus. Other studies [9, 10] also suggest that the presence of institutional public actors and their response to user emotions may affect the emotional dynamics, e.g. spur/diminish the emotional waves of users' dissent, while absence of institutional actors creates a policy-discussing vacuum in online talk and deprives the authorities of chances to influence the cumulative crises of trust.

Therefore, the purpose of our pilot study is to examine the patterns of emotional dynamics of socially-mediated discussions in two languages and on four social media platforms popular in Kazakhstan, namely Facebook, Telegram, Instagram, and YouTube. In particular, we will focus on accumulation of emotions: 1) emotional polarization (expression of positive vs. negative views); 2) expression of trust/confidence and sense of justice vs. distrust to public actors.

Given all the above stated, we have formulated the following research questions:

RQ1. How does emotional polarization (positive vs. negative emotions) show up in online discussions, and which emotions accumulate more in time?

RQ2. How do trust and distrust show up in user texts? Who is trusted more or who is doubted? Can one say that distrust is compensated by trust and sense of justice?

RQ3. Are representatives of public authorities present as discussants in the cases under our scrutiny? What is their role in shaping online emotions and attitudes, including trust and distrust?

Social networks and online media are integrated into the lives of Kazakhstanis. The Top Digital trends in 2023 report "State of Digital Technologies in Kazakhstan" provides data that at the beginning of 2023 there were 17.73 million Internet users in the country, when Internet penetration was 90.9%. These data allow us to understand the communication pattern of users with an average age of 29.5 years with digital information flows. According to the same very competent organization, 11.05 million users aged 18 years and older used social networks, which is equivalent to 86.3% of the total number of users at that time. An interesting architecture of demand for social networks is emerging. The most popular in Kazakhstan in 2023 are Instagram (10.45 million) and TikTok (10.41 million). The previously popular Facebook attracts only 2.20 million users. Even less for such social networks as LinkedIn (1.20 million), Snapshat (1.40 million). Twitter has the least number of users (384.9 thousand). Russian-language social networks such as Yandex (2 million, including in the Kazakh language) [11], and VK (VKontakte) according to data of 6 million [12] are also gaining in number of users. Telegram, popular in the world, is not so in demand in Kazakhstan, and is about 50 thousand [13]. According to the results of the study, the top three most popular social media in Kazakhstan at the end of October 2023 included Pinterest, YouTube and Facebook. The share of Pinterest and YouTube users increased by 28.1% and 20.64%, respectively, BaigeNews.kz reports.

2 Evolution of the Emotional Model of Communication

2.1 The Timeline of Emotional Development of Social Networks in Kazakhstan

The model of communication between users and social networks in Kazakhstan has developed ambiguously from the emotional and psychological side. Three periods can be distinguished.

The first period is *trust*, when the attitude towards information and comments posted online was sincere, with a degree of enthusiasm, surprise and admiration. Users identified and personalized themselves, unaware of such aggressive tactics as trolling, bullying, bolivar, flame, etc. During this period, the influencer's position was indisputable and in moments of scandals, his opinion outweighed all arguments. An example is one of the first scandalous cases, when one of the major businessmen of the southern region of Kazakhstan, provoked by a manipulative family quarrel, ended up deprived of both his property and business, and was also accused of the most serious crimes. If initially the opinions of users were half-hearted, then after a speech by a well-known public opinion leader who showed photographic evidence that caused emotional stress in society, the subsequent actions of the tough authorities against the businessman no longer aroused support in public opinion. At that time, this kind of manipulation was new to an inexperienced user and was probably one of the first emotional blows.

The second period is *doubt*. Because the user's opinions were subject to both bullying and open aggression, which forced the user to create fictitious accounts. Social networks have also changed their attitude towards users. For example, Facebook was able to limit the number of friends to such an extent that so-called "information bubbles" emerged, which included only positively communicating communities of people. The tone of communication has changed to a rational and balanced trend, in which there is no longer romance and enthusiastic initial knowledge of the secrets of online communication. People realized that their apparent anonymity in communication was in reality easily revealed and began to express their opinions on certain issues with greater caution. The legislative work of countries, including Kazakhstan, in the field of online media and social networks has also become significant. Nevertheless, users tend to social networks in search of useful information, create groups of friends with similar interests, and once in their "information bubble" they can behave quite boldly, but without breaking the laws of the country, speak out with their ideas and opinions [14]. A team of new social media personalities called bloggers is emerging. Most often, a blogger is not identified with a professional journalist; he hypes, that is, he creates situations and patterns of behavior among his subscribers that evoke positive emotions. Some of the bloggers with millions of subscribers were children like Aminka-Vitaminka (1.3 million), Enonchik (1.8 million).

The third period is most likely a period of *sanity*. The user has not become a cynic; he allows himself empathy, regulated anger, empathy or compassion. This is especially evident when users unite to defend their ideals, moral values and national priorities.

Currently, the amount of information that users receive through the network has expanded significantly. Events are taking place at the international and local levels that may not be as spectacular and bright, but nevertheless have a strong emotional impact on society, excite public opinion, and involve in the process not only ordinary people, but also major public figures and representatives of local authorities.

2.2 The Cases Under Scrutiny

How does emotional polarization (positive and negative emotions) manifest itself in online discussions, and which emotions accumulate more strongly over time?

Let's consider three cases that received the most vivid emotional outburst during 2023 and gave rise to discussions, conflicts and emotional stress of various levels in society.

The first case is related to a very sensitive topic, which the President of the country Tokayev asked "not to politicize" this state and the development of the Kazakh language in the country.

Background: Case 1. Before the independence of the Kazakh people, back in 1989, the Kazakh language received the status of the state language. In 1995, a constitutional decision was made in Article 7 of the country's Constitution: "In the Republic of Kazakhstan, the Kazakh language is the state language." However, the Kazakh language, which received the status of the state language thirty years ago, actually cannot achieve its real status. In 1993, only 37% of students studied in Kazakh. In 2014, their number increased to only 49% of the total number of children who received secondary education. However, in the 2022–2023 academic year, 120,439 graduates have already graduated from Kazakh-language schools. This is just over 70% of the total number of graduates. Thus, the situation is slowly but changing. Nevertheless, this topic finds many "patriots", for whom it is important to assert their rules through public scandals and "hate speech", dividing Kazakhs by place of residence, into aul and city, or by region, where the northern ones, in their opinion, are not always active speaking the Kazakh language, as well as division by zhuz, Zhuz is the tribal structure of the Kazakhs and consists of three zhuz: Senior Zhuz (Kazakh: Uly zhuz), Middle Zhuz (Kazakh: Orta zhuz) and Junior Zhuz (Kazakh: Kishi zhuz). In addition, Kazakhs from China, Mongolia, Uzbekistan, and Russia emigrated to Kazakhstan, who also have their own stereotypes regarding the Kazakh language in the country.

The topic of the Kazakh language is one of the most acute and sensitive in Kazakhstan. In 2023, a number of scandals occurred that shook social networks. One of these was a case involving businessman M., the founder of a number of popular businesses in the country [15]. A group of Mazhilis deputies joined the conflict that suddenly flared up in society, turning to the Prosecutor General to check the businessman's statements under Article 174, paragraph 1, of the Criminal Code of the Republic of Kazakhstan. Users of social networks began to massively refuse the services of mobile applications of the company M. As has become a tradition, the businessman made a public apology, and the scandal gradually subsided. However, the topic of the Kazakh language remains very sensitive and tense for society; it can suddenly flare up and create the fire of conflict and aggression.

Digital data measured by Yandexю.kz counting tools on this topic turned out to be the highest, both in terms of the number of users, responses on social networks, and demonstrate constant tension (Fig. 1).

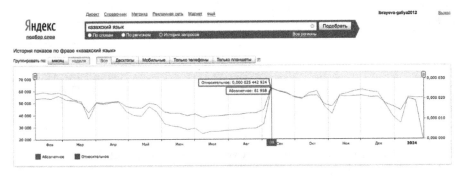

Fig. 1. Digital data on the topic "Kazakh language" in 2023

This graph shows that the topic "Kazakh language" is sensitive throughout 2023. From time to time, public opinion was fueled by domestic conflicts that occurred in the most unexpected places, such as on board an airplane in conflicts with flight attendants, to whom there were complaints regarding their knowledge of the Kazakh language or a cafe menu that was not provided in the state language. It should be noted that the video material from one of the television companies was commented on by the press service of the Almaty Police Department. They reported that a pre-trial investigation into this fact is being carried out under the article of the Criminal Code of the Republic of Kazakhstan "Inciting social, national, tribal, racial, class or religious hatred." Law enforcement officers added that measures will be taken against the townswoman in accordance with the legislation of the Republic of Kazakhstan.

Another surge in the increase in responses to the topic "Kazakh language" was the activity of the self-proclaimed public initiator of the so-called "language patrol", headed by A.K., even a criminal case was opened, and he hastily retired to another country. How did the authorities react to such initiatives? Deputy Head of the Presidential Administration of Kazakhstan Dauren Abaev criticized the "extremists" and called the "patrols" they created a manifestation of "cave nationalism."

Another aspect of the "Kazakh language" theme is the transition to the Latin script, that is, the creation of an alphabet in the Latin script. This was officially approved in 2017. The transition according to this alphabet is expected to be carried out during 2017–2025. Here public opinion is again divided into those who support these changes and those who are in favor. Earlier, in 1927, the KASSR officially announced the upcoming transition from Arabic script to a new alphabet; in 1929, such an alphabet was approved: it was Yanalif, a writing based on the Latin alphabet. Kazakhstan switched to Cyrillic in 1940. After various changes, the Cyrillic spelling was approved in 1957. The third transition of the alphabet from Cyrillic to Latin should be completed by 2025. The alphabet consists of 31 letters. Although society as a whole has calmed down and agreed with the changes, discussions flare up from time to time regarding the correctness of these actions, especially due to concerns for the country's cultural fund created in the Cyrillic alphabet (Fig. 2).

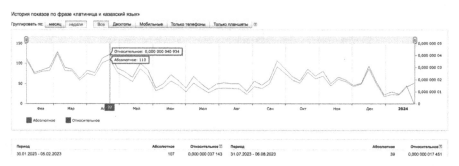

Fig. 2. Digital data on the topic "Cyrillic and Kazakh alphabet" in 2023

As the Yandex statistical table shows, a wary attitude towards the topic of switching to the Latin alphabet is constantly on the pulse of society. They are systemic and even the summer months of 2023 do not reduce the degree of aggravation and sensitivity to this topic.

The second case of this study is related to an image person who had a significant impact on the nation's self-esteem - this is the hero of the British cinema - "Borat".

Background: Case 2. The first film, 'Borat': Cultural Learnings of America for Make Benefit Glorious Nation of Kazakhstan," appeared back in 2006. The creator of the films about the fictional Kazakh journalist Borat Sagdiyev is the British comedian and director Sacha Baron Cohen. Analysts saw in the first "Borat" an order to undermine the image, and with it the political capital of the Kazakh elite. "Borat", which exposes Kazakhstan as a backward, deindustrialized and wretched country with shocking rules. The first reaction to the festival preview of the film was an article by the Ambassador of Kazakhstan to the UK, Erlan Idrisov, published on October 4, 2006 in The Guardian, where he stated that Sasha Cohen "created an entire fictional country - a cruel, primitive and oppressive place, which he called "Kazakhstan", but has nothing to do with real Kazakhstan", "the most striking character traits of Borat are his rudeness, ignorance, racism and chauvinism. This is a pig, not a man: stupid, hostile, disgusting". The prohibitive reaction gave the film "Borat" and Sacha Cohen additional impetus to "promote" the film. Kazakhstan's ambassador to Britain, Erlan Idrissov, has written a new article in the Times, pointing out that "Kazakhs owe a debt of gratitude to Sacha Cohen, who not only made many of us laugh heartily, but also brought Kazakhstan into the spotlight."

Only when Akorda turned the perception of what was happening into the format of a reaction to a stupid joke did the excitement subside. Any challenge or threat is also a stress test for management, information, ideological and PR services in order to determine their efficiency and effectiveness [16]. In 2012, the head of the republican Ministry of Foreign Affairs, Yerzhan Kazykhanov, said that, since the release of the film, the number of tours to Kazakhstan has increased sharply. "With the release of this film, the number of visas issued by Kazakhstan increased 10 times. This is a big victory for us, and I am grateful to "Borat" for helping attract tourists to Kazakhstan," he said.

The appearance of the second film in 2020 by British comedian Cohen sharpened the sense of national dignity of the Kazakhs. It is already clear today that Borat 2 for Kazakhstan will be comparable to the use of an information attack. Therefore, the audience of Kazakhstan was ready for the most incredible intrigues of the protagonist. The release of the film received a number of publications in the press of the United States and European countries. Public surveys conducted among young people showed that in Kazakhstan there remains a negative attitude towards the character of the imaginary journalist. Although in general the younger generation has forgotten this character, any mention of Borat causes a negative reaction. 3 years ago, the film "Borat 2" was accused of racism and a petition was launched against it.

An example would be a surge in negative reactions in a static diagram obtained through Yandex, that even without Cohen's new film, even the mention of Borat causes negative emotions in society. The mention of Borat's name by rapper 50 Cent caused a strong negative reaction, especially among the youth of Kazakhstan, after he posted on a social network: "Almaty, Kazakhstan, was incendiary. If it weren't for the Borat movie, you wouldn't know what I'm talking about. I am global." (Fig. 3).

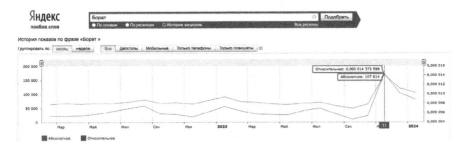

Fig. 3. Digital data on the topic of the film "Borat" in 2023

However, social network users reacted angrily to his post, "Borat has nothing to do with Kazakhstan!", "That was too much about Borat!" "We are not Borat. We are Kazakhstan with a rich culture and economy." - indignant users of social networks spoke out. The rapper's post also apparently surprised popular artist and rapper Busta Rhymes. He left a "brain explosion" emoji to indicate confusion and shock. The artist 50 Cent himself was also surprised by the reaction of young Kazakhstanis. This case, on the one hand, caused active actions on the part of the authorities and the government of Kazakhstan, which tried to maintain a positive image of the country, but the fight against humor must be waged with more subtle tools, among which time plays a role.

The third case is criminal. The topic of protecting women's rights in Kazakhstan is very pressing.

Background: Case 3. According to public organizations, dozens of women are subjected to abuse, low self-esteem, and assault, which sometimes ends tragically. Many cases raised waves in society after yet another mockery of the weaker half of humanity. Typically, conflicts in families arise due to social reasons, such as lack of housing, large families, low level of education, low communication culture. However, the case that stands out in the study stands out from the rest. The persons involved were the former adviser to the First President, ex-minister the national economy and his wife S., whom he mercilessly killed for a long time, and then tried to hide the crime. Expert S; Sadieva believes that "The case of the murder of Saltanat is a political matter. This is not just an everyday affair…. a stormy campaign is unfolding here in defense of the killer. Bishimbayev is the new Usenov in the new Kazakhstan" [17]. Maksat Usenov is a young man, who in 2013 hit six pedestrians with a BMW X6 and did not carry a name. After that, such cases began to be called "Usenovshchina." He managed to reconcile with the father of the deceased, which subsequently led to a change in the legislation of the Criminal Code of the Republic of Kazakhstan, and currently the method of resolving conflict as "reconciliation of the parties" is now prohibited. "Bishimbaev is also a marker for our elite. If you claim influence and status in society, … will you still run around buying positive posts? They don't convince anyone, they only highlight the horror of the situation," noted expert S. Sadieva (Fig. 4).

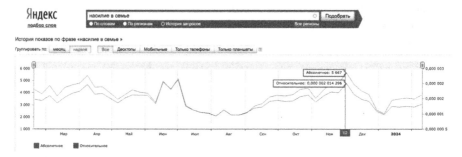

Fig. 4. Digital data on the topic "Domestic Violence" in 2023

In this case, which had a strong emotional impact on the public of Kazakhstan, new circumstances arose as attempts to influence public opinion through bloggers who had a certain authority in society, including journalists and public figures. If earlier the position of society was inclined to sympathize with the victim, but for the first time so-called "defenders" of the killer appeared, who, according to patterns incomprehensible to public morality, tried to convince society, whitewash the criminal, and give him positive qualities. The outright hypocrisy of some media personalities on social networks outraged the public. The fact that the reaction to this case was especially active was made decisive by the support of the President himself, who ordered that this case be taken carefully. Statistics show that one in three women in the world experiences physical or sexual violence from their partners. According to the General Prosecutor's Office, in Kazakhstan Every day the police receive 300 reports of domestic violence.

For this study, two online agencies in the Kazakh language and two in Russian were selected (although in principle they have three broadcast languages: state, Russian and English). These are Massaget.kz, Abai.kz Tengrinews.kz, informburo.kz. The peculiarity of these media was that they immediately posted their information on social networks, thereby increasing the audience and the number of comments. If we take two publications like Tengrinews.kz and informburo.kz, then the systematic approach to this case was unusually active. Typically, Tengrinews.kz publishes its information extremely selectively, trying to show mainly the activities of the government and large businessmen; even during popular campaigns, they are stingy with publication. However, in this case Tengrinews.kz has 42 materials. In Kazakh language Massaget.kz - 28 results. There are more than 12 thousand comments in Russian on the social network Facebook. Of which more than 9 thousand have a negative attitude towards the criminal. Search engine Google.com shows that this case in Kazakh has about 3,800 results (0.27 s), in Russian there are about 9960 results (0.32 s).

Content analysis of scanned comments shows that there are almost no neutral statements. All carry a strong positive or negative emotional connotation. The main result of this case led to the fact that provisions were adopted at the national level that had not been resolved for years [18].

However, among commentators there are many who do not approve of the victim's passive behavior and recommend that they behave more boldly and come under pressure and intimidation. However, it's easy to recommend! Just the day before, a video appeared on social networks of a man attacking his wife in a hairdresser and cutting her throat with a penknife. The police released the man. Another husband doused his wife, who was working in a bank, with gasoline and set her on fire. Again the criminal was reprimanded. There have been so many such cases that public organizations have been created to protect victims of family abuse. Not all foundations and public organizations are supported by the authorities, even persecuted. "The problem of domestic violence is becoming a painful wound in society. Every year, at least 80 women die in the country because of this immorality, about 150 are seriously injured, 200 are of moderate severity and more than 4 thousand are slightly injured. The police receive 300 reports every day," reports the head of the service for the protection of public interests of the General Prosecutor's Office, Marat Abishev. For example, in 2020, a petition to criminalize domestic violence and adopt a new law on domestic violence collected about 100 thousand signatures. In 2023, a similar petition collected 150 thousand signatures in just a couple of days.

In September 2020, the Parliament considered the bill "On combating domestic violence." But its acceptance was delayed. Only in January 2024 will the draft law be considered again "On issues of ensuring women's rights and ensuring the safety of children" was initiated by deputies of the Mazhilis. What is planned to change: In articles 106 (Intentional infliction of grievous bodily harm), 107 (Intentional infliction of moderate harm to health) and 110 (Torture) of the Criminal Code the type of punishment - restriction of freedom - is excluded.

According to expert Azhigulova, the decriminalization of physical violence in the past was a serious mistake. Because, according to her, over several years it has led to an increase in crime.

3 Sampling and Data Analysis

To tackle the RQs, we use data from the Telegram messenger and Yandex.ru statistics to analyze the statistics from social networks such as Facebook, Instagram, and YouTube for the period of 2023. Content analysis was applied, and software tools were used to download posts and comments from the platforms. 12,000+ comments and their corresponding posts on three cases were downloaded. Dictionaries were used based on word use frequency and expert reading. More than 3,000 negative comments openly expressed anger, indignation, fear, and social anxiety. Based on the statistical data, a curve was identified for the frequency of posts and comments on critical topics with the regard of their relevance; in each case, it showed a decline within 7–10 days from peak days, thus supporting previous findings on cumulative crises in online discussions [19]. The type of content (text, text + photo, text + video, etc.), the type of emotion (anger, sadness, rage, anger, joy, delight, etc.), the genre nature of the posts (informational, analytical, abstract), and the sentiment in the comments (positive, neutral, negative) were coded as variables. We have also employed process tracing to detect governmental action during cases, including legal action and the efforts in online communication.

4 Preliminary Results

The results of the study show that public sentiment reveals the distrust that has formed in the legal branch of government and the lack of confidence in the positive adoption of new laws that protect human rights. We reveal the inertia of government institutions in responding to public crises with cumulative emotional outbursts in user talk; the lack of official response to them gave rise to new emotional waves, no less disturbing to the public. At this background, though, unlike in previously studied Russian cases, a positive factor was the involvement of the Mazhilis of Parliament in public discussion of acute crisis events. The President's speech spread on social networks helped increase trust in the government and helped overcome internal conflicts on both the overall discussion level and on the micro-level of interpersonal interlocutions. This study reveals the gradual involvement of government and business in conflictual discussions on social networks, which increases the level of trust in society and casts a positive effect on cumulative public opinion, reducing the level of criticism and negativity. At the level of the Mazhilis of the Parliament of Kazakhstan, there is a serious discussion of changes in the country's legislation, which is the result of the active civil position of society partly formed by heated discussions on social networks. Taking into account all of the above, we formulated the following research results: How does emotional polarization (positive and negative emotions) manifest itself in online discussions, and which emotions accumulate more strongly over time? As the analysis shows, society is ready for active actions in order to defend those principles and ideals that preserve national integrity and identity. Trust and distrust were clearly demonstrated in user texts. People do not always trust, since even authoritative persons can change their beliefs and show their negative insides. There are fewer and fewer users who have begun to completely trust social networks, because critical thinking is developing, media literacy is increasing, and they are becoming resistant to fakes and disinformation. In each of the cases under consideration, representatives of government authorities are present, including as participants in discussions in the cases we are considering. Sometimes their position is wrong, but they are flexible in changing it if they see that they are wrong, as in the case of Borat. The President's attitude towards domestic violence also provided strong emotional support, which intensified the adoption of amendments to the Laws. In the online environment, they listen to the opinions of the authorities, at the same time they critically perceive the positions of the so-called influencers, who discredited themselves during the discussion of complex events of a criminal nature, which develops the user, making him emotionally sensitive in relation to trust and distrust.

Disclosure of Interests. The authors have no competing interests to declare that are relevant to the content of this article.

References

1. Bodrunova, S.S.: The concept of cumulative deliberation: linking systemic approaches to healthier normativity in assessing opinion formation in online discussions. J. Assoc. Inf. Sci. Technol., 1–15 (2023). https://doi.org/10.1002/asi.24850
2. Hong, S., Na, J.: How Facebook is perceived and used by people across cultures: the implications of cultural differences in the use of Facebook. Soc. Psychol. Pers. Sci. **9**(4), 435–443 (2018)
3. Bodrunova, S.S., Litvinenko, A.A.: Four Russias in communication: fragmentation of the Russian public sphere in the 2010s. In: Dobek-Ostrowska, B., Glowacki, M. (eds.) Democracy and Media in Central and Eastern Europe 25 Years On, pp. 63–79. Peter Lang (2015)
4. Bykov, I., Hradziushka, A., Ibrayeva, G., Turdubaeva, E.: Instant messaging for journalists and PR-practitioners: a study of four countries. In: Bodrunova, S. (ed.) Proceedings of the 5th International Conference, INSCI 2018, St. Petersburg, Russia, 24–26 October 2018, Proceedings (2018)
5. Akbari, A., Gabdulhakov, R.: Platform surveillance and resistance in Iran and Russia: the case of Telegram. Surveill. Soc. **17**(1/2), 223–231 (2019)
6. Bodrunova, S.S., Nepiyushchikh, D.: Unhealthy communication on health: discursive and ecosystemic features of opinion cumulation in the anti-vaccination discourse on Russian Telegram. World Media **1** (Accepted for publication for 2024)
7. Mickiewicz, E., Ibrayeva, G.: Elite Students in Kazakhstan: complexities of the internet and the international arena. In: Davydov, S. (ed.) Internet in the Post-Soviet Area, pp. 183–201. Springer, Cham (2023). https://doi.org/10.1007/978-3-031-32507-6_9
8. Kim, S., Kim, J.: The information ecosystem of conspiracy theory: examining the QAnon narrative on Facebook. Proc. ACM Hum.-Comput. Interact. **7**(CSCW1), 1–24 (2023). https://doi.org/10.31219/osf.io/wku5b
9. Smoliarova, A.S., Bodrunova, S.S., Blekanov, I.S.: Politicians driving online discussions: are institutionalized influencers top Twitter users? In: Kompatsiaris, I., et al. (eds.) Internet Science. LNCS, vol. 10673, pp. 132–147. Springer, Cham (2017). https://doi.org/10.1007/978-3-319-70284-1_11

10. Nigmatullina, K., Bodrunova, S.S., Rodossky, N., Nepiyushchikh, D.: Discourse of complaining on social networks in russia: cumulative opinions vs. decentering of institutions. In: Antonyuk, A., Basov, N. (eds.) Fifth Networks in the Global World Conference, vol. 663, pp. 3–20. Springer, Cham (2022). https://doi.org/10.1007/978-3-031-29408-2_1

11. Forbes Kazakhstan: "Yandex Kazakhstan" presented statistics on the use of "Search" in the Republic of Kazakhstan Users of social networks in Kazakhstan. https://forbes.kz//actual/technologies/yandeks_kazahstan_predstavil_statistiku_ispolzovaniya_poiska_i_drugih_ser visov_v_rk. Accessed 3 Feb 2024

12. How many VKontakte users by country. https://uchet-jkh.ru/i/skolko-polzovatelei-vkontakte-po-stranam. Accessed 3 Feb 2024

13. Telegram statistics in 2024 (updated) – Inclient. https://inclient.ru/telegram-stats. Accessed 3 Feb 2024

14. Hasebrink, U., Holig, S.: Audience-based indicators for news media performance: a conceptual framework and findings from Germany. Media Perform Times Media Change **8**(3) (2020)

15. Statement by businessman Mukhoryapov about the Kazakh language: the police opened a case under the article of "inciting hatred". https://rus.azattyq.org/a/32105480.html, Accessed 3 Feb 2024

16. Isakhanov, T.: Borat's new foray into the image of Kazakhstan. https://ia-centr.ru/experts/timur-isakhanov/noviy-nabeg-borata-na-imidzh-kazakhstana/Ia-centr.ru. Accessed 3 Feb 2024

17. Sadieva, S.: Expert: Bishimbayev is a stress test for justice and a marker for the elite. Lvdv, 11 November 2023. https://www.lada.kz/kazakhstan-news/116419-ekspert-bishimbaev-eto-stress-test-dlya-pravosudiya-i-marker-dlya-elity.html. Accessed 3 Feb 2024

18. Women changing the country: Will new laws be able to stop domestic abusers in Kazakhstan? 9 January 2024. https://tengrinews.kz/article/jenschinyi-menyayuschie-stranu-smogut-novyie-zakonyi-2290/. Accessed 3 Feb 2024

19. Rodicheva, A., Bodrunova, S.S., Blekanov, I.S., Tarasov, N., Belyakova, N.: Crisis communication and reputation management of Russian brands on social media. In: Digital Geography – Proceedings of the International Conference on Internet and Modern Society (IMS 2023). Accepted for publication in 2024 (in print)

Spatial and Temporal Patterns of Government – Citizen Interaction Online. Examining the Social Media Pages of the Russian Regional Authorities

Yury Kabanov[1,2]([✉]) [iD] and Anna Kuzmenko[1] [iD]

[1] HSE University, St. Petersburg, Russia
ykabanov@hse.ru
[2] ITMO University, St. Petersburg, Russia

Abstract. The current stage of e-participation development in Russia is associated with unification across the country as well as the institutionalization of social media (SM) as a channel of government-citizen communication. As a result, subnational governments are actively launching and utilizing their official SM pages. This pilot study attempts to explore some emerging patterns of their use by public authorities and citizens. The overview of 79 regions is complemented by a deep analysis of five cases. Overall, one may notice substantial variation in how actively these SM pages are used across the country, which may reflect the differences in regional e-governance performance as well as human capital development. In terms of content, the communication is mostly centered on non-politicized issues related to socioeconomic policies and public administration. This trend can be attributed to most of the regions, though some peculiar topics can be revealed in separate cases. While the focus of SM pages is on informing citizens, the latter seem to use these pages to communicate their problems to the public authorities, thus contributing to the institutionalization of SM as an e-participation mechanism. At the same time, the level of engagement remains low and does not show a certain positive or negative trend so far, despite the recent federal initiatives.

Keywords: E-Participation · Social Media · Russian Regions · Topical Modeling

1 Introduction

Since 2020, the system of e-participation in Russia has undergone significant changes towards centralization and unification across the country. The regions have joined the federal *Feedback Platform*, and the so-called *Regional Control Centers* (RCC) have been established to monitor the situation and intensify interaction with citizens via social media (SM) [4]. In line with federal regulations, regional and municipal organizations are actively launching their official SM pages: as of 2023, about 220,000 accounts have been created.[1] Thus, SM in Russia are in the active process of institutionalization as a channel of government-citizen communication, alongside specialized government-led portals [5]. By institutionalization here we may understand, following Criado and Villodre, «the formal decision to deliberately incorporate these technologies in the organization or routinize them into the organizational processes» [3, p. 2].

Due to the novelty of these changes, few studies have been carried out so far to investigate how these SM pages are used by regional governments and citizens. In this paper, we address this gap and present a pilot exploratory study to reveal some major patterns of SM use in 79 regions of Russia. We are interested in the dynamics of post and comment publication, as well as the main topics covered. Our general overview is then complemented by a deeper analysis of five cases.

The structure of the paper is as follows: Section 2 is devoted to the literature review and background of the study; in Sect. 3, we describe the data and techniques used, Sect. 4 reports the main findings. Some contributions and further steps are given in the conclusion.

2 Background

Public authorities across the globe are increasing their presence online, complementing government-led e-participation portals with the use of SM. Many scholars consider these efforts positively as an attempt to raise citizens' awareness of e-participation, foster civic engagement and community building, and provide more inclusive and effective e-participation ecosystems [12, 19, 23, 28]. Despite normative expectations and emerging empirical studies, the topic is still at an early stage of development, and more research is needed to learn how SM are utilized in various political contexts [1].

This is especially relevant, as the trend goes beyond Western democracies. A vivid example here is China. Numerous studies devoted to Internet politics in the country report that SM act as a useful tool for governance and political stability. The government collects information about citizens' views and shapes them online [7], controls the conduct of low-level bureaucracy, and mitigates public discontent [13]. The use of SM may provoke some responsiveness towards citizens' complaints [15] and provide space for limited public deliberation, generating extra legitimacy for authorities [8, 14].

The use of SM in public administration is not new to Russia either. However, up until recently, this practice has not been formally institutionalized. Early studies on this topic were mostly focused on the role SM played in mobilization, political discussions, and contention among various sociopolitical groups [18, 26], rather than in citizens' engagement in public policy issues. In this context, SM have gained popularity with politicians in Russia since the 2010s, mainly due to Dmitry Medvedev's proactive position towards the Internet [16]. Twitter and other SM became trendy among regional governors, who, as Toepfl put it, used them to gain extra input- and output- legitimacy [27]. Renz and Sullivan revealed a variety of roles governors' Twitter accounts actually

---

[1] The number of *gospubliki* in Russia has reached 220 thousand. D-Russia.ru. 02.11.2023. URL: https://d-russia.ru/kolichestvo-gospablikov-v-rossii-dostiglo-220-tysjach.html   (accessed: 10.11.2023) [in Russian].

played, from a symbolic tool to «an actual working instrument to run the administration» [17, p. 149]. However, when it comes to the subnational authorities' pages on SM, scholars would express serious skepticism about their capacity to become meaningful channels for government-citizen communication [11].

The current stage started in 2020, when the federal government announced significant changes in the e-participation system. Most of the subnational authorities were to join the federal *Feedback Platform* and create RCCs to coordinate regional authorities' activities related to SM and citizens' complaint processing. A special organization, *ANO Dialogue-Regions*, was established to facilitate these processes, provide subnational governments with technical assistance and education, and disseminate the best practices [4]. Official SM pages (*gospubliki*) became a crucial component of this new policy: in 2022, a federal law was adopted to oblige public authorities and organizations to create such pages in *VKontakte (VK)* and *Odnoklassniki* social networks.[2] What is also important is that regional authorities' performance on SM is further evaluated by the federal government, and regional rankings are formed [9].

With the new federal legislation, the use of SM by public authorities is becoming a formally institutionalized practice, while rankings and other enforcement mechanisms incentivize local authorities to comply with it. However, despite the efforts to unify the SM strategies of the regions, one may still find significant disproportions in their development [10]. It opens up new possibilities for regional comparisons, but so far, few studies have been carried out in this field. Though scholars are mostly positive about governments' endeavors to facilitate communication with citizens, they also notice the lack of citizens' engagement, as well as the prevalence of informing citizens rather than involving them in effective interaction [5]. Due to the dynamism of this process, new studies are needed to track regional performance in this sphere.

3 Data and Methods

Overall, this exploratory pilot study covers 79 SM pages of the Russian regional authorities for the period from January 1, 2022, to January 1, 2023. The dataset contains about 165 thousand posts and 1.49 million comments.

First, we analyze the data on the number of posts and comments in each region using the correlation analysis technique and some secondary data. It helps us define some spatial patterns of SM use. Then, we conduct topic modeling (LDA model) to build word clouds and topic profiles. Preprocessing of the raw textual data, such as lemmatization and tokenization, is conducted via Python 3.0. To remove stop-words, the 'nltk package' is used [30], as well as Pymystem3, the Python wrapper for the Yandex Mystem 3 morphological analyzer. Texts in Russian are subject to morphological analysis and lemmatization using the Mystem technique, which is often used in different natural language processing applications [25].

---

[2] Federal Law N 270-FZ On amendments to the Federal Law "On ensuring access to information on the activities of state bodies and local governments" and Article 10 of the Federal Law "On ensuring access to information on the activities of courts in the Russian Federation". 14.07.2022. URL: https://base.garant.ru/404992163/ (accessed 15.11.2023) [in Russian].

Also, we calculated cosine similarity measures between posts and comments for each region. This metric allows us to calculate the proximity of vectors and determine how similar text corpora are to one another. The closer the value to 1, the more similar are the texts [6, 31], which may indicate that comments are more relevant to posts and follow a similar topic [17].

Then, five cases are selected for a deeper analysis of temporal dynamics. In addition to the indicators mentioned above, we analyze the engagement rate (ER) using the analytical tool *Popsters* (https://popsters.ru/). For these cases, the period of analysis is extended for another year (till December 31, 2023).

4   Results of the Study

4.1   General Trends of SM Use in the Russian Regions

In general, we may observe significant disparities in how actively SM pages are utilized by regional governments and citizens. The number of posts in 2022 ranged from 295 in Ingushetia to 7550 in Sakha (Yakutia), with an average of about 2088. While the SM page of Khakassia had 443 comments from citizens, there were 234310 comments in Smolensk Oblast, with an average of about 18872. The cosine similarity measures also differed substantially across the country, from 0.22 in Tatarstan to 0.94 in Adygea, with an average of 0.53.

In order to reveal some patterns in the observed variance, we conducted a correlation analysis (Pearson's correlation). The development of e-participation in Russia is known to be uneven and dependent on both supply-side (regional capacity, resources) and demand-side (citizens' motivation, human capital) factors [9, 10]. For our analysis, we selected some of these 'usual suspects'. As for the supply-side factors, we use the data on e-participation and e-government (e-services) performance in the regions, as well as the general effectiveness of the regional administrations. The data on the Internet and VK penetration, as well as the quality of life and level of urbanization, are used to operationalize the demand-side variables. The data sources are described in detail in Table 1. The final sample for the correlation analysis consists of 77 cases; the cases of Sakha and Smolensk Oblast are omitted as outliers.

The results of the correlation analysis are presented in Table 2. The coefficients are not very high, so the links between the variables are not very strong; however, most of them are statistically significant. First of all, the numbers of posts and comments correlate significantly with each other (.496**)[3]: the more active the regional authorities are in SM, the more feedback they are likely to get from the public. An important variable for both posts and comments is the level of VK penetration in a region (but not the share of Internet users in general): the more people use VK in a region, the more actively a regional government's SM page is developing.

Furthermore, the number of posts is associated with such supply-side variables as the quality of e-participation and e-government provision and, to a certain extent, the general effectiveness of the regional administrations. If a region successfully develops its own channels of citizens' engagement and has the necessary expertise in digital governance

---

[3] Note: ** – correlation is significant at 0.01 level, * – correlation is significant at 0.05 level.

and regional capacity, it is more likely to be an active SM user. Statistically speaking, more urbanized regions also use SM more actively.

Table 1. Variables for Correlation Analysis

Variable	Indicator	Source
EPART	Quality of e-participation channels (2021)	ITMO University [2]
EGOV	E-Services provision quality (2021)	Ministry of Economic Development[a]
RQG	Rating of Governance Effectiveness in the Subjects of the Russian Federation (2021)	Agency of Political and Economic Communications[b]
VK	Penetration of VK authors (2023)	Brand Analytics[c]
INT	The share of broadband Internet users (2021)	Federal State Statistics Service (Rosstat)[d]
URBAN	Percentage of citizens living in cities (2021)	
IQL	Quality of life rating score in a region (2021)	RIA Rating Agency[e]

[a]Rating of regions by quality of electronic public services in 2021 is presented. D-Russia.Ru. URL: https://d-russia.ru/predstavlen-rejting-regionov-po-kachestvu-predostavlenija-jelektronnyh-gosuslug-v-2021-godu.html (accessed 20.04.2023). [in Russian].
[b]Rating of governance effectiveness in the subjects of the Russian Federation Agency of Political and Economic Communications. URL: http://www.apecom.ru/projects/list.php?SECTION_ID=91 (accessed 20.04.2023) [in Russian].
[c]Social media statistics. Brand Analytics. URL: https://brandanalytics.ru/statistics/am/vk/month (accessed 01.01.2024) [in Russian]. Note: due to the data availability, we use the scores for October 2023, assuming the measure to be quite stable.
[d]Regions of Russia: Socio-Economic Indicators – 2022. Rosstat. URL: https://rosstat.gov.ru/folder/210/document/13204 (accessed 10.04.2023). [in Russian].
[e]Rating of the Regions based on the Life Quality. 2021. RIA Rating. URL: https://riarating.ru/infografika/20220215/630216951.html (accessed: 20.11.2023) [in Russian].

Table 2. Results of the Correlation Analysis. Authors' Calculations

	EPART	EGOV	RQG	VK	INT	IQL	URBAN
POSTS	.308**	.295**	.287*	.382**	.061	.208	.318**
COMMENTS	.223	.162	.290*	.467**	−.141	.303**	.168
COSINE	.086	.042	.155	.076	−.132	.119	.058

Notes: ** – correlation is significant at 0.01 level, * – correlation is significant at 0.05 level, the number of cases is 77.

As for the number of comments, apart from the share of VK users, they may also be linked to the quality of life in a region. This composite indicator, combining economic, social, environmental, and other conditions, may be considered a proxy for the level of human development. In this context, this finding is in line with previous studies, which emphasize the importance of human development in fostering e-participation [20].

Additionally, correlations were calculated with the dummy variables for the federal districts (FD) the regions belong to. Here, some weak but significant correlations are also observed: positive for the Northwestern FD (.265* for posts and .282* for comments) and negative for the North Caucasian FD (−.261* for posts and −.253* for comments) and the Far Eastern FD (−.274* for comments). None of the other correlations are significant.

Correlations cannot tell us anything about the causal relationship between the variables, but they might be a good starting point for further analysis. The pilot study indicates some spatial variations in how regional governments and citizens use SM channels. As a hypothesis in this regard, the activities of the administrations themselves are more dependent on the supply-side factors related to their e-participation and e-government performance, while the demand-side factors, like human capital, might explain the use of SM by the citizens.

The score of cosine similarity does not correlate significantly with any of the variables, including the number of posts and comments. So far, we may hypothesize, first, that the variance reflects the peculiarities of the regional SM strategies: for example, some regions focus on visual content, while others post more textual information. It may lead to differences between the texts of posts and comments. Secondly, it might be explained by how communities are formed around these SM pages and how people use these new avenues of communication with the government. Low cosine similarity may imply that the topics of comments are not related to the content of posts [17, 29]. For example, citizens use a post as a trigger to raise other issues of concern, to draw attention to other problems in the region, to start a discussion on another topic, etc. Some anecdotal evidence of such cases has been revealed during our screening of the SM pages, but a deeper analysis is required to understand this phenomenon.

Another part of our analysis is devoted to the topics often covered by the regional authorities. All posts are processed as a single text corpus, so the topics reflect some general patterns of the discourse generated by the government, which can be attributed to multiple regions. However, it should be noted that individual topic profiles may (and do, in fact) deviate from this overall picture.

In 2022, the most prominent topic was COVID-19, followed by various issues, mostly related to the area of social and economic policy, like sports, education, social support, family and children, healthcare, culture, local tourism, regional development, and some other topics (see Table 3). On average, government-citizen communication online is dominated by non-politicized discourse on local public policy and public administration issues. As the screening of these SM pages suggests, the regional authorities often use them to report on some developments, achievements, events, new decisions, or public officials' activities in one of the abovementioned areas.

This observation corresponds to the general idea of e-participation as citizens' engagement in policymaking, rather than politics [24]. The topic profile we observe in the case of the Russian regions indicates this trend as well: the SM seem to convert into a platform of so-called technocratic or administrative political participation, which

Table 3. Topic Weights. Authors' Calculations

Topic	Weight	Topic	Weight
Sport	0.07	Education	0.06
Forest fires	0.06	Healthcare	0.06
Agriculture	0.10	Victory Day celebration	0.06
Coronavirus	0.11	Weather and environment	0.06
Family and children	0.07	Media communication	0.06
Local tourism	0.05	Culture	0.07
Federal program for regional economic development	0.06	Social support for families with children	0.06
Regional development	0.06		

is introduced to «transform conflicts into issues of policy refinement and implementation» [27, p. 810]. The fact that many topics are shared by various regions also provokes the assumption that there might be some general information policy affecting regional media agendas. This assumption is plausible, given the new centralized approach towards e-participation, but further empirical studies in this regard are needed.

4.2 Comparison of Cases

The overall picture presented above is to be complemented by the analysis of cases, for which we have selected five regions: the Republic of Sakha (Yakutia), the Republic of Adygea, as well as Smolensk, Ryazan and Tomsk Oblasts. They represent various geographical areas and federal districts. What is more important is that these regions demonstrate different dynamics of SM use. In 2022, Sakha had the highest number of posts, while Smolensk Oblast had the highest number of comments. Ryazan, and Tomsk Oblasts were the regions with a median number of posts (1877) and comments (12146), respectively. For this study, we first build individual topic profiles based on posts and comments in 2022 and then analyze the trends of the engagement rate (ER) in 2022–2023.

Table 4 represents the regional topic profiles, based on the posts published in 2022. If a topic is revealed, it is marked gray. It can be seen that some topics resemble the overall agenda depicted in Table 3. These topics are also found in five regions, for example, the questions of regional development and construction (e.g., road construction), the issues of culture and art (including cultural events, holidays, and entertainment), and healthcare (in particular, the news about COVID-19 and vaccination). Another topic common to most of the regions is policymaking and governance: posts that describe decisions of the regional administrations, activities to solve regional problems, etc. The federal program for regional economic development was also revealed as an important topic for three regions, as were the issues of urban projects and housing services. Some topics are quite unique to particular regions in the sample but nevertheless have been identified in the overall agenda: for instance, the issue of forest fires in Sakha and the question of agriculture in Ryazan Oblast.

Table 5 presents the topic profiles of the comments. A topic found in all the regions is related to the citizens' appeals, complaints, and addresses to public administration organizations. We can say that this is one of the most popular topics, which proves that these SM pages are identified by citizens as a channel to articulate their problems to the government and raise issues they find important. So, SM pages may indeed become a new channel of e-participation. Responsiveness to these appeals by the regional administrations is yet another question, requiring further studies. It should be added that in some regions, citizens' appeals are also complemented by the expression of gratitude as well as patriotic statements.

Another frequent topic, which resonates with the governmental agenda, is regional development and construction (including road repairs). The same pattern applies to the topic of urban projects and housing development problems. On the contrary, federal projects on development are not often identified as a separate topic. The third issue, found in all the regions, is devoted to social support and government support in general, implying government spending to support families, social groups, enterprises, etc. In three regions, the topic of education was also profound, including the issues of schools and enlightenment. Other topics (like healthcare) are not so widespread, especially when compared to the topic profiles of posts.

Table 4. Topic Profiles of Posts in the Selected Regions. Authors' Calculations

Topics	Adygea	Smolensk	Sakha	Ryazan	Tomsk
Federal program for regional development					
Regional development, construction					
Social support, social projects					
Healthcare (vaccination, doctors)					
Sport (sport for children)					
Children, child policy					
Culture, art, local events, entertainment					
Victory Day celebration					
Weather and environment					
Media communication					
Urban projects, housing					
Official news					
Policymaking and governance					
Local sights					
Issues of the Far Eastern District					
Forest fires					
Agriculture					
Budget					
Communication with Governor					
Key personalities of the region					

In general, we can see that individual topic profiles to some extent follow the overall agenda, emphasizing the issues of social and economic policy as well as public administration, while particular problems of the regions are also highlighted. At the same time, the topic profiles of posts and comments are not exactly identical. In the latter, citizens'

Table 5. Topic Profiles of Comments in the Selected Regions. Authors' Calculations

Topics	Adygea	Smolensk	Sakha	Ryazan	Tomsk
Citizens' appeals and complaints					
Regional development, construction					
Social support, government support					
Urban projects, housing					
Education, school education					
Family and children					
Retirement					
Expression of gratitude					
Healthcare					
Patriotism					
Holidays and celebrations					
Media communication					
Federal projects					

appeals are a profound topic, which may indicate that SM have become an e-participation tool to collect citizens' feedback.

Finally, we need to evaluate the temporal patterns of SM use in the selected regions. We are especially interested in possible changes that have occurred since December 2022, when the federal regulations mentioned in Sect. 2 came into effect. In order to do this, we use the data on the daily ER provided by the *Popsters*.

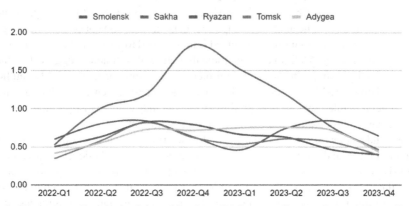

Fig. 1. Engagement Rate in the Selected Regions, by Quarters. **Source**: Popsters (https://popste rs.ru/)

Based on these data (Fig. 1), it is hard to identify a single trend of citizens' engagement, whether positive or negative: in all the regions, the ER is very volatile and seemingly dependent on particular posts. The type of content may also matter. According to the data from the *Popsters*, for example, video content attracts more attention in Sakha, Ryazan, and Smolensk Oblasts, while for Tomsk Oblast and Adygea, the highest ER is generated by images. At the same time, most of the posts published contain textual information, followed by images.

The highest average ER is found in Sakha (1.06), followed by Smolensk Oblast (0.69), Adygea (0.63), Ryazan Oblast (0.61), and Tomsk Oblast (0.55). Overall, the scores are not high and demonstrate rather low engagement of citizens. Since December 2022, when all public organizations were obliged to launch their official SM pages, the average ER has even slightly declined, except for Adygea. In sum, the data we have suggest that the new policy does not seem to have affected citizens' involvement so far, though it may also be due to its novelty.

5 Conclusion

The pilot study presented above should be considered an initial stage towards a more thorough analysis of government-citizen communication patterns, emerging in the context of changes in the overall e-participation ecosystem. As in the case of other e-participation institutions in Russia [9, 10], the development of the official SM pages is not even across the country. Our preliminary analysis shows that possible drivers of regional governments' performance may be due to supply-side factors, for instance, the quality of e-participation and e-government provision. At the same time, the level of citizens' engagement may be associated with the social characteristics of the regions, including human capital development. Further studies are needed to confirm the significance of these factors.

Currently, we may agree with previous studies [4], that the level of engagement remains at a rather low level. As the selected cases show, it is quite volatile and dependent on particular posts. The recent federal requirements do not seem to have significantly affected this situation. The analysis of topics reveals that these SM pages are used to generally inform citizens about non-politicized issues related to socio-economic policy and public administration. Additionally, the topic modeling of comments suggests that these pages are used by citizens to raise their problems and communicate them to the authorities. Based on how SM pages are used by governments and citizens, as well as given the recent federal regulations, we may preliminarily conclude that the institutionalization of SM as a new e-participation platform in Russia is going on.

The study opens up some avenues for further research on this topic. Firstly, it is crucial to understand the impact these SM pages will have on the level of government responsiveness, as well as other effects on governance and citizen participation reported for similar political systems. Secondly, another aspect of this topic is related to the deep analysis of emerging discourse. Our study has revealed substantial differences in the degree of similarity between posts and comments, and the explanation of this variance may give valuable insights into the nature of government-citizen communication and government responsiveness. This analysis may also be complemented by the study of post and comment tonality, and their spatial and temporal patterns. Thirdly, given the trends towards unification, it will be interesting to compare the degrees of centralization and decentralization in the formation of regional social media agendas and explore the impact of federal requirements on the level of citizens' engagement. Finally, overall, the analysis of the case of Russia may help to understand the features, drivers, and barriers of SM institutionalization as an e-participation channel [3]. This research should be complemented by a qualitative analysis of particular cases. These steps, in our view, will significantly contribute to the role SM play in politics and governance in general, and particularly in Russia.

Acknowledgements. The research was supported by the Russian Science Foundation grant No. 22-18-00364 "Institutional Transformation of E-Participation Governance in Russia: A Study of Regional Peculiarities" (https://rscf.ru/project/22-18-00364/).

References

1. Alarabiat, A., Soares, D.S., Estevez, E.: Electronic participation with a special reference to social media - a literature review. In: Tambouris, E., et al. (eds.) Electronic Participation. LNCS, vol. 9821, pp. 41–52. Springer, Cham (2016). https://doi.org/10.1007/978-3-319-450 74-2_4

2. Chugunov, A., et al.: Regional e-participation portals evaluation: preliminary results from Russia. In: Virkar, S., et al. (eds.) Ongoing Research, Practitioners, Posters, Workshops, and Projects of the International Conference EGOV-CeDEM-ePart, EGOV-CeDEM-ePart 2020, 31 August 2020–2 September 2020, pp. 71–78. CEUR, Virtual, Linkoping (2020)

3. Criado, J.I., Villodre, J.: Revisiting social media institutionalization in government. An empirical analysis of barriers. Gov. Inf. Q. **39**(2), 101643 (2022). https://doi.org/10.1016/j.giq.2021. 101643

4. Filatova, O., et al.: Transformation of the electronic participation system in Russia in the early 2020s: centralization trends. In: Bolgov, R., et al. (eds.) TIPG 2021. Springer Geography, pp. 309–319. Springer, Cham (2023). https://doi.org/10.1007/978-3-031-20620-7_27

5. Filatova, O., Chugunov, A.: Development of the E-participation ecosystem in Russia in the early 2020s: the role of social media and regional governance centers. Polit. Expert. Politex. **18**, 2, 120–137 (2022). https://doi.org/10.21638/spbu23.2022.201. (in Russian)

6. Gunawan, D., et al.: The implementation of cosine similarity to calculate text relevance between two documents. J. Phys. Conf. Ser., 12120 (2018). https://doi.org/10.1088/1742-6596/978/1/012120

7. Gunitsky, S.: Corrupting the cyber-commons: social media as a tool of autocratic stability. Perspect. Polit. **13**(1), 42–54 (2015). https://doi.org/10.1017/S1537592714003120

8. He, B., Warren, M.E.: Authoritarian deliberation: the deliberative turn in Chinese political development. Perspect. Polit. **9**(2), 269–289 (2011). https://doi.org/10.1017/S15375927110 00892

9. Kabanov, Y., et al.: Drivers of E-participation performance from a supply-side perspective: the case of the Russian regions. In: Getschko, D., et al. (eds.) ICEGOV 2023: Proceedings of the 16th International Conference on Theory and Practice of Electronic Governance, pp. 191–196. Association for Computing Machinery, New York, NY, USA (2023). https://doi.org/10.1145/3614321.3614347

10. Kabanov, Y.A., Chugunov, A.V.: Peculiarities of E-Governance in Russian regions: preliminary analysis of regional rankings and statistics. Int. J. Open Inf. Technol. **11**(12), 138–142 (2023). (in Russian)

11. Karyagin, M.: Russian large cities authorities' pages in social media: a platform for expert communication? In: Chugunov, A.V., Bolgov, R., Kabanov, Y., Kampis, G., Wimmer, M. (eds.) Digital Transformation and Global Society. CCIS, vol. 674, pp. 14–21. Springer, Cham (2016). https://doi.org/10.1007/978-3-319-49700-6_2

12. Lin, Y., Kant, S.: Using social media for citizen participation: contexts, empowerment, and inclusion. Sustainability **13**(12), 6635 (2021). https://doi.org/10.3390/su13126635

13. Lorentzen, P.: China's strategic censorship. Am. J. Pol. Sci. **58**(2), 402–414 (2014). https://doi.org/10.1111/ajps.12065
14. Medaglia, R., Zhu, D.: Paradoxes of deliberative interactions on government-managed social media: evidence from China. In: Duenas-Cid, D. et al. (eds.) Proceedings of the 17th International Digital Government Research Conference on Digital Government Research (DG.O 2016), pp. 435–444. Association for Computing Machinery, New York, NY, USA (2016). https://doi.org/10.1145/2912160.2912184
15. Meng, T., Yang, Z.: Variety of responsive institutions and quality of responsiveness in cyber China. China Rev. Rev. **20**(3), 13–42 (2020)
16. Moen-Larsen, N.: 'Dear Mr President'. The blogosphere as arena for communication between people and power. Communist Post-Communist Stud. **47**(1), 27–37 (2014). https://doi.org/10.1016/j.postcomstud.2014.01.007
17. Mozafari, M., et al.: Content similarity analysis of written comments under posts in social media. In: Jararweh, Y., Alsmirat, M. (eds.) 2019 Sixth International Conference on Social Networks Analysis, Management and Security (SNAMS), pp. 158–165. IEEE (2019). https://doi.org/10.1109/SNAMS.2019.8931726
18. Nechai, V., Goncharov, D.: Russian anti-corruption protests: how Russian Twitter sees it? In: Alexandrov, D.A., Boukhanovsky, A.V., Chugunov, A.V., Kabanov, Y., Koltsova, O. (eds.) Digital Transformation and Global Society. CCIS, vol. 745, pp. 270–281. Springer, Cham (2017). https://doi.org/10.1007/978-3-319-69784-0_23
19. Pflughoeft, B.R., Schneider, I.E.: Social media as E-participation: can a multiple hierarchy stratification perspective predict public interest? Gov. Inf. Q. **37**(1), 101422 (2020). https://doi.org/10.1016/j.giq.2019.101422
20. Pirannejad, A., et al.: Towards a balanced E-participation index: integrating government and society perspectives. Gov. Inf. Q. **36**(4), 101404 (2019). https://doi.org/10.1016/j.giq.2019.101404
21. Renz, B., Sullivan, J.: Making a connection in the provinces? Russia's tweeting governors. East Eur. Polit. **29**(2), 135–151 (2013). https://doi.org/10.1080/21599165.2013.779258
22. Rodan, G., Jayasuriya, K.: The technocratic politics of administrative participation: case studies of Singapore and Vietnam. Democratization **14**(5), 795–815 (2007). https://doi.org/10.1080/13510340701635662
23. Sæbø, Ø., Rose, J., Nyvang, T.: The role of social networking services in eParticipation. In: Macintosh, A., Tambouris, E. (eds.) Electronic Participation. LNCS, vol. 5694, pp. 46–55. Springer, Heidelberg (2009). https://doi.org/10.1007/978-3-642-03781-8_5
24. Sæbø, Ø., et al.: The shape of eParticipation: characterizing an emerging research area. Gov. Inf. Q. **25**(3), 400–428 (2008). https://doi.org/10.1016/j.giq.2007.04.007
25. Segalovich, I.: A fast morphological algorithm with unknown word guessing induced by a dictionary for a web search engine. In: Proceedings of the International Conference on Machine Learning; Models, Technologies and Applications, MLMTA 2003, 23–26 June 2003, Las Vegas, Nevada, USA, pp. 273–280. CSREA Press (2003)
26. Sherstobitov, A.: The potential of social media in Russia: from political mobilization to civic engagement. In: EGOSE 2014: Proceedings of the 2014 Conference on Electronic Governance and Open Society: Challenges in Eurasia, pp. 162–166. Association for Computing Machinery, New York, NY, USA (2014). https://doi.org/10.1145/2729104.2729118
27. Toepfl, F.: Blogging for the sake of the president: the online diaries of Russian governors. Eur. Asia Stud. **64**(8), 1435–1459 (2012). https://doi.org/10.1080/09668136.2012.712261
28. Vicente, M.R., Novo, A.: An empirical analysis of e-participation. The role of social networks and e-government over citizens' online engagement. Gov. Inf. Q. **31**(3), 379–387 (2014). https://doi.org/10.1016/j.giq.2013.12.006

29. Wang, J., et al.: Diversionary comments under political blog posts. In: Chen, X. (ed.) CIKM 2012: Proceedings of the 21st ACM International Conference on Information and Knowledge Management, pp. 1789–1793. Association for Computing Machinery, New York, NY, USA (2012). https://doi.org/10.1145/2396761.2398518

30. Yao, J.: Automated sentiment analysis of text data with NLTK. J. Phys. Conf. Ser. **1187**(5), 52020 (2019). https://doi.org/10.1088/1742-6596/1187/5/052020

31. Ye, J.: Cosine similarity measures for intuitionistic fuzzy sets and their applications. Math. Comput. Model.Comput. Model. **53**(1–2), 91–97 (2011). https://doi.org/10.1016/j.mcm.2010.07.022

Learned Futility: How Social Learning Can Lead to the Diffusion of Ineffective Strategies

Veronika Kurchyna[1]([✉]), Lilian Kojan[2], Jan Schneider[3], Bernd Wurpts[4],
Anastasia Golovin[5], André Calero Valdez[2], Jan Ole Berndt[1],
and Ingo J. Timm[1]

[1] German Research Center for Artificial Intelligence, Cognitive Social Simulation,
Trier, Germany
veronika.kurchyna@dfki.de
[2] University of Luebeck, Lübeck, Germany
[3] Wroclaw University of Science and Technology, Wrocław, Poland
[4] Wrocław, Poland
[5] Max Planck Institute for Dynamics and Self-Organization, Göttingen, Germany

Abstract. When facing a crisis, such as a novel type of disease, individuals need to learn about effective health measures and practices to prevent the spread of illness. They do so both through reflection about their own actions as well as the communal experience of their peers. Here, we present an agent-based model to examine the resulting dynamics in the diffusion of health behaviours and practices. In the model, we employ reinforcement learning and bounded confidence opinion dynamics to model varying degrees of external, e.g. social, and internal knowledge gains in the context of protective measures against a novel disease as use case. Our study shows that social influence is critical for the adoption of potentially effective low-cost strategies, while individual learning modes limit the spread of potentially harmful high-cost strategies. On the downside, social learning also facilitates the spread of ineffective or even harmful health measures and practices. Our findings suggest that cultural variation emerges in times of crisis among learning individuals.

Keywords: Agent-based Modelling · Multi-Agent Reinforcement Learning · Opinion Dynamics · Social Simulation

1 Introduction

The recent COVID-19 pandemic is the reflection of a broader pattern in the evolution of human history: increaseing numbers of emerging diseases. In the decades after the Second World War, hundreds of new diseases were identified, including dangerous pathogens that caused serious epidemics [24]. Increasing health threats through diseases call for a better understanding of the human responses that mediate the harmful impact of pathogens. While many of the

---

B. Wurpts—Independent Researcher.

emergency responses in modern societies are coordinated by governments and international organisations, in times of crisis, people frequently draw on their own knowledge and learn from their social environment. Lacking the knowledge about effective health measures and practices, individuals fall back on established measures from other contexts or develop health strategies in coordination with their social contacts. These micro-interactions and social learning experiences can produce cultural variation in the societal responses to epidemic diseases. This paper uses agent-based modelling to uncover some of the conditions under which effective and ineffective cultural variation emerges during times of crisis. Often certain groups display health behaviour that strongly differs from the majority. In the past, as example for effective group practices, we observed Jewish hygiene customs that safeguarded during the Black Death [27]. A contemporary example of ineffective or even harmful actions is the questionable use of anti-parasitic drugs during the recent COVID-19 pandemic [26]. In social simulation, such phenomena are typically framed as processes of opinion spread and assimilation [12], which could be interpreted as peer pressure, a contagion of fear, or behavioural imitation. At the same time, it is self-evident that individuals are not solely imitating the behaviour of others but are also capable of accumulating and evaluating their own experiences and will adjust their behaviour accordingly, something represented in agent-based modelling as agent learning [30].

In this paper, we combine both mechanisms to describe how cultural practices spread in the context of disease prevention. The distinctive innovation of our method lies in its capacity to facilitate the co-learning of various actions, encompassing a wide range of effectiveness, from potentially harmful to highly effective. In contrast to traditional reinforcement learning, this allows a convergence towards cultural practices that are actually ineffective in preventing diseases. Through this novel approach, we investigate the interplay of learning processes, social influence dynamics, and the propagation of diseases, with a particular emphasis on the emergence of seemingly ineffective strategies, despite the potential for knowledge acquisition.

2   Background, Motivation and Research Question

To understand the current relevance of this research, it is important to consider it in its historical and social context.

2.1   Epidemic Diseases and Societal Responses

While epidemic diseases played only a minor role in social scientific research for many decades, the recent COVID-19 pandemic led to new efforts to improve public health and investigate the change of societies. Social scientists widely agree that many factors drive social change. They are related to social and technological innovations, changing demographics, revolutions, wars, or economic crises. Infectious diseases are also increasingly recognised as contributors towards change. Major killers such as plague, cholera, smallpox, HIV/AIDS and other illnesses were important causes in the generation of different forms of organised social responses and the advancement of methods in public health [24].

Historically, epidemics are distinct from other, less destructive and widespread forms of disease, such as chronic or genetic ones. Infectious diseases are ongoing threats and human societies stay susceptible to the transmission of known and novel pathogens. Records of responses to epidemics are indicative of human creativity and diversity across societies and periods. As the dominant frameworks on the causes of diseases changed, so did the ways individuals and groups responded to changing health threats [24]. Reactions are intrinsically tied to dominant medical doctrines and prevalent structures of power. As an example, the handling of the reduced mortality among patients of homeopathic practitioners during a cholera outbreak illustrates two phenomena: For one, although homeopaths might attribute success to homeopathic treatments, it was likely due to differing hygiene and rehydration practices. It is difficult to identify effective practices in the absence of rigorous scientific methods, since individuals typically engage in multiple practices concurrently. For another, the medical establishment outright disregarded the success of the homeopaths without investigating the reasons of success [9]. Regardless of success, people are more likely to adopt practices of similar individuals than those perceived as different.

Jumping to the 21st century, the COVID-19 pandemic marks an important contemporary case signalling the importance of dominant medical paradigms of disease and power structures. In the immediate pandemic period, individuals in the U.S. and many other countries applied various non-pharmaceutical interventions to confront the disease, partially because effective pharmaceutical interventions (e.g. medications and vaccines) were not yet available. The disease spread largely depended on the personal behavioural choices. Physical distancing measures (such as self-isolation) in combination with hygienic practices (including frequent hand-washing or wearing face masks) were highly effective. However, social distancing through contact reduction was also associated with major social and economic costs. Isolation negatively impacted mental health and disrupted the daily lives of individuals across the globe. Additionally, we observed various processes of social contagions in the dissemination of misinformation, fear and health advice. Observable behaviours, such as mask wearing, influenced group behaviour. Misinformation about cures caused many cases of self-injuries because harmful substances such as bleaching agents were praised as potent solutions. Less harmful home remedies such as eating garlic or drinking ginger tea were also falsely named effective on social media [7].

These examples suggest that societal responses to epidemic diseases are highly contingent on social context. Political authorities play an active role by coordinating measures and drawing from experiences with previous epidemics. However the success of public health policies relies on compliance and the active decisions of individuals. During times of crisis, individuals try to protect themselves and their closest contacts using various private and public sources as well as spiritual and non-spiritual goods and services to cope with the various consequences of epidemic diseases.

2.2 Diffusion and Learning of Cultural Practices

The theory of contagion was initially developed to explain diseases, but core ideas were also adopted by social sciences to study the diffusion of behaviours, beliefs, or cultural practices through social reinforcement. An important approach to the explanation of social change is therefore dedicated to the structures of social networks, defined as sets of relations among individuals [6, 8].

A fundamental assumption is that the structural characteristics of social networks are significant for transmission processes. Research shows that human networks are defined by connectivity (average degree of edges above 1) and short paths, referred to as the small world property. These traits provide important structural conditions for the diffusion of diseases, information, or practices [29].

As mobility and the range of contacts increased, so did the potential for epidemic diseases to spread rapidly and widely [18]. Research on the most deadly disease in human history, the Black Death, indicates that the fear response in the form of testaments and wills generated large connected networks that provided opportunities for information transmission and knowledge transfer [31].

Going beyond empirical studies of diseases, social scientists developed a set of learning models that incorporate network dynamics and foster a better understanding of general patterns in decision making processes. Through repeated interaction, information gathering and updating of beliefs, a social network converges towards shared beliefs. Commonly, the emerging consensus depends on the initial opinions of individuals and the degrees of nodes in the network [18].

While consensus may form in many contexts, opinions about health measures such as vaccinations are not homogeneous and large variations can be found in countries such as the United States where groups of "anti-vaxxers" emerged in several regions. Research based on agent-based modelling shows that these types of variation in cultural beliefs are not dependent on social network structures, but rather related to cognitive processes such as the interpretations of the relations among cognitive objects, i.e., associative diffusion rather than social contagion. This research shifts the focus from durable relationships in many network studies of social influence, to short-term observations of behaviours. It is argued that assumptions about balkanised worlds and segregated groups do not sufficiently explain cultural differentiation [13].

Research Questions and Approach. In summary, our research is motivated by the observation that both historically and concurrently, cultural practices in the context of infectious diseases are strongly tied to the patterns of interaction in social groups. Thus, the central research question revolves around investigating the mechanisms through which reinforcement learning and opinion dynamics collectively contribute to the propagation of ineffective practices through incorrect beliefs (or opinions) about their effectiveness.

This is achieved by combining three fundamental mechanisms: Multi-action reinforcement learning, wherein multiple actions can be chosen in parallel; opinion dynamics, were agents can adapt their opinions about the effectiveness of practices based on the opinions of other agents; and an epidemiological model in which effective actions curb disease transmission. This approach enables us to explore how a lack of understanding regarding the actual significance of individual actions in shaping the overall outcome fosters the development of suboptimal strategies. This view does not imply malice or ignorance on the part of the agents - however, during a pandemic, a successful agent will not be inclined to conduct systematic experiments to determine which of the different preventive measures contributed to their continued health. As such, the multi-agent perspective introduced through opinion dynamic and cooperative multi-agent reinforcement learning is necessary to mimic the way real people learn or abandon practices.

3   Foundations and Related Works

As an introduction to the methods used in this work, we give a brief presentation of basic epidemiological modelling and the modelling of learning agents using reinforcement learning, opinion dynamics and the way they can be combined.

3.1   Epidemiological Modelling

Both equation- and agent-based models can be used to examine questions related to epidemics, typically represented by a type of a Susceptible-Infected-Recovered (SIR) model [21]. The acronym stands for compartments characterising the progression of diseases in different stages. Reinfectability can be introduced by returning to Susceptible after a period of immunity, leading to an SIRS model [16].

3.2   Modelling Learning Agents

Characteristics of agency [30] such as autonomy, social interaction and adaptation to environments are often necessary to portray human behaviour. Some models achieve the simulation of behaviour using routines such as workplaces or education [25] without entering the complexity of human decision-making, while others focus on needs to implement goal-directed agent behaviour [14]. Finally, social components such as pressure or support [5] may also influence behaviour.

Reinforcement Learning. Reinforcement Learning (RL) is a method of machine learning rooted in mechanisms observed in nature. *Operant Conditioning* examines behaviour beyond simple stimulus-response pairs and instead considers behaviour a result of rewards and punishments for actions emitted by the actor [28]. Through these responses from the environment, individuals learn which behaviours lead to desirable feedback, increasing the likelihood of repetition.

RL functions on similar principles: learning agents explore the action-state-space, gathering information about the attractiveness of certain actions (or practices) depending on the current state and possible subsequent states [19]. Contrary to goal-directed agents, reinforcement agents seek to maximise their rewards. As such, the definition of states, actions and the balancing of rewards is crucial to the outcome of the learning process. Typically, implementations of RL will use some form of so-called Q-learning. In Q-learning, agents learn the utility of an action in a certain state - either learning ahead of the actual simulation (Monte Carlo Learning) or during runtime (temporal difference learning). While so far, only a single learning agent was spoken of, the same principle can be expanded to multi-agent reinforcement learning [32] in which agents either cooperatively explore different strategies or each agent learns on their own in competition against others.

Opinion Dynamics. This field examines the way social influence leads to emergent patterns of opinion formation in populations. The basis of these models is social influence [11]. In short, agents will adapt their opinion to the opinion of other agents so overall, opinions will assimilate. That is, when two agents interact, either one or both of them will move their own opinion to be closer to the opinion of the other agents. An important extension is that similarity makes assimilation more likely, e.g., by including a bounded confidence mechanism [15]. That means that an agent will only adapt their opinion to that of another agent if the difference between their opinions is below a certain threshold, the confidence level. Conversely, opinion dynamic models can also be extended to include repulsive influence where under certain circumstances, agents actually move their opinion to be further away from the opinion of another agent [11].

Bounded Confidence and Social Learning. Bounded confidence models can easily be applied to the concept of social learning. In learning by observing others, individuals will not just imitate any behaviour, but only that of sufficiently similar other individuals [3]. This minimum degree of similarity can be understood as the confidence level. However, while in the opinion dynamics literature, opinions are often examined independent from related behaviour, the social learning literature is concerned with behaviour and its consequences. Behaviour is imitated when these consequences are evaluated positively. So while bounded confidence models of opinion dynamics serve to describe *if* we learn from others, including some processing of behavioural outcomes serves to narrow down *what* we learn from others [22].

3.3   Related Work

Most generally, it is acknowledged that both social learning as well as learning based on individual experience can be described as a trade-off. Less costly strategies of information acquisition come with the risk of forming superstitions or false beliefs [20]. Works like these do not attribute this trade-off to specific theories or algorithmic approaches such as operant conditioning and social cognitive learning or reinforcement learning and bounded confidence opinion dynamics. Even so, they show that a link between learning strategies and 'superstitious' behaviour is not an entirely novel idea. In particular, social influences facilitating the establishment of irrational beliefs and superstitions is already well-established from psychological and sociological perspectives. The notion that such beliefs are a byproduct of learning processes [4], as opposed to lack of insight or knowledge, supports this work's assumption that collective learning *supports* the formation of superstitions or ineffective strategies. Further, research also has shown that in situations of risk, stress and danger, these effects are particularly likely to emerge [23]. As such, a novel disease with associated health risks is a suitable use case to demonstrate the rise of ineffective actions despite learning agents.

Some research already applied reinforcement learning to examine the relationship of learning and superstition, noting that low-cost actions are particularly susceptible to the formation of superstition [1]. However, we are unaware of any such works combining reinforcement learning with social components or a multi-action learning algorithm. Generally, related work suggests that while the theoretical link between the different forms of learning and the emergence of superstitious behaviour is established in theoretical research, agent-based simulation is rarely used to incorporate these learning strategies to observe how specific habits of strategies are propagated in a community.

4 Conceptual Model and Mathematical Description

Agents interact and spread diseases in a simple infection model. Agents can reduce the transmission risk by engaging in different practices, each associated with costs and objective effectiveness ratings. The set of practices an agent is currently implementing is that agent's *strategy*. Agents hold *subjective beliefs* about the effectiveness of each practice and communicate about these beliefs. While they correspond to opinions in classical models of opinion dynamics, we will use the term *belief* going forward to emphasise that these cognitions are subjective views 'about' specific practices and their effects. A belief is formed through the combination of individual learning based on success so far, as well as communicated experiences of others.

Before proceeding with a detailed mathematical description, we present a schematic of how one agent interacts with another and updates their beliefs. In Fig. 1, one can observe how a blue agent (b) changes their disease status, beliefs and strategy based on their interaction with a red (r) agent. Numbers are for illustration purposes only. Also, for easier presentation, exogenous random influences on beliefs are not depicted.

At the outset of each step (1a), all agents hold a set of subjective *beliefs* about the effectiveness of the practices: Hand-washing, praying, physical distancing, and drinking bleach. If that belief is 0.5 or larger, the respective practice is active and part of the *strategy*. The practice *costs* are the same for all agents. Agents also have a disease status: Susceptible, infectious, or recovered. Here, b is susceptible and engages in praying and drinking bleach, while r is infected and engages in physical distancing and drinking bleach.

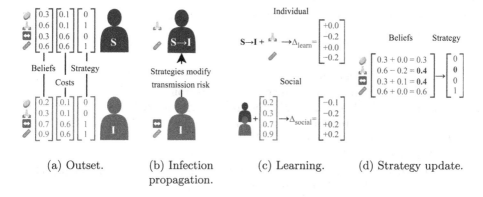

(a) Outset.   (b) Infection propagation.   (c) Learning.   (d) Strategy update.

Fig. 1. Schematic sequence of one model step and one agent interaction.

In the infection propagation phase (1b), if a susceptible and an infected agent interact, there is the risk of disease transmission. This risk is decreased based on the effectiveness of the practices in the agents' strategies. Here, r infects b.

In the learning phase (1c), both individual learning and social learning take place. Since b got infected, individual learning leads to b decreasing the belief in the practices that were active. Because b and r have similar enough beliefs, social learning leads to b's beliefs moving closer to r's beliefs.

In the strategy update phase (1d), individual and social learning combined change b's belief vector sufficiently that b's strategy also changes. The belief in praying is below the threshold of 0.5, so the new strategy no longer includes it.

Our goal is to observe the interplay of individual-level learning and collective learning moderated by bounded confidence. Thus, a number of abstractions were made to allow focusing on the core mechanisms of the model:

- Agents do not have a spatial network or activity-based routine. In each time step, agents choose a single other agent they are connected to for interaction.
- While agents know the costs of practices, there is no explicit budget, and the costs are not reflected in the initial belief value. It does, however, impact how agents evaluate their strategies.
- When calculating the payoff of a practice, the only reward weighed against the cost of a practice is the subjective belief about the effectiveness of that practice in protecting from disease. Other rewards, like social rewards for assimilating, are not explicitly modelled.
- The agents encounter a novel disease for which no established knowledge or best practice recommendations exist at the beginning of the simulation. Communication is limited to personal contacts - information and disease travel at the same speed in this simplified model.
- Beliefs are the main basis for social comparisons - our agents are traitless apart from their health status and their individual belief vector.

To facilitate the reading of mathematical expressions, we define the following notations and model parameters:

1. n, m - for agents n and m by unique numeric identifier,
2. i, j - for practices i and j,
3. t, s - for time steps t and s.

- N: Number of agents/nodes in the graph
- i_c: Base probability that an infection spreads from n to m
- i_{cs}: Probability that m is randomly infected without contact
- t_i: Time an agent remains in the I state
- t_r: Time an agent remains in the R state
- r: Weight for individual learning vs. social learning
- β: Magnitude of assimilation of m to n, even if n may have a lower payoff.
- k_b: Similarity threshold for bounded confidence
- k_a: Activity threshold
- r_b: Base payoff agents receive for remaining healthy while doing nothing
- A: Action Space, consisting of $(i, e_i, c_i), i \in \{1 \ldots I\}$
- d: Parameter which controls the influence of random, stochastic perturbation
- c_i: cost associated with the practice of measure i
- e_i: degree of true effectiveness of practice i

4.1 Agent Environment and Network

As described in Sect. 2.2, most individuals (referred to as *agents*) have a small number of contacts with local clustering. To model an appropriate network topology, we employ a Watts-Strogatz model with small-world properties [29].

The probability for an agent n to randomly meet another given agent m at time t is uniform among its network neighbours and 0 if they are not neighbors.

In this model, contacts are not reciprocal. While not reflective of reality, this design choice ensures analytical exactness, in which interactions between agents cannot be doubled by agents choosing each other and interacting twice.

4.2 Disease Modelling

To model the spread of an infectious disease across the network, a SIRS model is used. Each agent's health status is at any time one of the three: either susceptible S, infected I or recovered R. Once a susceptible agent gets infected, it remains in the state I for a fixed amount of time (days) t_i before moving on to the status recovered R. This status provides a temporary immunity period t_r after which it transitions back into the S state and may be infected again.

An individual's probability of getting infected is a function of the agent's strategy, i.e., the set of active practices, with effective practices lowering the risk of infection. The degree to which a given practice is effective may be quantified as on a continuous scale between 0 (*no effect at all*) and 1 (100% *effective*). We number the practices $i = 1 \ldots I$ with a degree of effectiveness e_i attributed to each practice i and define a vector of *true* effectiveness:$E := (e_1, e_2, e_3, \ldots, e_I)$.

This vector describing the degree of protection (which we call *true effectiveness*) of each practice is global and the same for all agents, and doesn't change over the course of the simulation time. The same goes for the cost vector $C := (c_1, c_2, \ldots, c_i)$.

We assume first a universal probability of infection per contact with an infected person: i_c, which holds when no effective practices at all are being taken by a given agent. This unprotected probability is then reduced individually for each agent n and at each time step t dependent on which practices are implemented by the agent at the time. With E the vector of true effectiveness of practices given in (4.2) and A the time dependent activity vector (3) the individual protected infectibility of each *susceptible* agent is modelled by Eq. 1 with i_{cs} as the chance of n being randomly infected without contact.

$$i_c(n, t) = i_c \cdot \prod_{i=1}^{I} \left(1 - a_{(n,t,i)} e_i\right) + i_{cs} \tag{1}$$

4.3 Agent Beliefs and Strategy

Each agent holds *subjective beliefs* about the effectiveness of different practices. As in the case of true effectiveness e_i, believed effectiveness $q_{(n,t,i)}$ of each measure i is quantified on a continuous scale between 0 and 1 as expressed in Eq. (2). This *believed effectiveness* can differ from $e_i(4.2)$, and agents can either over- or underestimate the effectiveness of different practices.

$$Q(n, t) := (q_{(n,t,1)}, q_{(n,t,2)}, q_{(n,t,3)}, \ldots, q_{(n,t,I)}), \quad q_{(n,t,i)} \in [0, 1] \tag{2}$$

Beliefs can change over time due to interaction with other agents, due to an agent's own experience, or due to exogenous random influences. These three mechanisms are introduced in the next section. At the beginning of the simulation, the belief values in the agents' belief vectors are randomly generated. Accordingly, agents explore a broad range of strategies which are reduced over the runtime through experience and interaction with others.

To implement a practice, agents need to have a sufficient level of faith in the effectiveness of that practice. This level is expressed by the static threshold k_a. Once at belief value falls beneath the given threshold degree the agent ceases to exercise the practice. Hereinafter, we refer to the vector of those practices which an agent actively pursues as it's *strategy*, denoted by $A(n, t)$

$$A(n, t) := (a_{(n,t,1)}, a_{(n,t,2)}, a_{(n,t,3)}, \ldots, a_{(n,t,I)}), \quad a_{(n,t,i)} \in \{0, 1\}. \tag{3}$$

where $a_{(n,t,i)} := \begin{cases} 1 & q_{(n,t,i)} \geq k_a, \\ 0 & q_{(n,t,i)} < k_a. \end{cases}$

Just as real people typically can take multiple protective measures at the same time, such as wearing masks in public spaces while also observing a strict personal hygiene and taking homeopathic supplements, agents are also able to choose multiple practices to implement simultaneously. The higher the effort (cost) necessary to exercise a given practice, the less willing (ready) any agent will be to adopt it. If taking up a new practice takes a lot of effort, then the agent will be reluctant to take that step. On the other hand: If the effort (necessary cost) to try out a new practice is sufficiently low, then an agent, put simply, *might as well decide to try it out* - cost and readiness to adopt are inversely proportional to each other.

4.4   Learning Mechanisms

As laid out above, agents beliefs about practice effectiveness can change due to three mechanisms, described mathematically in 4:

1. **Social Learning:** Agents assimilate beliefs of others, provided their overall beliefs do not conflict too much.
2. **Individual Learning:** Agents draw on their own experience and evaluate whether their strategy was successful in protecting them from infection.
3. **Exogenous Random Influences:** Agents randomly adjust beliefs. This represents unaccounted-for external influences apart from social contacts.

$$Q(n, t+1) = Q(n,t) + r \cdot \Delta_{social}Q(n,t) + (1-r) \cdot \Delta_{learn}Q(n,t) + \Delta_{stoch}Q(n,t) \quad (4)$$

with the model parameter r setting the ratio of influence between social and individual learning. In our definitions of the two learning effects, Δ_{learn} and Δ_{social}, we make use of the two concepts of *bounded confidence* between two agents and of the *payoff function* related to each agent at each time.

Bounded Confidence in Interactions. As described previously, agents have a network on which contacts occur randomly. During these interactions, each agent's beliefs about the effectiveness of protective measures is transparent to others. While selective information-sharing is an interesting phenomenon to examine, it is not part of the current study.

Agents will not be inclined to accept the beliefs of others when the degree of disagreement exceeds a threshold k_b. In our model this degree of disagreement is measured by the Euclidean distance between their respective belief vectors.

$$dist(m, n, t) = \sqrt{\sum_{i=1}^{I} \left(q_{(m,i,t)} - q_{(n,i,t)} \right)^2} \quad (5)$$

Agents must acknowledge at least a minimum of similarity to each other before being willing to consider the experiences of one another. If the distance of beliefs between them exceeds the model threshold k_b, then no social learning interaction between the two agents will take place. This may be modelled by the following threshold function:

$$b(n, m, t) = \begin{cases} 1 & dist(n, m, t) > k_b, \\ 0 & dist(n, m, t) \le k_b. \end{cases} \quad (6)$$

Payoff Function. We further introduce the *payoff* $u(n, t)$, an index which incorporates the costs incurred by a given agent when exercising a given strategy at time t, and at the same time imposes a penalty of -1 for the time the agent is infected. At time $t = 0$, before agents start exercising any practices this index $u(n, 0) = r_b$, that is a base value. During the simulation, the payoff index goes through a trajectory dependent on changes in strategy and health status:

$$u(n, t) = r_b - \sum_i^I c_i \cdot a_{(i,n,t)} - h(n, t), \tag{7}$$

where $h(n, t) = \begin{cases} -r_b & \text{if the agent is infected at time } t, \\ 0 & otherwise. \end{cases}$

This ensures that the payoff of agents who pursue only few or only low-cost practices will be higher than that of agents who engage in *all* possible practices.

When two agents m and n interact, the difference in payoffs determines how strongly m will assimilate their own beliefs to n - meaning that agents who either chose very effective low-cost strategies or who were plain lucky so far will exert a stronger influence on their peers than agents who remained healthy due to intense self-protection efforts.

This is modelled mathematically by the following weight function $w(n, m, t)$:

$$w(m, n, t) = 1 \,/\, (1 + e^{-\beta \cdot [u(m,t) - u(n,t)]}) \tag{8}$$

Using the individual agents' payoffs $u(m, t)$ and $u(n, t)$ defined as in (7), which in turn define the weight function $w(n, m, t)$ (8) as well as the bounded confidence threshold function $b(n, m, t)$ (6), the $\Delta Q(n, t)_{social}$ for agent n interacting with m is computed for each practice as follows:

$$\Delta_{social}\, q_{(n,t,i)} = b(n, m, t) \cdot w(m, n, t) \cdot \big(q(m, i, t) - q(n, i, t)\big), \tag{9}$$

$$\Delta_{social}\, Q(n, t) = \big(\Delta_{social}\, q_{(n,t,1)}, \Delta_{social}\, q_{(n,t,2)}, \ldots, \Delta_{social}\, q_{(n,t,I)}\big). \tag{10}$$

Multi-action Reinforcement Learning. In this use case, agents distinguish between two states: being healthy (S or R) and being sick I.

Each day an agent succeeds to remain healthy, their belief in active practices is reinforced by a fraction until the degree of certainty $= 1$ is reached. Since agents cannot discern which of the practices in their strategy truly led to continued health, all active practices are being reinforced.

Once the agent gets infected, belief in the effectiveness of their strategy is penalised. This means that the belief values of the active practices decrease, while the values for inactive measures remain unchanged. These penalties on failing practices occur in function of their implementation cost - expensive practices will be met with more criticism in case of failure.

Depending again on the agent's payoff function $u(n, t)$ the change in belief may occur in either direction: up or down. This direction is established by (11) which leads to (12)

$$dir(n,t) = \left(e^{\beta \cdot u(n,t)} - 1\right) / \left(e^{\beta \cdot u(n,t)} + 1\right) \tag{11}$$

$$\Delta_{learn}\, q_{(n,t,i)} = dir(n,t) \cdot a(n,i,t) \cdot (1 - q(n,i,t)) \cdot 0.5, \tag{12}$$

but to ensure that the resulting belief degree $q(n, t+1, i)$ stays within the limits $0 \le q(n, t+1, i) \le 1$ we define (13) and (14).

$$
\begin{aligned}
&\Delta_{learn}\, q_{(n,t,i)} \\
&= \begin{cases} \min\left(dir(n,t) \cdot a(n,i,t) \cdot \frac{1-q(n,i,t)}{2}, 1 - q_{(n,t,i)}\right) & \text{if } dir(n,t) \ge 0, \\ \max\left(dir(n,t) \cdot a(n,i,t) \cdot \frac{1-q(n,i,t)}{2}, -q_{(n,t,i)}\right) & \text{if } dir(n,t) \le 0, \end{cases}
\end{aligned}
\tag{13}
$$

$$\Delta_{learn}\, Q(n,t) = \left(\Delta_{learn}\, q_{(n,t,1)}, \Delta_{learn}\, q_{(n,t,2)}, \dots, \Delta_{learn}\, q_{(n,t,I)}\right). \tag{14}$$

Exogenous Random Influences. We assume that agents may change their beliefs not only due to social interactions and their own experience, but also due to other outside influences not explicitly included in our model. Example of such outside influences could happen when listening to a radio broadcast, watching a TV show, or just walking the streets and seeing street signs with related messaging. The model sometimes gives a random nudge in either direction for beliefs towards individual practices, with the stochastic update Δ_{stoch} being a random value on the interval $[-d, d]$ added to beliefs. The value of this nudge is, as defined in 15, limited to values that would not result in $q(n,t,i)$ exceeding 1.

$$\Delta_{stoch} = \min\left(U[-d,d], 1 - q(n,t,i)\right) \tag{15}$$

5   Methodology and Design of Experiments

We perform experiments to examine the model behaviour in three tiers:

1. *Experiment 1*: Development of Transmission and Agent Behaviour with **one** possible effective practice - in this use case, agents only can choose to engage in regular *Hand-washing* or not.
2. *Experiment 2*: Development of Transmission and Agent Behaviour with **two** practices - one effective (*Hand-washing*) and one ineffective (*Praying*). Agents can choose to engage in both practices concurrently, in only one of the practices, or in none of the two.
3. *Experiment 3*: Development of Transmission and Agent Behaviour with **four** practices: *Hand-washing* is cheap and effective, *Praying* is cheap and ineffective. *Physical Distancing* is effective but also costly. *Drinking Bleach* is both ineffective and costly. In their strategy, the agents can choose to activate any combination of these practices.

Each action space option is combined with the following parameter variation:

1. The ratio of individual and social learning is *balanced* with $r = 0.5$.
2. Agents favour individual learning over social learning with $r = 0.8$
3. Agents favour social learning over individual learning with $r = 0.2$

Thus, we are looking at 9 different experimental setups to examine the way reinforcement-based learning and social learning interact and impact the results. Each of these experimental setups is tested on an agent-based model with 200 agents and a model run duration of 700 model steps representing days passed. We record the number of infected agents as well as the number of agents performing available practices at each time step. Further, we run 300 replicates for each setup to rule out coincidence and randomness skewing the results.

6 Results

In *Experiment 1*, we observe that a high value for r, i.e., individual learning being favoured over social learning, leads to significantly higher numbers of infections compared to even a moderately higher degree of social learning, as shown in Figs. 2a and 2b. Through the inclusion of social learning, the effective strategy is adopted across the population rapidly, greatly reducing the number of infections early into the simulation.

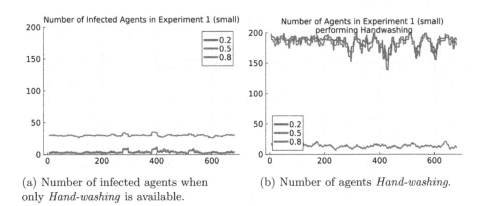

(a) Number of infected agents when only *Hand-washing* is available.

(b) Number of agents *Hand-washing*.

Fig. 2. Experiment 1 (single low-cost effective practice): Infection and behaviour results averaged over 300 model runs.

Neither of the two practices reaches widespread adoption under individual learning, though the effective practice is slightly more common than the other one, as seen in Figs. 3a and 3b. Again, the implementation rates for both practices are very similar for high rates of social learning regardless of effectiveness.

Interestingly, this pattern is not universal. While this is not visible when averaging over 300 model runs, there appears to exist a 'break point' after which

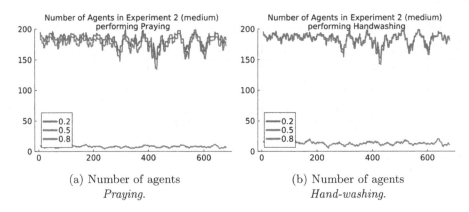

(a) Number of agents
Praying.

(b) Number of agents
Hand-washing.

Fig. 3. Experiment 2 (two low-cost practices of different effectiveness): Behaviour results averaged over 300 model runs.

agents adopt a practice even for a high r, such as shown in Figs. 4a and 4b. We see a clear point where most agents will cross k_a in favour of hand-washing consistently, leading to an exponential rise in agents performing that action.

Simultaneously, hardly any agent performs the ineffective action, which aligns with the results shown in Fig. 3a. This result shows that such outlier results may occur. Still, self-learning agents remaining largely inactive appears to be the dominant outcome of most repetitions.

Finally, in *experiment 3*, we can observe that the degree of social learning has a strong impact on the system dynamics in the presence of high-cost options. The two low-cost practices show broadly similar trajectories with low and medium r-values leading to high adoption independent of effectiveness. High r-values hinder widespread adoption, though the effective practice is chosen slightly more often. For the high-cost practices, the trend is almost reversed: Balanced learning methods will reduce the choice of high-cost practices, regardless of their effectiveness, while social learning being favoured will lead to an ongoing propagation of high-cost practices, albeit to a lesser degree than low-cost ones (Fig. 5).

A major factor in these observations is the overall dynamic of the infections which remains similar to the one shown in Fig. 2a. Social learning, even to a moderate degree, will help flatten the curve rapidly, while purely individualistic learning is slower to reach similar levels of protection in the population.

The results are clearly influenced by model design and protective measures - in the presence of effective low-cost practices, there is hardly a significant benefit to choosing high-cost measures of similar effectiveness instead. Likewise, overly effective methods that stop spread altogether will also eradicate the disease rapidly, preventing the establishment of 'common knowledge'.

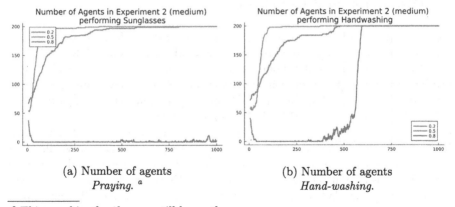

(a) Number of agents
Praying. [a]

(b) Number of agents
Hand-washing.

[a] This graphic of early runs still bears the
placeholder action name.

Fig. 4. Experiment 2 (two low-cost practices of different effectiveness): Behaviour
results of an individual sample model run with 1000 ticks.

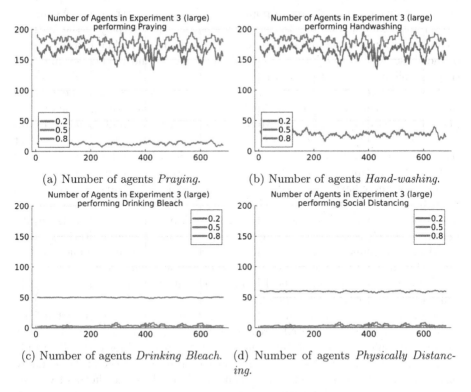

(a) Number of agents *Praying.*

(b) Number of agents *Hand-washing.*

(c) Number of agents *Drinking Bleach.*

(d) Number of agents *Physically Distancing.*

Fig. 5. Experiment 3 (four practices of different cost and effectiveness): Behaviour
results averaged over 300 model runs.

7   Discussion and Conclusion

Throughout history, social context and past experience have shaped individual and societal response to crises such as epidemics. By combining RL and BCOD, we have presented a model which can explain how mixed learning types can lead to the propagation of ineffective strategies for disease prevention. Our experiments show, cycling back to this work's title, how agents 'learn futility' - especially when it comes to largely benign superstitions.

From a methodological point of view, this combination of two different learning techniques is novel in the space of agent-based social simulation. While Opinion Dynamics are commonly used, reinforcement learning is typically found in other domains of multi-agent systems research. However, this system still needs further refinement. When examining the results of the three different experiments, we can observe that the true efficacy of a practice is overall less important for its adoption than the practice costs and how strongly an agent relies on others' experience. This observation matches not only the historical examples cited at the outset [9,27], it also fits phenomena observed today. Individual learning is slow to catch on to cheap practices and rapidly eliminates expensive ones, while a high social degree of learning leads to a fast adoption of cheap practices and maintains a certain degree of popularity for expensive strategies. As such, a more refined model is needed to better understand the interplay of the learning techniques by providing an environment in which the individual characteristics of the chosen concepts get to showcase their strengths and weaknesses and how they complement each other as a result.

However, these results still hold some interesting findings - the original hypothesis of this work, that social learning can increase the propagation of ineffective strategies, holds true. Moreover, a balanced ratio of social and individual learning seems to perform best in encouraging the adoption of low-cost strategies while also reducing the spread of potentially harmful high-cost options such as bloodletting, without fully eliminating potentially useful practices.

While we now have advanced scientific methodology that allows us to better infer the health benefits of different interventions, this does not translate into the universal acceptance of beneficial interventions. A prominent example is vaccine hesitancy which is strongly tied to one's social context and narratives about the risks of vaccination, i.e., its potential costs [10]. Conspiracy beliefs about, inter alia, vaccinations are strongly tied to intergroup behaviour [17]. And in a fragmented society, conflicting health practices that are central to group identity will only exacerbate existing fault lines.

In future work, we could adapt our model to even better reflect such a fragmented society with segregated streams of information. An increased tendency to polarise could be modelled by reducing the confidence threshold. This would result in an agent having less other agents to learn from and therefore having to rely more on individual learning. An open question is how the effects of varying the confidence threshold differ from the effects of varying the ratio of individual to social learning.

Beyond the theoretical implication of comparing the effects of changes in these two parameter values, it is obvious that the model is highly sensitive to changes in the parameter values in general. A systematic sensitivity analysis can aid in understanding the central mechanisms of the model. This will not only provide improved insights into the underlying patterns and dependencies between parameters, but also help explaining the model observations from a better validated position.

Overall, computer simulations provide a promising tool set in the exploration of dynamic interaction and the formation of social phenomena. An important line of research on the dissemination of culture demonstrated that individual preferences and exposure in micro-interactions cannot only explain patterns of convergence, but also divergence among individuals and groups [2]. This paper extended this classical research by using more elaborate social learning models, but widely confirms that processes of local convergence can generate cultural variation for the context of biological and social crisis. During epidemics, social learning cannot only explain the spread of effective health interventions, but also destructive cultural variation and the diffusion of ineffective or even harmful health behaviours. Future research should expand and refine our efforts to study the sources of destructive learning behaviours using models that incorporate more complex patterns of seasonality, social structure, and associations among cultural practices.

Acknowledgements. We thank Michael Maes for his substantial support in developing the original version of this model. Bernd Wurpts is grateful for financial support from the University of Lucerne research committee (FoKo). Supported by SEMSAI (German Federal Ministry of Education and Research, Code: 031L0295A) and Optim-Agent (German Federal Ministry of Education and Research, Code: 031L0299D).

References

1. Abbott, K.R., Sherratt, T.N.: The evolution of superstition through optimal use of incomplete information. Anim. Behav. **82**(1), 85–92 (2011). ISSN 0003-3472
2. Axelrod, R.: The dissemination of culture: a model with local convergence and global polarization. J. Confl. Resolut. **41**(2), 203–226 (1997)
3. Bandura, A.: Social Foundations of Thought and Action: A Social Cognitive Theory. Prentice-Hall, New York (1986)
4. Beck, J., Forstmeier, W.: Superstition and belief as inevitable by-products of an adaptive learning strategy. Hum. Nat. **18**(1), 35–46 (2007). ISSN 1936-4776
5. Berndt, J.O., Rodermund, S.C., Timm, I.J.: Social congtagion of fertility: an agent-based simulation study. In: 2018 Winter Simulation Conference (WSC), pp. 953–964 (2018)
6. Centola, D.: How Behavior Spreads: The Science of Complex Contagions, vol. 3. Princeton University Press, Princeton (2018)
7. Christakis, N.A.: Apollo's Arrow: The Profound and Enduring Impact of Coronavirus on the Way We Live. Hachette UK, Paris (2020)
8. Christakis, N.A., Fowler, J.H.: Connected: The Surprising Power of Our Social Networks and How They Shape Our Lives. Little, Brown Spark (2009)

9. Dean, M.E.: Selective suppression by the medical establishment of unwelcome research findings: the cholera treatment evaluation by the General Board of Health, London 1854. J. Roy. Soc. Med. **109**(5), 200–205 (2016)

10. Dubé, E., et al.: Vaccine hesitancy. Hum. Vaccin. Immunother. **9**(8), 1763–1773 (2013). ISSN: 2164-5515. PMID: 23584253

11. Flache, A., et al.: Models of social influence: towards the next frontiers. J. Artif. Soc. Soc. Simul. **20**(4), 2 (2017). ISSN: 1460-7425

12. Funk, S., et al.: The spread of awareness and its impact on epidemic outbreaks. Proc. Natl. Acad. Sci. USA **106**(16), 6872–6877 (2009). ISSN: 1091-6490

13. Goldberg, A., Stein, S.K.: Beyond social contagion: associative diffusion and the emergence of cultural variation. Am. Sociol. Rev. **83**(5), 897–932 (2018)

14. Gramoli, L., et al.: Needs model for an autonomous agent during longterm simulations. In: 2021 IEEE International Conference on Artificial Intelligence and Virtual Reality (AIVR), pp. 134–138. IEEE (2021)

15. Hegselmann, R., Krause, U.: Opinion dynamics and bounded confidence: Models, analysis and simulation. JASSS **5**(3) (2002)

16. Hethcote, H.W.: Qualitative analyses of communicable disease models. Math. Biosci. **28**(3), 335–356 (1976). ISSN: 0025-5564

17. Hornsey, M.J., et al.: Individual, intergroup and nation-level influences on belief in conspiracy theories. Nat. Rev. Psychol. 1–13 (2022). ISSN: 2731-0574

18. Jackson, M.O.: The Human Network: How Your Social Position Determines Your Power, Beliefs, and Behaviors. Vintage, New York (2019)

19. Kaelbling, L.P., Littman, M.L., Moore, A.W.: Reinforcement learning: a survey. J. Artif. Intell. Res. **4**, 237–285 (1996)

20. Kendal, R.L., et al.: Trade-offs in the adaptive use of social and asocial learning. Adv. Study Behav. **35**, 333–379 (2005). ISSN: 0065-3454

21. Kermack, W.O., McKendrick, A.G.: A contribution to the mathematical theory of epidemics. Proc. Roy. Soc. London Ser. A Containing Papers Math. Phys. Charact. **115**(772), 700–721 (1927)

22. Kurchyna, V., et al.: Health and habit: an agent-based approach. In: Bergmann, R., et al. (eds.) KI 2022: Advances in Artificial Intelligence. LNCS, vol. 13404, pp. 131–145. Springer, Cham (2022). https://doi.org/10.1007/978-3-031-15791-2_12

23. Mandal, F.B.: Superstitions: a culturally transmitted human behavior. Int. J. Psychol. Behav. Sci. **8**(4), 65–69 (2018). ISSN: 2163-1956

24. Snowden, F.M.: Epidemics and Society: From the Black Death to the Present. Yale University Press, New Haven (2019)

25. Tapp, L., et al.: School's out? Simulating schooling strategies during COVID-19. In: Lorig, F., Norling, E. (eds.) MABS 2022. LNCS, vol. 13743, pp. 95–106. Springer, Cham (2022). https://doi.org/10.1007/978-3-031-22947-3_8

26. Temple, C., Hoang, R., Hendrickson, R.G.: Toxic effects from ivermectin use associated with prevention and treatment of Covid-19. N. Engl. J. Med. **385**(23), 2197–2198 (2021). ISSN: 0028-4793. PMID: 34670041

27. Teplitsky, J.: Imagined immunities: medieval myths and modern histories of jews and the black death. AJS Rev. J. Assoc. Jewish Stud. **46**(2), 320–346 (2022)

28. Touretzky, D.S., Saksida, L.M.: Operant conditioning in Skinnerbots. Adapt. Behav. **5**(3–4), 219–247 (1997)

29. Watts, D.J.: Small Worlds: The Dynamics of Networks Between Order and Randomness, vol. 36. Princeton University Press, Princeton (2004)

30. Wooldridge, M., Jennings, N.R.: Intelligent agents: theory and practice. Knowl. Eng. Rev. **10**(2), 115–152 (1995). ISSN: 1469-8005, 0269-8889

31. Wurpts, B.: Networks into institutions or institutions into networks? evidence from the medieval hansa. Ph.D. Dissertation, Department of Sociology, University of Washington (2018)
32. Zhang, K., Yang, Z., Başar, T.: Multi-agent reinforcement learning: a selective overview of theories and algorithms. In: Vamvoudakis, K.G., et al. (eds.) Handbook of Reinforcement Learning and Control. Studies in Systems, Decision and Control, pp. 321–384. Springer, Cham (2021). https://doi.org/10.1007/978-3-030-60990-0_12

Build Your Campus Image Together: Media Memory Shaping Campus Culture

Jida Li[✉], Mingyang Su, Junfan Zhao, Xiaomei Nie, and Xiu Li

Tsinghua Shenzhen International Graduate School, Shenzhen, China
lijd22@mails.tsinghua.edu.cn

Abstract. In the digital information age, it is crucial to use digital media technology to expand the forms of campus culture construction. This study proposes a digital media visualization method for campus cultural construction, using images posted by campus teachers and students on social media platforms as raw data. The data is processed through dimensionality reduction and clustering analysis and then visualized using generative artificial intelligence and visual programming software to produce digital images. Campus teachers and students can control the color, shape, and other information generated by digital images by adjusting the generation parameters. At the same time, as campus teachers and students add more original images, the generated digital images will also change accordingly. This method transforms concrete media memory into abstract data visualization through visual co-construction and dynamically influences visual form through people's behavior in the media. The method proposed by this research institute provides a participatory way for campus teachers and students to create visual digital images of the campus, which is a new way to experience campus culture and also an interactive installation of art of the campus.

Keywords: Campus Culture · Digital Media · Visualization

1 Introduction

Campus culture, as the spiritual foundation of the school community, is critical to enhancing students' cohesion and sense of belonging. In a student-centered campus, a supportive school culture fosters a sense of shared identity and belonging among students and helps build strong bonds between students and their learning environment [1]. It can significantly enhance the reputation and overall image of a school. With the advent of the digital age, new opportunities have emerged to develop campus culture [2]. Students have more options for self-expression thanks to digital tools and social media technologies, which enable them to co-create and disseminate campus culture.

Campus culture building focuses on using multimedia and diverse forms of content [3]. In traditional campus culture buildings, text and images are the main traditional media types. Due to the rapid development of digital technology, communication methods are now available in a broader range of formats,

© The Author(s), under exclusive license to Springer Nature Switzerland AG 2024
A. Coman and S. Vasilache (Eds.): HCII 2024, LNCS 14705, pp. 140–153, 2024.
https://doi.org/10.1007/978-3-031-61312-8_10

including campus pictures and short videos. However, these formats and content are relatively dispersed and need a media piece that can mobilize the collective memories and emotions of the student body. While these media formats evolve, they typically follow a one-way communication model in which the school communicates content to students and audiences. This one-way communication model limits audience engagement, makes it challenging to evoke profound emotional experiences, and fails to emphasize student participation and interaction.

Efforts were made to use multimodal media formats to collect and archive content produced by users for campus culture. Media memory theory emphasizes the fundamental function of media in storing and transmitting information [4]. This function includes collecting, organizing, editing, storing, extracting, and distributing information [5]. We use this concept to help co-create and disseminate campus culture. This theory has been widely used in creating national historical and cultural narratives.

Specifically, we collected campus photo resources independently generated by campus faculty and students on social media and, subsequently, analyzed this information in terms of downscaling and clustering, from which we extracted features to represent campus culture information and grouped them. Next, we used the visual techniques of Touch Designer software and Stable Diffusion to present the encoded memory information to create a collective memory image of the users, which could be disseminated outwards. In the process of information dissemination, users can continue to add new photo resource information, continuously update visual images, and thus establish a virtuous cycle of campus culture promotion. Our research not only provides digital visualization ideas for campus culture but also promotes users to integrate personal behavior into the collective construction of campus culture, thereby promoting innovation and dissemination of campus culture.

Our research aims to provide insights into how media memory methods can contribute to the construction of campus culture and open up new channels for the visual expression and dissemination of school culture. We also provide an example of cutting-edge digital technology applied to the development of school culture. In addition, this study opens up new opportunities for building social identity and encouraging collaborative building of school culture.

2   Related Work

In the Internet era, the relationship between the development of new media technology and the construction of campus culture is getting closer and closer. In 2013, Pang Guoqing pointed out that the campus culture of colleges and universities presents new characteristics and development trends under the environment of new media, and the campus culture is developing in the direction of informatization, diversification, virtualization, and personalization [6]. In 2015, Yin Ziqiang pointed out that the new media makes the campus culture of colleges and universities present diversity, autonomy, dynamism, interactivity, autonomy, dynamics, interactivity, and other characteristics [7]. In 2016, Xu Jian et al.

believed that university campus culture embodies openness, plurality, richness, and interaction under the influence of new media. The campus culture is more closely exchanged with the external social culture, and the convenient dissemination of information makes the campus culture of colleges and universities more open [8]. In 2019, Kausha et al. found through empirical analysis that the cultural image of schools has both direct and indirect effects on student loyalty behavior [9]. In 2020, Polyorat et al. pointed out the relationship between the brand image and personality of universities, while providing theoretical guidance for building university brands [10].

Although the current new media works of campus culture have opened up new ideas for spreading campus culture through new technological means, there are still some shortcomings. First, the interactive technology and means of the works are not perfect enough, and most of the works are still based on display, lacking the interactive mode in which the users can participate; second, the information source of the works is the static primary mode, the medium of information transmission is relatively single, and the transmission mode is primarily one-way communication, which makes it difficult to form a more immersive and three-dimensional experience mode; third, the spirit and content of the campus culture conveyed by the works are relatively fragmented, and it is difficult to let the students produce collective memory effect in the group.

This study constructs a new form of campus culture construction in the form of digital media visualization to compensate for and solve the current problems of lack of user participation and static and single information sources in campus cultural works. Visualization is a process of transforming abstract concepts into graphics and images that can be intuitively perceived by people, in order to better understand and convey information. It can help people better understand and grasp information and can stimulate their imagination. In a broad sense, "visualization" is a change in the way humans perceive the world, rather than just transforming complex information into simple graphics or images. Visualization is a new way of expressing media information, and it is also an essential way of expression with the advent of the big data era and the era of integrated media. Due to the development of technology, visual presentation methods have become more diverse, often presented in various forms such as charts, graphics, audio, video, etc.

This study constructs a new form of campus culture construction in the form of digital media visualization to compensate for and solve the current problems of lack of user participation and static and single information sources in campus cultural works. Visualization is a process of transforming abstract concepts into graphics and images that can be intuitively perceived by people to better understand and convey information. It can help people better understand and grasp information and can stimulate their imagination. In a broad sense, "visualization" is a change in the way humans perceive the world, rather than just transforming complex information into simple graphics or images. Visualization is a new way of expressing media information, and it is also an essential way of expression with the advent of the big data era and the era of integrated media.

Due to the development of technology, visual presentation methods have become more diverse, often presented in various forms such as charts, graphics, audio, video, etc.

In recent years, with the continuous development of digital media technology, research on the visual design of digital media has also been deepening. Ren Liu proposed an innovative research method for the collaborative development of digital integrated media and visual design based on the Kruskal algorithm, aiming to explore the innovative development of the collaboration between digital media and visual design [11]. In 2012, the giant ball screen film "Butterfly Transformation" opened up a new channel for music appreciation through the use of 3D animation technology to visually interpret hearing [12]. In 2014, at the TONALI performance in Hamburg, Germany, Marinovsky and his music visual design works used an animation renderer as the implementation path, and set different conceptual architectures on the mapped visual images to complete the overall dynamic effect [13]. According to the needs, use visual concepts of expansion, growth, digestion, and other movements, as well as the comparison of object and image sounds, to form abstract forms for a unique experience of concrete "viewing". However, current visualization research in the field of campus is mostly focused on serving the construction of smart campuses or the maintenance of data management systems, with less application in the promotion of campus culture.

This study is based on the theory of media memory to produce digital media works for campus culture. Media memory was first proposed by American scholar Caroline Cage in 2005 as a cross disciplinary research concept between media research and memory research, attempting to explore the role of memory construction in media operation and how media memory can have corresponding impacts on other fields [14]. Some scholars believe that "media memory encompasses not only the content of pre-existing memory, or media represented as a reference framework, but also refers to some phenomena that exist within the media itself [15]. In 2011, Garde Hansen explored how cultural memory was integrated with media forms in his research process [16]. In the field of media, media memory and collective memory have a bidirectional interaction function, and media is not only a channel but also a phenomenon [17]. Media based memory has a continuous growth trend, and media technology enables memory to have multiple forms of formation and sharing [18]. In the process of building campus culture, using digital media to condense campus culture can better shape the emotions and memories of teachers and students. Therefore, this study aims to expand the dissemination form of campus culture by using digital media to produce campus cultural content independently produced by teachers and students based on the theory of media memory (Fig. 1).

3   Research Methodology

Our system collects pictures of campus culture from various social media platforms, posted by teachers and students independently, and a total of 100 pictures

Fig. 1. A Model of Campus Culture Co-construction Platform Based on Media Memory Theory.

were collected in this study. Firstly, we used the PCA tool to reduce the dimensionality of these pictures. After processing, we obtained 50 low-dimensional features for each photo, representing each image's critical information. After that, K-means clustering analysis with n = 5 was performed for these 100 pictures with features, and after the analysis was completed, five labels were obtained. After that, color features were assigned to these five labels according to the theme color of the research subject campus, and the scatterplot was plotted through Touch Designer, interfered with, and rendered with different formation functions of Touch Designer to form a visual image. Finally, Stable Diffusion was performed with the representative flowers of the research subject campus as the prompt for picture drawing, and finally the digitized flower visualization image representing these campus culture pictures (Fig. 2).

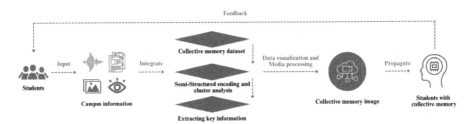

Fig. 2. The Construction Process of Campus Collective Memory Images with Student articipation.

PCA. Principal Component Analysis (PCA) is converting high-dimensional data into a low-dimensional space while retaining the most essential information in the data. PCA can analyze the data more intuitively by converting the original variables into a set of linearly independent representations of the dimensions through linear transformations. The advantage of PCA lies in the fact that the main features of the data can be extracted, and the data can be projected into a set of linearly independent representations of the dimensions. Main features and project the data into a low-dimensional space while preserving the variance in the data. In the digital visualization of campus culture, the PCA tool can perform dimensionality reduction for complex campus image information, aiming to simplify the data's complexity while preserving the data's main features.

Its main functions include:

1. Reducing data complexity: Campus culture pictures contain many features such as color, shape, and texture. Using PCA, these features can be compressed into a few principal components, thus greatly simplifying the complexity of the data.
2. Highlighting the main features: PCA can extract the main features that can represent the characteristics of the pictures, which facilitates the use of lower dimensional data to represent the photo information.
3. Improve processing efficiency: Reducing the dimensionality of the data can significantly improve the efficiency of data processing and analysis, enabling us to process and analyze the data quickly in a low-dimensional space.
4. Convenient visualization: Reducing the dimensionality of the data allows us to visualize the campus culture data more efficiently. Displaying the data in two-dimensional or three-dimensional space allows us to visualize the distribution and pattern of the data.

K-Means. K-means is a commonly used unsupervised learning algorithm mainly used for data clustering analysis. The basic principle of K-means is to divide n points (data points, sample points, or observations) into k clusters. Hence, each point belongs to the cluster corresponding to the mean (i.e., the center of the cluster) closest to it. Typically, the clustering results in a spherical or ellipsoidal shape.

The main reasons for using K-means in photo classification of campus culture are as follows:

1. Cluster analysis: The K-means algorithm can automatically classify pictures with similar characteristics into the same group, thus achieving the classification of campus culture for display. This classification method can better reveal the patterns and themes in the pictures so that viewers can more intuitively understand the thematic content embedded in the campus culture.
2. Unsupervised learning: K-means is an unsupervised learning algorithm. It does not require a pre-labeled training dataset but automatically performs classification through computation and comparison. In the processing of campus cultural data and information, the data is often large, fragmented, and

constantly generated; in this data characteristic, unsupervised learning can more quickly complete the classification task.

3. Visualization friendly: After classification by K-means, we can visualize the results to show campus culture's diversity and characteristics more intuitively and improve the presentation and understanding.

Visualization. Touch Designer, a powerful node-based visualization programming software, has significant advantages in its real-time multimedia content creation capabilities within digital arts and technology applications. Its integrated full-media functionality, including data processing, sensor-signal interaction, 2D/3D graphic rendering, image recognition, and virtual reality simulation, provides users a wide range of in-depth creative possibilities.

In this study, the construction of campus culture is mainly characterized by the following features:

1. The data modality of campus culture is diversified.
2. The content of campus culture needs to be presented in the form of digital media visualization.
3. The content of visualization needs to follow the changes in the data.

Touch Designer provides a more suitable solution than traditional development tools. Touch Designer's node-based programming approach allows users to organize complex logic and data flows in an intuitive, modular way, which is ideally suited to dealing with the diverse data modalities of campus culture. Its powerful graphic rendering and multimedia output capabilities ensure that campus culture content is presented visually, whether it is a 2D image, a 3D model, or an interactive virtual reality experience. Touch Designer's real-time rendering technology ensures that the content can be instantly updated as the data changes, ensuring the timeliness and accuracy of the display content. Therefore, in the context of campus culture construction, the choice of Touch Designer as a system development tool is not only a recognition of its technical capability but also an affirmation of its innovative value within the digital art and technology applications field.

4 Data Collection and Processing

Taking the International Graduate School of Tsinghua University Shenzhen as an example, we collected data on the picture information produced and uploaded independently by campus teachers and students on social media. In order to have a comprehensive understanding of the cultural memory information of campus teachers and students on social media, we chose several time points, including the New Year, the beginning of the semester, the school festival, holidays, and other key time points, and downloaded the image content on social media respectively.

In the first stage of data collection and collation, we obtained 100 campus culture pictures from the independent production of campus teachers and students, which cover a wide range of aspects such as campus architecture, activity chronicles, and weather environment, which reflect the daily life and learning status of campus teachers and students, as well as representing their own unique campus culture perspectives.

PCA Downscaling. Our system first processes the campus culture information according to the PCA dimensionality reduction method. First, we perform a standardization operation for the original data to ensure that the mean of each feature is 0 and the standard deviation is 1. Then, we calculate the covariance matrix, eigenvalues, and eigenvectors of the covariance matrix. In this study, we selected the first 50 principal components as the dimensions were reduced. Finally, the original data is transformed into a projection on a low-dimensional space.

K-means Classification. After completing the previous step, each image is stored with a lower dimension value, containing 50-dimensional information. Based on this, we perform a K-means clustering analysis for these data. In this study, we randomly select 5 points in the dataset as the initial clustering centers, then calculate the distance of each data point to these five song clustering centers, assign each data point to the category of the clustering center closest to it, divide the dataset into five categories, and for each category, re-calculate the centers of all the data points, and then take them as the new clustering centers, and repeat the calculation of clustering centers until the clustering center no longer changes significantly. Finally, we divided the 100 images into five groups, representing the five categories of campus culture data we selected at this stage.

Plotting the Scatterplot. After completing the K-means classification, we selected the first two dimensional features of each data as the x-axis and y-axis coordinates of that data, respectively, to draw the scatterplot. After the scatterplot is plotted, the data of different groups are colored according to the results of the K-means classification.

5   Digital Media Visualisation

After completing the data processing, we process the data information artistically to form digital media images to store the campus culture information.

Colour Selection. In the previous section, we divided the data into five categories, and we selected five different colors to represent each category of data according to the visual identity system of Shenzhen International Graduate School of Tsinghua University. The specific color and data correspondences are shown in the following table (Table 1):

In the process of color selection, we fully consider the core content of campus culture. "Tsinghua Purple", the school color of Tsinghua University, is chosen as the first label color; "Rose Red," the auxiliary color of Tsinghua Purple, is chosen as the second label color; "Creative," the color of Tsinghua International Shenzhen Graduate School, is chosen as the second label color; and "Creative," the color of Tsinghua International Shenzhen Graduate School, is chosen as the first label color. Graduate School of Tsinghua University, "Creative Blue," "Vibrant Orange," and "Fresh Green" for the third, fourth, and fifth label colors.

Table 1. Table of Colors with Hexadecimal Values

Number	Color	Hexadecimal
1	Purple	#660874
2	Rose	#D93379
3	Blue	#418CFF
4	Orange	#FF3C32
5	Green	#D4EC8D

Colour Filling. We use Touch Designer software for digital processing. First, we store the processed data in RGB information storage, where R is the first eigenvalue of the principal component information after PCA dimensionality reduction, G is the second eigenvalue of the principal component information after PCA dimensionality reduction, and B is the label after K-means classification. We extract the B value separately and normalize it to form a data bar with a value range of 0-1 and a length of 100, and then fill that data with color according to our color scheme (Fig. 3).

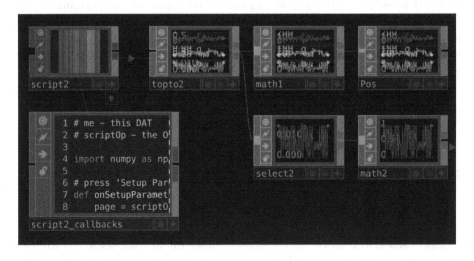

Fig. 3. Colour Filling.

Reference Drawing. We combine this part of the data with its R and G data for image drawing. For image plotting, we plot a scatter plot with five different colors in the coordinate system using a circle as the plotting unit and render it afterward (Fig. 4).

Noise Interference. Based on this rendered image, we add noise to interfere with the data to avoid it being too discrete, forming a more fuzzy abstract effect (Fig. 5).

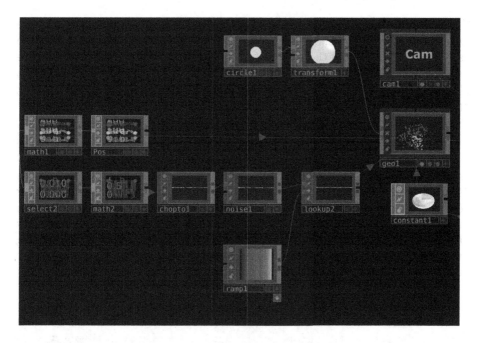

Fig. 4. Reference Drawing.

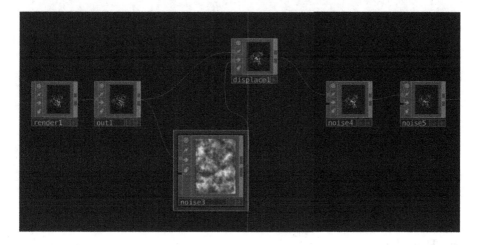

Fig. 5. Noise Interference.

Stable Diffusion Rendering. After the interference is completed, we use the Stable Diffusion tool to generate the flower image in Touch Designer using the rendered image after interference as the shape reference and the preset prompt for text generation. The flower image generated will be somewhat different depending on our parameter settings.

The flower image serves as a collective memory of the content produced by the students and faculty of the campus during the period we selected. By storing the self-produced content of the students and faculty in the form of digital media, we provide a new way of looking at campus culture for the students and faculty. At the same time, as the data changes, the data classification and image drawing processes carried out in this system will also change to form dynamic media works.

Visual Co-construction and Interaction. In this study, we simulated the changes that occur in the media work after users add data information. Figure 6 shows the results generated by different numbers of pictures. It can be seen that as the number of pictures increases, there will be changes in the drawing of scatter plots and clustering analysis of the data, the image effect after noise interference, and the shape of the final generated digital image. This can allow users to better experience the visual experience brought by the image changing with their own operation after adding campus pictures, making campus culture more participatory and dynamic.

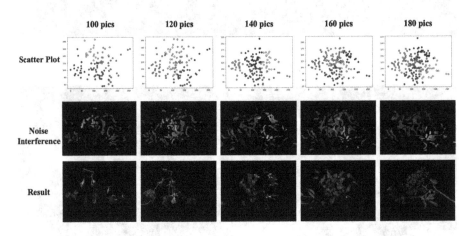

Fig. 6. The Results Generated by Different Numbers of Pictures.

6   Results

In this study, photo information produced by teachers and students independently on social media platforms is processed through data dimensionality reduction, classification, and visualization steps and combined with campus theme colors and campus representative flowers to produce visual digital flower images with collective characteristics of the campus.

The color composition of the flowers is represented by the campus theme colors specified by the system. In contrast, the distribution and proportion of the colors are determined by the classification results of the original data. The generated shape of the flowers is related to the degree of discrete and aggregated data classification. Therefore, the flowers can represent the campus culture information embedded in the original data.

When using Stable Diffusion to generate flowers, adjusting the size of random seeds can result in different images. Figure 7 shows the changes in the image generated by adjusting the size of the random seed while keeping it unchanged from the data.

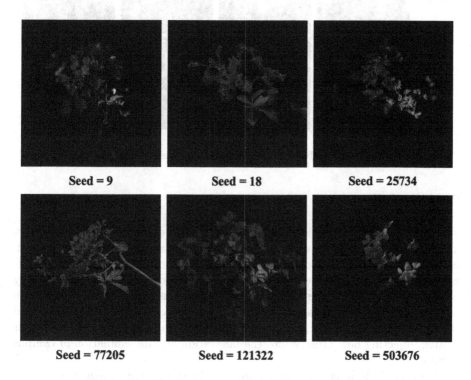

| Seed = 9 | Seed = 18 | Seed = 25734 |
| Seed = 77205 | Seed = 121322 | Seed = 503676 |

Fig. 7. The Results Generated by Different seed Values.

The structure of the generated flowers will also change by adjusting the value of n for PCA dimensionality reduction and the value of k for K-means (Fig. 8).

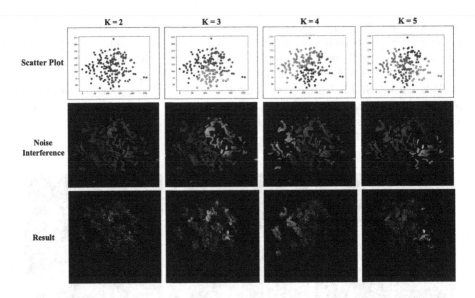

Fig. 8. The Results Generated by Different k Values.

7   Conclusion

Through in-depth exploration and analysis of photo resources generated by users of on-campus social media, we not only reveal users' unique perspectives on campus memory but also successfully present this information using visual technology, creating digital media images of campus memory. This process not only provides a technological demonstration for creating campus cultural information in the form of digital media but also provides a method for campus teachers and students to visually participate in the process of cultural information content editing, injecting new vitality into the innovation and dissemination of campus culture.

The digital visualization method provided by this research institute can serve as a visualization tool, which can be combined with different themes and time points of campus culture in the construction process. This method is also a kind of interactive installation art on campus, which can encourage teachers and students to participate in creation by adjusting data, promoting interaction and communication, not only enriching campus cultural forms but also enhancing the vitality of campus public spaces, providing a new and creative artistic experience platform for teachers and students. At the same time, this method also provides digital solutions for the construction of campus culture in the future media era.

In summary, our work not only has certain foresight but also has broad practical application value and significance. We believe that with the continuous development and improvement of relevant technologies, our work will provide more possibilities and opportunities for the inheritance and innovation of campus culture.

Acknowledgement. This work was supported by a research grant from Shenzhen Key Laboratory of next generation interactive media innovative technology (Funding No: ZDSYS20210623092001004) and the Center for Social Governance and Innovation at Tsinghua University, a major research center for Shenzhen Humanities & Social Sciences Key Research Bases.

References

1. Han, L.: Research on campus culture construction based on university's core values. Res. Mod. High. Educ. **3**, 81–85 (2017)
2. Ning, K.: Discussion on the construction of campus culture in the environment of new media based on computer network. BCP Soc. Sci. Humanit. **14**, 119–123 (2021)
3. Weng, A.: Research on construction of campus culture under new media environment. Adv. Mater. Res. **926**, 4713–4716 (2014)
4. Erll, A.: Media and the dynamics of memory: from cultural paradigms to transcultural premediation. In: Handbook of Culture and Memory (2017)
5. Neiger, M.: Theorizing media memory: six elements defining the role of the media in shaping collective memory in the digital age. Sociol. Compass **14**, e12782 (2020)
6. Guoqing, P.: On the characteristics and development trends of campus culture in universities under the new media environment. J. Henan Univ. Educ. Philos. Soc. Sci. Ed. **32**, 3 (2013)
7. Ziqiang, Y.: Construction of campus culture in universities based on new media. J. Changchun Inst. Educ. 2 (2015)
8. Wen, X. Suqiang, Y.: On the construction of university campus culture from the perspective of new media. School Party Building and Ideological Education, pp. 84–87 (2016)
9. Kaushal, V., Ali, N.: University reputation, brand attachment and brand personality as antecedents of student loyalty: a study in higher education context. Corp. Reput. Rev. **23**, 254–266 (2020)
10. Kawpong, P., Walee, P.: University branding: the impact of University personality on University distinctiveness and University identification. J. Crit. Rev. (2020)
11. Liu, R.: Innovative research on synergistic development of digital integrated media and visual design based on kruskal algorithm. Appl. Math. Nonlinear Sci. (2023)
12. Xia, T., Zhu, Z.: Visual design and cultural expression of guizhou miao folk songs. Hunan Packag. **38** (2023)
13. Wentao, Z.: A systematic study on the concept and design methods of "music visualization". Creat. Des. (2021)
14. Carolyn, K.: Chapel Hill, Pages of the Past: History and Memory in American Magazines. University of North Carolina Press (2005)
15. Neiger, M., Meyers, O., Zandberg, E.: On Media Memory: Collective Memory in a New Media. Palgrave Macmillan, London (2011)
16. Garde-Hansen, J.: Memory studies and media studies. Media Mem. (2011)
17. Motti, N., Eyal, Z.: On Media Memory: Collective Memory in a New Media. Age Palgrave Macmillan (2011)
18. Pinchevski, A.: Archive, media, trauma. In: Neiger, M., Meyers, O., Zandberg, E. (eds.) On Media Memory: Collective Memory in a New Media Age, p. 253. Palgrave Macmillan, Basingstoke (2011)

Bridging the Gap: A Case Study of Utilizing Social Media to Accelerate Recovery and Structuring Disaster Management

Suzad Mohammad[1,3]($\boxtimes$), Abdullah Al Jobair[2], Fairuz Shaiara[1], and Sadia Sharmin[1]

[1] Bangladesh University of Engineering and Technology, Dhaka, Bangladesh
{0423052030,0423052027}@grad.cse.buet.ac.bd,
sadiasharmin@cse.buet.ac.bd
[2] United International University, Dhaka, Bangladesh
jobair@cse.uiu.ac.bd
[3] International University of Business Agriculture and Technology, Dhaka, Bangladesh

Abstract. The widespread availability of the internet and smartphones and active participation in social media platforms reflect a substantial advancement in information and communication technology. Despite Bangladesh's economic progress and widespread technology adoption, recurring natural disasters disrupt lives and hinder development. Using a mixed-method approach, our study examines the effectiveness of social media in disaster management activities in Bangladesh with the goal of aiding the traditional approaches with social media to alleviate post-disaster suffering. The research involves analyzing official social media data from Facebook and Instagram using CrowdTangle. This quantitative analysis is followed by semi-structured interviews with 57 people affected by the 2022 floods in Sylhet. Additionally, our study involves interviews with disaster management organizations in Bangladesh to gather valuable insights from an organizational standpoint. According to the CrowdTangle analysis, most social media activity on Facebook and Instagram during the Sylhet flood was related to the disaster itself. Around 65% of Facebook posts and 70% of Instagram posts were directly linked to the flood. The interviews highlight the difficulties faced during such crises, as well as the potential of social media in managing disasters. The study sheds light on the difficulties faced during disaster management in developing countries such as Bangladesh and offers a path toward faster recovery from the aftermath of such disasters.

Keywords: Social Media · Disaster Management · Sylhet Flood 2022 · Disaster Affected People · Disaster Management Organizations · CrowdTangle · Facebook · Instagram

1 Introduction

Natural disasters pose significant challenges to communities worldwide [8], and Bangladesh ranked ninth among the countries grappling with the multifaceted impacts of such calamities [3]. Bangladesh, situated in the deltaic region of South Asia, is vulnerable to a variety of natural disasters such as cyclones, floods, earthquakes, and riverbank erosions. The geographical location and dense population exacerbate the country's susceptibility to these catastrophic events [15].

Bangladesh's people confront many challenges stemming from the frequent occurrence of natural disasters, such as cyclones, floods, riverbank erosions, and earthquakes [17]. Coastal areas are hit hardest by cyclones, which often cause extensive damage to livelihoods. In rural regions, where agriculture is a primary source of income, riverbank erosions, and floods frequently lead to the displacement of communities and disrupt traditional ways of life. Natural disasters, such as cyclones and floods, can have a devastating impact on the agricultural sector, damaging crops, reducing land availability, and causing financial hardship for farmers. [22]. The vulnerability is further compounded by limited access to early warning systems in some remote areas, hindering timely preparation and evacuation. Furthermore, the increasing impacts of climate change, including rising sea levels and changing rainfall patterns [6], add complexity to disaster management, necessitating adaptive measures.

Natural disasters, occurring with alarming regularity, disrupt communities, upend livelihoods, and strain existing infrastructures. Traditional methods face formidable challenges in meeting the urgent demands imposed by the unpredictable nature of these catastrophes [9]. The need for robust disaster management strategies is evident to mitigate the limitations of traditional disaster management methods in timely communication, resource mobilization, and coordination [26]. Under such circumstances, the pervasive use of social media has emerged as a potentially transformative force in disaster management, opening up new avenues for communication, information dissemination, and community engagement [13].

This study aims to unravel the dynamics between technology and disaster resilience, with a specific focus on the role played by social media platforms. We aim to contribute valuable insights to the evolving field of disaster management by incorporating a combination of qualitative and quantitative research methods, including CrowdTangle[1] data analysis (a tool by Meta which provides official data of social platforms), interviews, and story-based content analysis. We consider the massive Sylhet flood of 2022[2,3] in Bangladesh as the case study to conduct this research. The research study has been organized into the following five research questions (RQ) -

1. **RQ-1: What is the propensity for social media usage during the natural disaster occurrence in Bangladesh?**
   The aim is to explore the frequency and nature of social media engagement by individuals and communities when faced with natural calamities, shedding

---

[1] https://www.crowdtangle.com/.

[2] https://bdrcs.org/wp-content/uploads/2022/06/20220618Flash-Flood_SitRep-3_BDRCS.pdf.

[3] https://www.thedailystar.net/environment/climate-crisis/natural-disaster/news/tk-1238cr-lost-flood-sylhet.

light on the role and impact of these platforms in the context of disaster occurrence in Bangladesh.

2. **RQ-2: What are the perceptions and experiences of affected individuals regarding the role of social media in natural disaster communication and response?**
   This research question explores the thoughts and firsthand encounters of individuals affected by natural disasters, focusing on how they perceive and experience the role of social media in communication and response during such incidents. It seeks insights into the effectiveness and impact of social media in aiding affected communities and shaping their disaster-related experiences.

3. **RQ-3: How do various stakeholders (Disaster Management agencies, NGOs, etc.) involved in disaster management leverage social media platforms for information dissemination and coordination?**
   This research question investigates how key stakeholders, such as disaster management agencies and NGOs, utilize social media platforms to disseminate information and coordinate efforts in the realm of disaster management.

4. **RQ-4: What are the main challenges and limitations of using social media for disaster management?**
   We identify and understand the obstacles and constraints that impede the effective utilization of social media platforms in managing and responding to disasters.

5. **RQ-5: How can the influence of social media be enhanced for faster recovery from post-disaster agony?**
   Lastly, we explore ways to amplify the impact of social media in expediting recovery from post-disaster distress. The focus is to identify strategies and mechanisms to enhance the positive influence of social media platforms for a quicker and more effective recovery process following a disaster.

The study findings revealed that the Sylhet flood generated over 157 million interactions across 362,036 posts. The disaster was the most shared and commented topic in Bangladesh, with 65% of all posts related to it. The peak of the event coincided with a surge in Facebook activity. Our interview result demonstrates that During flood events, a majority of interview participants (68%) reported frequent social media usage. Facebook was the most commonly used platform (62%), followed by YouTube (17%), WhatsApp (13%), and TikTok (8%). Participants rated the efficacy of social media in crisis management as 4.2 out of 5. The primary challenge to using social media during floods was connectivity concerns, as reported by 58% of participants. In addition, our study identified that using social media for disaster management in Bangladesh poses several challenges. These include information verification and misinformation, privacy concerns, digital divide, limited reach of certain platforms, platform reliability and connectivity issues, lack of standardized protocols, and overwhelming volume of information. To address these challenges, comprehensive strategies, guidelines, and protocols are needed to enhance the utility of social media in disaster management in Bangladesh.

To enhance recovery efforts after disasters in Bangladesh through social media, we recommend a multifaceted approach. This includes strengthening collaboration among disaster management stakeholders on social media platforms, customizing information dissemination strategies to reach specific demographics and vulnerable populations, fostering public-private partnerships to expedite recovery efforts, utilizing social media for real-time communication to provide updates and address concerns, and implementing crowdsourcing strategies to empower communities to participate in recovery efforts. Bangladesh is facing an increasing frequency and severity of natural disasters, and incorporating social media into established disaster management frameworks is crucial. This study highlights the importance of effectively utilizing social media to strengthen the nation's preparedness, accelerate response efforts, and facilitate a quicker recovery in the aftermath of disasters. Ultimately, our research aims to provide guidance to policymakers, practitioners, and the wider community in building a more resilient and adaptive society in the face of natural adversities.

2 Motivation

Bangladesh has witnessed an unprecedented surge in social media usage, marking a transformative shift in the country's digital landscape [4]. Fueled by increasing internet accessibility and the widespread adoption of smartphones, platforms like Facebook, YouTube, WhatsApp, etc., have become integral components of daily life for millions of Bangladeshis [25]. Mobile data packages and Wi-Fi accessibility have become more widespread and affordable, breaking down barriers to entry and enabling a broader cross-section of society to engage in online platforms. Currently, it is one of the top three countries for the growth of active Facebook users [1].

Moreover, the COVID-19 pandemic further accelerated the reliance on social media as a primary source of information, communication, and entertainment [12]. With lockdowns and physical distancing measures in place, individuals turned to digital platforms to stay connected, access news updates, and mitigate the sense of isolation.

While Bangladesh is swiftly advancing in technology and embracing social media, a significant obstacle to its rapid development is the recurring natural disasters that cause the loss of lives and resources and economic setbacks [2]. Our objective is to explore the connection between these two aspects. We seek to investigate the role of social media in managing disasters in Bangladesh and assess its potential as an effective tool for swift recovery from the aftermath of such calamities.

With the country prone to frequent natural disasters, we aim to investigate how social media platforms contribute to swift information dissemination, community mobilization, and stakeholder coordination. By examining the real-time dynamics of social media use during disasters, the research seeks to uncover insights into its effectiveness in facilitating timely responses, aiding relief efforts, and enhancing overall disaster resilience. The findings could inform strategies for leveraging social media as a dynamic tool in the rapid and efficient management of disasters, offering valuable insights for policymakers, disaster management agencies, and communities alike.

3   Literature Review

Researchers, policymakers, and practitioners have shown a growing interest in the convergence of social media and disaster management in recent years [11,16,24]. The increasing use of digital technologies and social networking platforms has led to a significant trend in utilizing these tools to improve disaster readiness, response, and recovery efforts [14]. Researchers have become more aware of the possibilities of social media as a dynamic means of communication [5]. It allows for the immediate spread of information, engagement with communities, and coordination of relief efforts during emergencies [7]. However, despite the growing interest, there is still a noticeable lack of understanding of the intricate dynamics of social media usage in disaster management, especially in locations prone to frequent natural disasters like flooding. Although previous research has examined the general impact of social media in disaster situations, there is still a requirement for more focused studies that investigate the specific circumstances, attitudes, actions, and technical difficulties that influence the effectiveness and resilience of disaster management strategies that utilize social media [23]. Although extensive study has been carried out in Western nations such as the USA, China and Japan, [28] there has been significantly less focus on countries like Bangladesh, which encounter distinctive difficulties and prospects in disaster management. This section aims to thoroughly examine previous studies, emphasizing significant findings, research methods, and upcoming patterns while also clarifying the particular gaps of knowledge that this study attempts to fill.

A study by A. Shandraseharan et al. [29] explores the use of social media in disaster management (DM) in Sri Lanka, emphasizing its potential for early warnings. While acknowledging challenges like information reliability and financial constraints, the research underscores social media's role in efficient emergency communication. The choice of social media platforms for direct messaging in Sri Lanka depends on public preferences. However, the study's limitation lies in its broad focus, lacking specificity to a particular catastrophic event, which may impact the depth and applicability of its findings.

Research reveals a limited inclination for social media use in underserved areas focusing on African-Americans in southeast Texas by utilizing surveys and structural equation modelling [27]. It establishes a direct correlation between individual effort and social media use, an inverse correlation with task complexity, and underscores the moderating effect of an underprivileged population. The study contributes to understanding social media use in disaster management, with implications for theory and practice. Further research is needed to explore additional socioeconomic variables and validate the framework in diverse settings.

Kobiruzzaman [18] analyzes Bangladeshi social media's impact on COVID-19 disaster management, highlighting both benefits (citizen journalism, awareness) and drawbacks (misinformation). The study suggests educational, verification, and policy strategies to mitigate adverse impacts using content analysis from diverse sources. However, it solely focuses on secondary data and overlooks primary data collection and broader perspectives beyond journalism.

Ogie et al. [21] fill a research gap by comprehensively reviewing the literature on social media in disaster recovery. They analyze temporal trends, preferred platforms, and recovery aspects like donations, mental health, and reconstruction. Weaknesses include a limited overview of the current landscape and a need for in-depth method analysis. The research leans heavily on the USA, Japan, and China.

Another study by Mavrodieva et al. [20] presents a concise summary of the existing literature on the use of social media in disaster management, including the many types, applications, advantages, and potential risks and difficulties. A comprehensive analysis of pertinent case studies aims to discover effective and ineffective approaches and extract valuable insights. Ultimately, the article identifies the specific and essential messages that practitioners and policy-makers should note, aiming to determine the best course of action for the future. The work was mostly based on theoretical aspects rather than any practical incident, and it focused on the context of practitioners and policy-makers rather than the disaster-affected people.

Dahal et al. [10] explores how Nepali youth leveraged Facebook to organize earthquake relief in 2015. Through field notes and interviews, the study shows social media's success in mobilizing volunteers, coordinating aid packages, and highlighting needs. However, it omits specific data collection methods and overlooks potential downsides of social media in disaster response.

The study of Lovari et al. [19] explores the role of social media in South Carolina's flood disaster, focusing on government agencies and public sector involvement in emergency management. It investigates communication techniques, challenges faced, and ethical considerations. Emphasizing the need for specialized staff, resources, and ethical communication, the authors stress the importance of countering misinformation during disasters. The study also advocates for qualitative assessments to gauge the effectiveness of social media in meeting the needs of media personnel and citizens during the flood. Challenges identified include coordination issues, varying social media expertise among communication managers, and the complexity of managing rumours and preventing misinformation spread.

The overall gap analysis demonstrates that although Bangladesh is ranked ninth among the nations with the most significant risk of natural disasters worldwide [3], very little or no research has been done in the field of disaster management using social media in the context of Bangladesh. A recent study on social media use in disaster recovery [21] states that 55.6% of research in this context is focused on the USA, which can also be seen in the related works above. Moreover, the disparity in social media usage between the underprivileged and affluent communities [27] prompted us to explore the evolving role of social media in disaster management in Bangladesh.

4   Methodology

The study employs both qualitative and quantitative analyses. The investigation starts with a quantitative analysis of data obtained from *CrowdTangle*, a social media data analytics tool developed by Meta, which offers official data from social platforms like Facebook and Instagram. Following the quantitative analysis, we conducted interviews with disaster-affected people and various stakeholder organizations such as disaster management agencies and NGOs. The study uses the 2022 Sylhet flash flood as a case study for qualitative analyses. These analyses are explained in detail in the following subsections, with an illustration of the methodology provided in Fig. 1.

4.1   Quantitative Analysis on CrowdTangle Data

CrowdTangle is a social media analytics tool developed by Meta, formerly known as Facebook. It is designed to provide insights and analytics on social media performance across various platforms, primarily focusing on Facebook and Instagram. The platform offers a range of features that allow researchers to monitor, analyze, and track content performance on these social networks. Critical features of CrowdTangle include the ability to track public posts, measure engagement metrics such as likes, shares, and comments, and identify trending content. It provides a comprehensive dashboard that enables researchers to visualize and understand the reach and impact of social media content.

We conducted a comprehensive analysis utilizing CrowdTangle to delve into the intricacies of social media usage during disasters, with the primary objective of providing a quantitative response to RQ-1. Throughout this analytical process, our focus extended to two major social platforms, Facebook and Instagram, given that CrowdTangle offers official data. The analysis started with identifying a recent disaster incident in Bangladesh, centring our attention on the substantial Sylhet flash flood in 2022.

We adopted a meticulous approach to establishing search criteria to scrutinize the specific case of the Sylhet flood in 2022. This involved the selection of specific parameters, including language, duration, social media account type, location, post type, and the aggregation of a targeted set of keywords. These criteria were strategically chosen to provide a nuanced and comprehensive understanding of the social media landscape surrounding the Sylhet flood.

The differentiation of post types enabled us to distinguish between various forms of content, such as textual posts, images, videos, and other media formats. Finally, accumulating a carefully curated set of keywords facilitated a targeted and comprehensive search, ensuring that our analysis captured relevant and meaningful data related to the Sylhet flood on social media platforms.

A brief overview of these search criteria is depicted in Table 1.

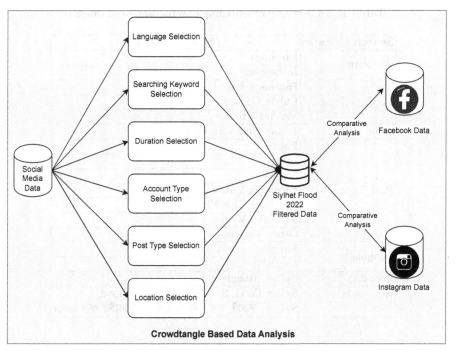

Crowdtangle Based Data Analysis

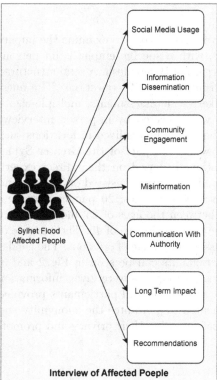

Interview of Affected Poeple

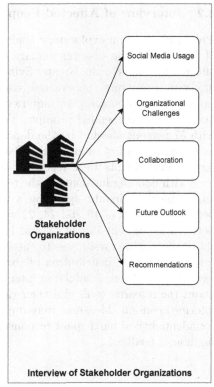

Interview of Stakeholder Organizations

Fig. 1. An overview of methodology.

Table 1. An overview of searching criteria on CrowdTangle.

Search Criteria	Search Value
Platform	Facebook
	Instagram
Account Type	Facebook Page
	Public Groups
	Verified Profiles
Timeframe	1 May 2022 - 31 July 2022
Post Type	Photos
	Links
	Statuses
	Facebook Videos
	Facebook Live Videos
	YouTube Videos
	Other Videos
Language	Bangla
	English
Location	Sylhet, Bangladesh
Keywords	Sylhet flood, Sylhet flood 2022, Flood, Sylhet, সিলেট, বন্যা, সিলেটের বন্যা, সিলেটের বন্যা ২০২২

4.2   Interview of Affected People

This study used an exploratory qualitative methodology to examine the impact of social media on disaster management, with a specific emphasis on persons affected by floods in the Greater Sylhet region of Bangladesh. A semi-structured interview procedure was created, comprising a set of 25 questions. The questions included demographic inquiries, Likert-scale assessments, multiple-choice queries, and open-ended prompts. Data was collected by in-person interviews with 57 persons affected by the flood. These individuals lived in locations such as Habiganj, Sylhet, and Moulvi Bazar, which are part of the Greater Sylhet region. Participants were recruited intentionally based on their direct experience with flooding incidents in the region. The sample consisted of 31 male and 26 female participants, spanning a wide variety of ages: 20 participants were between the ages of 15 and 24, 22 were between the ages of 25 and 34, 8 were between the ages of 35 and 44, and 7 were beyond the age of 45. The purpose of this demographic variety was to encompass a wide range of opinions. The gender ratio and the age distribution of the participants can be seen in Fig. 2 and 3, respectively. Before conducting interviews, participants were given information about the research goals and their rights as subjects. All participants provided informed consent. Measures were implemented to guarantee the anonymity and confidentiality of participant responses, safeguarding their privacy and promoting honest feedback.

Participants

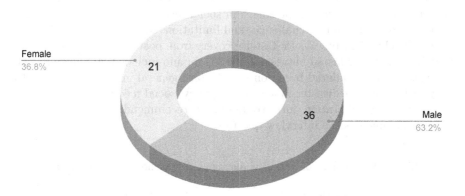

Fig. 2. Gender distribution of interviewee.

Number of Participants

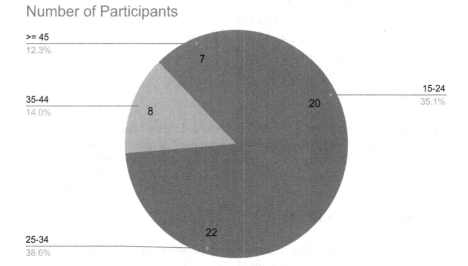

Fig. 3. Age distribution of flood affected interviewee.

4.3   Interview of Stakeholder Organizations

Bangladesh has an active network of disaster management agencies, organizations, NGOs, and other entities working together to mitigate and respond to crises. The Bangladesh Disaster Management Bureau (BDMB) is the national apex body coordinating disaster-related activities, while international organizations and NGOs collaborate with local counterparts to enhance disaster resilience and provide relief. Academic institutions, research centers, and grassroots organizations also play vital roles in fostering innovation and knowledge dissemination for effective disaster management in Bangladesh.

We formulate a semi-structured interview with three stakeholder organizations to understand their involvement in social media for disaster management (RQ-3), enlist the primary challenges and limitations in using social media (RQ-4) and thereby identify ways for faster recovery from post-disaster agony (RQ-5).

Every interview lasted between 25 to 35 min and included 20 questions. The questions were formulated based on six sections: general information about the organization and its disaster management policy, social media usage, challenges and concerns, collaboration, future outlook, and recommendations. The following Table 2 summarises the interview questions.

Table 2. Summary of interview questions of stakeholder organizations.

Question Section	No. of Question
General information	2
Social media usage	8
Challenges and concerns	3
Collaboration and partnership	2
Future outlook	2
Recommendation	3

The interview responses are carefully noted down to ensure that no crucial information is overlooked. A content-based manual analysis is conducted on the open-ended question responses to extract any concealed information. Finally, the gathered information is synthesized to address RQ-3, RQ-4, and RQ-5.

5   Result and Analysis

The methodology adopted in this research paper serves as a guiding framework, leading us systematically toward the answers to our research questions. The subsequent sections discuss the results obtained from the proposed research questions.

5.1   Result of RQ-1

Our investigation into the propensity for social media usage during natural disasters in Bangladesh yielded significant insights. The acquired outcome can be deliberated in two segments: one dedicated to analyzing Facebook data and the other focusing on Instagram.

CrowdTangle Analysis of Facebook: Throughout the Sylhet flood in 2022, a comprehensive analysis revealed a total of 157,097,717 interactions across 362,036 posts. Within this extensive dataset, the fourth most commented post, accumulating 15,000 comments, pertains to the disaster. Additionally, the sixth most viewed post, amassing 8.55 million views, focuses on the flood. Notably, the first most shared (164,900 shares) and interacted post is associated with the Sylhet disaster. Remarkably, during this timeframe, 65% of all posts originating from Bangladesh are linked to the significant Sylhet flood event.

The illustration in Fig. 4 vividly illustrates a pronounced surge in the volume of posts and interactions from June 16, 2022, to June 30, 2022, coinciding with the peak of the disaster. The abrupt increase during this period signifies a notable upswing in Facebook activity during the national crisis.

Fig. 4. Propensity of total posts and interactions on Facebook during Sylhet flood 2022.

CrowdTangle Analysis of Instagram: Like the surge observed in Facebook posts, Fig. 5 illustrates a corresponding increase in Instagram interactions. Throughout this period, Instagram recorded 7,007,086 interactions across 3,811 posts. While the number is comparatively lower than Facebook interactions, it holds significance, especially considering the relatively minor user base of Instagram in Bangladesh.

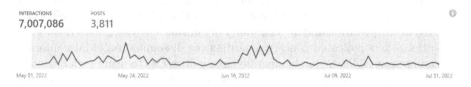

Fig. 5. Propensity of total posts and interactions on Instagram during Sylhet flood 2022.

During this period, the post related to the Sylhet flood secured the fourth-highest viewership with 213,000 views. The post with the highest number of comments (1,200 comments) and interactions vividly highlights the severity of the flood disaster. The fact that 70% of the platform's total posts during the disaster occurrence period is indicative of the devastation caused by the flood serves as a strong indication of the widespread use of social media during such crisis periods.

5.2   Result of RQ-2

The quantitative analysis of Likert-scale and multiple-choice responses of interviews offered additional and complementary perspectives on participants' attitudes and behaviors toward the use of social media during floods. During flood events, a significant majority of participants (68%) indicated frequent social media usage, as illustrated in Fig. 6. Among the various platforms, Facebook was the most commonly used (62%), followed by YouTube (17%), WhatsApp (13%), and TikTok (8%), as can be seen from Fig. 7. Participants evaluated the efficacy of social media in crisis management using a Likert scale that ranged from 1 (Not Effective) to 5 (Highly Effective). The average score was 4.2, suggesting a generally favorable assessment of its usefulness. When questioned about the categories of information they sought on social media during floods, participants indicated their preference for real-time news on flood conditions (68%), guidelines for safety (52%), and access to resources and aid (46%). The primary challenge to using social media during floods was connectivity concerns, as reported by 58% of participants who saw network congestion and inadequate internet connectivity as major issues.

The qualitative study provided comprehensive insights into how flood-affected citizens in the Greater Sylhet region use social media for disaster management. Several notable topics surfaced from the interview data. Participants emphasized the crucial significance of social media platforms like Facebook and WhatsApp in spreading the latest news during flood occurrences. These platforms played a vital role as communication channels for disseminating information about flood conditions, evacuation alerts, and relief activities. Social media helped the fast mobilization of community-based activities, with participants reporting instances where online networks were utilized to coordinate rescue operations, provide relief goods, and provide emotional support to affected persons. Although social media is commonly used for disaster communication, different degrees of trust and effectiveness were noticed. While several individuals believed in the precision and dependability of information disseminated via social networks, others indicated concern regarding the dissemination of false information and rumours. Participants identified many obstacles to using social media in disaster management, such as connectivity problems, language limitations, and the digital divide, significantly impacting underprivileged communities.

5.3   Result of RQ-3

Although two out of three organizations have their Facebook page where they actively post about disaster incidents and dos and don'ts while encountering a disaster, there is a limited scope of their work directly incorporating social media. All three organizations claimed disaster management work is more physical than online virtual. According to them, social media can play a significant role in

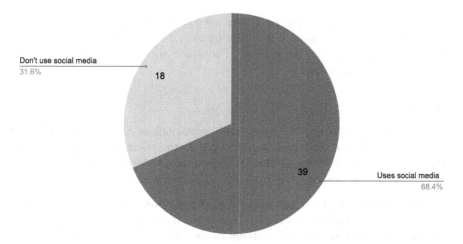

Fig. 6. Usage of social media during disaster encounter period.

Social Platform Wise User

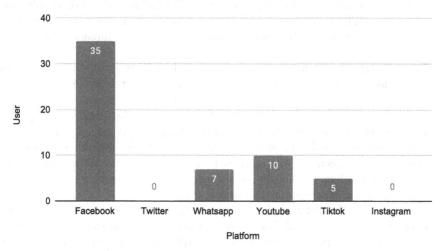

Fig. 7. Platform wise social media user.

providing moral support and information dissemination. However, the actual job of disaster management, including evacuation, relief management, etc., is to be done physically.

Collaboration was a prevalent theme, with 80% of respondents acknowledging social media's role in fostering collaborative initiatives. Notably, 75% of organizations reported active participation in joint efforts on social platforms, demonstrating the collaborative nature of disaster response through social media. Statistically, 75% of respondents recommended developing comprehensive guidelines for responsible social media usage during disasters. Digital literacy programs were suggested by 60%, emphasizing the need for enhanced public understanding. Moreover, 70% emphasized establishing clear protocols for information verification, underscoring the importance of accurate and trustworthy information dissemination during crises.

5.4   Result of RQ-4

Our investigation into the challenges and limitations of using social media for disaster management in Bangladesh brought forth crucial insights from interviews with affected people and disaster management stakeholder organizations. The primary challenges identified can be summarized as follows:

- **Information Verification and Misinformation:** A notable respondent expressed concerns about the rapid spread of misinformation during disaster events. The challenge lies in verifying the accuracy of information circulating on social media platforms, as false or unverified information can potentially lead to panic and hinder practical disaster response efforts.
- **Privacy Concerns:** Privacy concerns have been highlighted as a significant challenge by interviewees. Balancing the need for real-time communication with respect for individuals' privacy emerged as a delicate issue, prompting disaster-affected people and stakeholder organizations to navigate this terrain cautiously.
- **Digital Divide:** The digital divide posed challenges, with respondents acknowledging disparities in internet access and digital literacy. This limitation hampers the effectiveness of social media as a communication tool, especially in reaching vulnerable populations during disasters.
- **Limited Reach of Certain Platforms:** Despite the popularity of platforms like Facebook, YouTube, and WhatsApp, a notable interviewee indicated that reaching specific demographics, particularly older or rural populations, remains a challenge. This limitation emphasizes the need for a diversified communication strategy during disaster events.
- **Platform Reliability and Connectivity Issues:** Respondents reported concerns about the reliability of social media platforms during crises, with issues such as server outages or connectivity problems hindering effective communication and information dissemination.
- **Lack of Standardized Protocols:** The interview outcome highlighted the absence of standardized protocols for using social media in disaster management. Establishing clear guidelines for information sharing, collaboration, and verification emerged as a critical need to enhance the effectiveness of social media in disaster response.
- **Overwhelming Volume of Information:** Dealing with overwhelming information on social media platforms during disasters was cited. Streamlining relevant information and managing the influx of data poses a challenge, impacting the ability to prioritize and respond promptly.

Addressing these challenges will require a concerted effort from the government and every other entity to develop comprehensive strategies, guidelines, and protocols that mitigate risks and enhance the utility of social media in disaster management in Bangladesh.

5.5 Result of RQ-5

Enhancing the influence of social media for faster recovery from post-disaster agony in the context of Bangladesh requires a multifaceted approach. Based on our research and insights gathered from interviews with stakeholders and affected people, the following strategies can be recommended:

- **Strengthening Collaboration:** Encouraging collaborative efforts among Disaster Management agencies, NGOs, and communities on social media platforms can enhance recovery initiatives. Establishing coordinated response networks and sharing resources through collaborative campaigns can amplify the impact of recovery efforts.
- **Targeted Information Dissemination:** Tailoring information dissemination strategies on social media to target specific demographics and vulnerable populations is crucial. Employing geotargeting and language-specific content can ensure that information reaches those who need it most, facilitating a more inclusive and effective recovery process.
- **Public-Private Partnerships:** Fostering partnerships between the public and private sectors on social media can expedite recovery. Encouraging businesses and corporations to actively participate in relief efforts, donate resources, and engage in community-building initiatives through social media can significantly contribute to post-disaster recovery.
- **Real-Time Communication:** Leveraging social media for real-time communication is essential. Disaster Management agencies should utilize platforms to provide instant updates, share recovery progress, and address public concerns promptly. This real-time communication fosters transparency and builds trust within the affected communities.
- **Crowdsourcing for Recovery Efforts:** Implementing crowdsourcing strategies on social media can empower communities to participate actively in recovery. Social media can be utilized to crowdsource information about damaged areas, identify immediate needs, and mobilize volunteers for targeted recovery actions.
- **Digital Skill Development:** Investing in digital literacy programs is crucial for enhancing the influence of social media in recovery. Equipping communities with the necessary digital skills will empower them to access information, connect with resources, and actively engage in recovery efforts through various social media platforms.
- **Storytelling for Empathy and Support:** Utilizing storytelling on platforms like Instagram and YouTube can humanize the recovery process. Sharing personal stories, images, and testimonials from affected individuals creates empathy and encourages a supportive online community, fostering a sense of solidarity that accelerates recovery.

- **Government Engagement and Support:** Active engagement from government entities on social media is pivotal. Establishing official profiles to disseminate accurate information, address concerns, and solicit public input enhances government-citizen communication, contributing to a more coordinated and efficient recovery process.

By implementing these strategies and adapting them to the unique socio-cultural context of Bangladesh, the influence of social media can be harnessed effectively to expedite recovery and alleviate post-disaster agony. The key lies in fostering collaboration, leveraging technology, and prioritizing community engagement through targeted and empathetic communication.

6   Threats to Validity

While our research strives for rigor and reliability, certain aspects may pose potential threats to validity. To ensure that the research outcome is both accurate and unbiased, it is crucial to identify these aspects and take measures to mitigate or eliminate their impact on the research findings.

- The study's focus on Bangladesh and specific disaster events may limit the generalizability of findings to other contexts or types of disasters. Bangladesh's unique socio-cultural and geographical aspects may not align with other regions.
- Responses from interviewees, especially stakeholders, may be influenced by social desirability or organizational agendas. The potential for interviewee bias could impact the accuracy and objectivity of the information gathered.
- The analysis is limited to Facebook and Instagram data due to their availability on CrowdTangle. Including other widely used platforms such as YouTube and WhatsApp could have uncovered additional dynamics within the research.

Despite these potential threats, efforts were made to mitigate biases and enhance the robustness of our research.

7   Conclusion

Our study demonstrates the transformative effect of social media on disaster management in Bangladesh. The use of CrowdTangle data analysis and interviews with affected individuals and stakeholders highlights the crucial role played by social media in such situations. Social media acts as a real-time communication lifeline and amplifies community voices, thereby promoting resilience. While challenges such as misinformation and privacy concerns coexist, social media also offers opportunities for targeted information dissemination. Our research quantifies the impact of social media and lends a human touch to disaster response, providing a comprehensive narrative for informed strategies. Our recommendations include the need for standardized protocols, initiatives for digital literacy, and collaborative frameworks. As Bangladesh moves forward, social media emerges as a technological advancement that will play a key role in creating a more resilient and interconnected future.

References

1. Bangladesh among top 3 countries for Facebook active user growth: Meta — thedailystar.net. https://www.thedailystar.net/news/bangladesh/news/bangladesh-among-top-3-countries-facebook-active-user-growth-meta-3238806. Accessed 24 Jan 2024
2. Bangladesh lost $11.3b due to natural disasters last year: UN — tbsnews.net. https://www.tbsnews.net/bangladesh/environment/climate-change/bangladesh-lost-113b-due-natural-disasters-last-year-un-321319. Accessed 24 Jan 2024
3. WorldRiskReport 2022: Focus: Digitalization — preventionweb.net. https://www.preventionweb.net/publication/worldriskreport-2022-focus-digitalization. Accessed 24 Jan 2024
4. Al Hasibuzzaman, M., Noboneeta, A., Begum, M., Hridi, N.N.C.: Social media and social relationship among youth: a changing pattern and impacts in Bangladesh. Asian J. Soc. Sci. Legal Stud. **4**(1), 01–11 (2022)
5. Appel, G., Grewal, L., Hadi, R., Stephen, A.T.: The future of social media in marketing. J. Acad. Mark. Sci. **48**(1), 79–95 (2020)
6. Barde, V., Sinha, P., Mohanty, U., Panda, R.: Reversal nature in rainfall pattern over the Indian heavy and low rainfall zones in the recent era. Theoret. Appl. Climatol. **146**, 365–379 (2021)
7. Bingqing, L., Zhang, X., Jin, W.: Real world effectiveness of information and communication technologies in disaster relief: a systematic review. Iran. J. Public Health **49**(10), 1813 (2020)
8. Cahyono, S.T., Kuntjorowati, E., Hermawati, I., Rusmiyati, C., Purnama, A., et al.: Disaster risk management based on local wisdom in handling natural disaster victims. In: IOP Conference Series: Earth and Environmental Science, vol. 1109, p. 012023. IOP Publishing (2022)
9. Cox, L.A., Jr.: Decision theory challenges for catastrophic risks and community resilience. In: Cox, L.A., Jr. (ed.) AI-ML for Decision and Risk Analysis: Challenges and Opportunities for Normative Decision Theory, pp. 157–183. Springer, Cham (2023). https://doi.org/10.1007/978-3-031-32013-2_5
10. Dahal, L., Idris, M.S., Bravo, V.: "it helped us, and it hurt us" the role of social media in shaping agency and action among youth in post-disaster Nepal. J. Contingencies Crisis Manag. **29**(2), 217–225 (2021)
11. Dong, Z.S., Meng, L., Christenson, L., Fulton, L.: Social media information sharing for natural disaster response. Nat. Hazards **107**, 2077–2104 (2021)
12. Dubbelink, S.I., Herrando, C., Constantinides, E.: Social media marketing as a branding strategy in extraordinary times: lessons from the covid-19 pandemic. Sustainability **13**(18), 10310 (2021)
13. Faisal, M.R., Budiman, I., Abadi, F., Haekal, M., Delimayanti, M.K., Nugrahadi, D.T., et al.: Using social media data to monitor natural disaster: a multi dimension convolutional neural network approach with word embedding. Jurnal RESTI (Rekayasa Sistem dan Teknologi Informasi) **6**(6), 1037–1046 (2022)

14. Gupta, K., Oladimeji, D., Varol, C., Rasheed, A., Shahshidhar, N.: A comprehensive survey on artifact recovery from social media platforms: approaches and future research directions. Information **14**(12), 629 (2023)
15. Haque, S.E., Nahar, N.: Bangladesh: climate change issues, mitigation, and adaptation in the water sector. ACS ES&T Water **3**(6), 1484–1501 (2023)
16. Huang, Q., Xiao, Y.: Geographic situational awareness: mining tweets for disaster preparedness, emergency response, impact, and recovery. ISPRS Int. J. Geo Inf. **4**(3), 1549–1568 (2015)
17. Kabir, M.E., Kamruzzaman, P.: Exploring the drivers of vulnerability among disadvantaged internal migrants in riverbank erosion prone areas in north-west Bangladesh. J. South Asian Dev. **17**(1), 57–83 (2022)
18. Kobiruzzaman, M.: Role of social media in disaster management in Bangladesh towards the covid-19 pandemic: a critical review and directions. Int. J. Educ. Knowl. Manag. (IJEKM) **4**(2), 1–14 (2021)
19. Lovari, A., Bowen, S.A.: Social media in disaster communication: a case study of strategies, barriers, and ethical implications. J. Public Aff. **20**(1), e1967 (2020)
20. Mavrodieva, A.V., Shaw, R.: Social media in disaster management. In: Media and Disaster Risk Reduction: Advances, Challenges and Potentials, pp. 55–73 (2021)
21. Ogie, R., James, S., Moore, A., Dilworth, T., Amirghasemi, M., Whittaker, J.: Social media use in disaster recovery: a systematic literature review. Int. J. Disaster Risk Reduct. **70**, 102783 (2022)
22. Parker, L., Bourgoin, C., Martinez-Valle, A., Läderach, P.: Vulnerability of the agricultural sector to climate change: the development of a pan-tropical climate risk vulnerability assessment to inform sub-national decision making. PLoS ONE **14**(3), e0213641 (2019)
23. Pfefferbaum, B., Van Horn, R.L., Pfefferbaum, R.L.: A conceptual framework to enhance community resilience using social capital. Clin. Soc. Work J. **45**(2), 102–110 (2017)
24. Phengsuwan, J., et al.: Use of social media data in disaster management: a survey. Future Internet **13**(2), 46 (2021)
25. Prasad, M., Islam, M.M.U.: A quantitative study on usage measure of social media platforms in Bangladesh. In: Information Literacy Skills and the Role of Social Media in Disseminating Scholarly Information in the 21st Century, pp. 121–130. IGI Global (2023)
26. Ramakrishnan, K., Yuksel, M., Seferoglu, H., Chen, J., Blalock, R.A.: Resilient communication for dynamic first responder teams in disaster management. IEEE Commun. Mag. **60**(9), 93–99 (2022)
27. Ramakrishnan, T., Ngamassi, L., Rahman, S.: Examining the factors that influence the use of social media for disaster management by underserved communities. Int. J. Disaster Risk Sci. **13**(1), 52–65 (2022)
28. Ray, A., Bala, P.K.: Social media for improved process management in organizations during disasters. Knowl. Process. Manag. **27**(1), 63–74 (2020)
29. Shandraseharan, A., Kulatunga, U.: Social media for disaster management: the Sri Lankan context. Int. J. Constr. Manag. **23**(4), 648–655 (2023)

Local vs. Global Risk Perception's Effect in Dampening Infectious Disease Outbreaks – An Agent-Based Modeling Study

Sydney Paltra[(✉)] and Jakob Rehmann

Technische Universität Berlin, FG Verkehrssystemplanung und Verkehrstelematik,
10623 Berlin, Germany
paltra@vsp.tu-berlin.de

Abstract. This work explores two key dimensions of the dissemination of information on disease prevalence during an outbreak. First, we point out the necessity of prevalence data to be collected (and communicated) in different scopes, ranging from direct contacts to the whole population. Second, we emphasize the need to minimize the time between the beginning of contagiousness and case reporting, striving for near real-time reporting. To demonstrate the significance of these two dimensions, we introduce an agent-based toy model with an SEIR scheme on a variety of network topologies (random, regular, small-world, and scale-free networks). We compare four different disease mitigation strategies: A base strategy, which allows uncontrolled spread, a global strategy, where susceptible agents reduce their infection probability according to the system-wide prevalence and two local strategies, where susceptible agents reduce their infection probability according to the prevalence among either their first-order or their first-and-second-order neighbors. Across all four network types, we find that the local strategies better reduce both the outbreak's peak height and total size, with the first-order local strategy proving most effective. However, when a lag between becoming contagious and reporting one's disease state is introduced, the prevalence information of one's first order neighbors becomes less useful. In this scenario, the first-and-second-order local strategy performs as good as or better than the first-order local strategy in terms of reducing outbreak size, in all networks except the random network.

Keywords: Infectious disease modeling · Risk perception · Mitigation strategies

1 Introduction

The COVID-19 pandemic is accompanied by an inundation of information [1–3]. People form beliefs on COVID-19 and self-protective measures based on available information, which is not necessarily accurate or accessible in real-time. These

© The Author(s), under exclusive license to Springer Nature Switzerland AG 2024
A. Coman and S. Vasilache (Eds.): HCII 2024, LNCS 14705, pp. 173–189, 2024.
https://doi.org/10.1007/978-3-031-61312-8_12

beliefs motivate engagement in self-protective behaviors (or lack thereof) [4], which, in turn, can mitigate disease spread; this dynamic underscores the importance of rapid dissemination of accurate information in the context of infectious diseases in the 21st century [5]. In this paper, we explore disease surveillance, and two vital characteristics to make it useful in disease suppression and mitigation, both for individuals and governments. First, prevalence data should be collected (and communicated) in different scopes, ranging from direct contact network to the entire population. Second, disease surveillance data must be communicated in near real-time to unfold its full potential. Shorter reporting lags—time between begin of contagiousness and the registration of the case—improves the effectiveness of surveillance in mitigating disease spread.

Regarding scope, we differentiate between local and global information, both of which influence individuals' self-protective behaviors. Global information relates to the disease prevalence in the entire population (i.e. city, state, country); this can be spread through governmental channels or social and traditional media. [6] found that global COVID-19 infection and mortality rates drive future vaccination uptake, indicating that individuals' self-protective behavior is influenced by the disease's national prevalence. Furthermore, [7] found that respondents from countries with the lowest rates of COVID-19 infections, at the time of the survey, engaged in fewer self-protective behaviors than respondents from countries with high COVID-19 infection rates.

Local information, on the other hand, regards communication about disease prevalence within a contact bubble; for example in a neighborhood, family or friend group. It can also include knowledge on the disease prevalence of second-degree (or k-degree) neighbors through secondhand information. Several survey-based studies regarding the COVID-19 pandemic indicate that individuals adapt their behavior voluntarily (as opposed to state-mandated) based on the prevalence of the disease among their contacts: [8] found that survey participants who had infected family members or close friends were more likely to test themselves, and [7] concluded from their multi-country survey that awareness of exposure both in one's "close family" and "other networks" induced self-protective behavior.

Novel bluetooth-based smartphone applications ("apps") were introduced to improve both the disease information transfer between strangers and to reduce the reporting time-lag between infectiousness and registration. Examples include 1) the "Corona-Warn-App" (Germany), a decentralized open-source platform [9] that informed users near-instantaneously about their contacts' positive test results, 2) the "COVID Symptom Study smartphone-based app" (UK/USA), which allowed real-time tracking of disease progression through self-reported health information [10,11], and 3) the software "DiKoMa" (Germany) [12,13], which tracked index cases and their contacts, and collected users' diagnosis reports and symptom diaries. These technological innovations allowed rapid dissemination test result information within a contact network; however, the *presymptomatic* phase in COVID-19's disease progression—wherein an individual is contagious but doesn't show symptoms—continues to present a hurdle for all Test-Trace-Isolate strategies and the above mentioned technologies.

To demonstrate that it is advantageous to quickly provide individuals with local and global information, we built an agent-based toy model that explores the effect of different disease information strategies (in the following called mitigation strategies) on the spreading dynamics. We first explore how the mitigation strategies affect the disease spread when infections are reported immediately (no-lag scenario). Second, we implement a lag between becoming infectious and being registered by the reporting system (lag scenario), thus coming closer to the example of COVID-19 and the common cold.

This paper is structured as follows: We begin by laying the theoretical groundwork and give an introduction to the classic SEIR model, combine it with network theory, and motivate our interest in global and local disease mitigation strategies. In the methods section, we describe our model and the lag scenario extension in detail and formulate the mathematical details of the different disease mitigation strategies. In the results section, we explore the effect of said strategies on disease outbreaks for a random, a regular, a small-world, and a scale-free network. Finally, the discussion section summarizes the results for the different network topologies and encourages future work in this research direction.

2   Theoretical Foundation

The toy-model developed in this paper is based on three different modeling types: network-based, agent-based, and the *Susceptible-Exposed-Infected-Recovered* (SEIR) model. In the SEIR model [14], the population is divided into four disjoint groups: 1) *Susceptible* "S" individuals do not have disease, but can contract it. 2) Exposed "E" individuals have contracted the infection, but cannot yet infect others with it. 3) Infectious "I" individuals are infected with the modeled disease, and can transmit it to *susceptible* agents. 4) Recovered "R" individuals no longer have the disease, and are immune from being reinfected with it.

While SEIR models are usually utilized in compartmental models, we implement this disease progression in an agent-based model (ABM). At their core, ABMs consist of three main elements: First, a collection of "agents" who have at least one, possibly multiple, attributes that may change upon interaction with other agents or the environment. Second, an "environment", the space the agents inhabit and third, a "set of rules" that define the interaction between agents and their environment, agents and agents and how agents' attributes may change [15,16]. Among agents' attributes may be their disease state ("S", "E", "I", "R") as well as their ability to self-protect (later called the "reduction factor").

The ABM presented in this paper is modeled on a network structure, wherein a single agent inhabits a single node, and both information and disease spread across the connecting links. Network-based models are based on an observable finite contact structure, allowing the study of the interplay between contact networks, (non)-pharmaceutical interventions and disease spread [17,18]. Relevant network characteristics for the epidemic outbreak include average shortest path—average distance (jumps) between all pairs of nodes in a graph—and clustering coefficient, which quantifies the degree to which nodes form tightly interconnected groups. In this paper, we consider four network topologies. In the random network, links are randomly added between each pair of nodes, resulting in low clustering and a small average shortest path. The regular network, on the other hand, has a high clustering coefficient and a high average shortest path, as nodes are connected in a lattice structure of dimension one. The small-world network rewires links in the regular network so as to add "short-cuts" between previously far-flung nodes; thus, the average shortest path is reduced while maintaining a high clustering coefficient. The scale-free network is created through "preferential attachment", in which higher degree nodes are more likely to receive new links than less connected nodes; this creates hub nodes, which are not naturally formed in the previous three networks [19, 20].

2.1 Related Work

We are aware of two studies that integrate local and global information into disease spread models. [21] present a metapopulation SIR model, which considers two types of *susceptible* populations: risk-averse, which adapts their behaviour in response to the outbreak on a day-to-day basis, and risk-neutral, which does not. Nodes, representing communities, are connected to nearby communities by local links; long-distance links, on the other hand, connect disparate nodes for sporadic travel. Risk-adverse individuals use local disease prevalence information to adapt local behavior and use global disease prevalence information to curtail their long-distance travel. Our model differs from [21] in that we examine how both local *and* global disease prevalence affect local connections, i.e., the information on national incidence impacts how you interact with your local community. On the other hand, [22] discuss an SIR model on a network with exponential degree distribution, a regular network, and a Barbási-Albert scale-free network. Agents can adopt one of three strategies for instantaneous protective action: First, a local count strategy, for which agents simply count their infected neighbors. Second, a local fraction strategy, for which agents take into account the fraction of their neighbors who are sick and third, a strategy, for which agents consider the global prevalence. They find that the local count strategy offers the greatest protection, as it benefits from the herd effect. Our strategies presented in Sect. 3.2 follow a similar pattern, except that we add a second-order local strategy (neighbors' neighbors). However, we differ significantly from [22] in protective action taken in response to perceived risk. In [22], taking protective action amounts to moving to the recovered compartment, which irreversibly removes the agent from the infection dynamic (i.e. decision to receive vaccination). In our model, agents reevaluate the daily (local or global) prevalence and implement self-protective behavior in an adaptive manner (i.e. reduction of contacts or mask-wearing). Our model expands on the available literature in that it examines status of second-order neighbors, which could arrive at an agent through secondhand information. Furthermore, our model examines the impact of temporal delay between when an agent is infectious and when the community adapts their behavior accordingly (through the presymptomatic state).

3 Methods

3.1 SEIR Setup

For all disease mitigation strategies we discuss in this work, we assume an underlying network structure (N, L), where N denotes the set of nodes and L denotes the set of links. We further assume that each node is inhabited by a single agent and thus use the terms "agent" and "node" interchangeably. On the network (N, L), we implement a SEIR dynamic (see Sect. 2 for introduction and Fig. 1 for illustration). Consequently, "disease state" is added as an agent attribute. We assume the disease states to be mutually exclusive, meaning $N = S \cup E \cup I \cup R$. A *susceptible* agent n, who is infected by one of their neighbors in time step t, immediately moves to the set of *exposed* nodes ($n \in E$), before becoming *infectious* ($n \in I$) in the following time step $t + 1$. The introduction of E ensures that agent n cannot infect their neighbors in the same time step as they have become infected. Every time step, an infectious agent has the chance to recover and thus move to the set of *recovered* nodes R. When extending the model as part of the lag scenario, we introduce the additional disease state P. This set of nodes contains contagious, but *presymptomatic* agents. Whenever an agent's disease state is equal to P, they are contagious, but not yet detectable, and are thus unable to inform their neighbors or the system about their disease state (see Fig. 1 for illustration of connection of the different disease state sets). Due to the underlying network structure, in every time step, every agent n only comes into contact with their k neighbors. We assume that the network is static; thus, the number of neighbors remains constant over time. Consequently, in each time step t, the probability for the *susceptible* agent n to become infected, depends on π, the infection probability per single contact, on red, an infection probability reduction factor that depends on the considered mitigation strategy, as well as k_i, the number of infectious neighbors of agent n:

$$1 - (1 - red \cdot \pi)^{k_i}.$$

Finally, the probability to recover is denoted by τ and is equal for all agents.

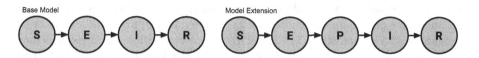

Fig. 1. Left: SEIR model used in the no-lag scenario, where susceptible individuals become exposed for one time step, before becoming symptomatic and infectious. Infectious agents move on to the recovered group. Right: SEPIR model used in the lag scenario. Here, the exposed state E is followed by a presymptomatic but contagious state P. While an agent's disease status is equal to P, their contagiousness cannot be detected.

3.2   Considered Mitigation Strategies

The main contribution of this work is the comparison of three self-protective and, in consequence, disease-mitigating strategies to one another and to a base strategy on different network topologies. The susceptible agents hereby base their decision to self-protect on their perceived epidemiological risk. The contagious agents, however, do nothing to decrease their transmissibility. The base strategy and the three mitigation strategies are modeled as follows:

Base. We assume that the agents' behavior is not affected by the local or global prevalence: No matter how far the disease has spread and no matter how many agents are currently infectious, susceptible agents do not reduce their probability of infection. Consequently, $red = 1$ and the probability of infection reads

$$1 - (1 - \pi)^{k_i}.$$

Reduction Based on Global Prevalence. For this scenario we assume that each agent n, at each time step, has full knowledge of the global prevalence $|I|/|N|$. A susceptible agents reduces their infection probability per single contact with $red = exp(-\frac{|I| \cdot \langle k \rangle}{|N|})$, such that if they have k_i infected neighbors, their infection probability reads

$$1 - \left(1 - exp\left(-\frac{|I| \cdot \langle k \rangle}{|N|}\right) \cdot \pi\right)^{k_i}.$$

Local$_1$, Reduction Based on Local Prevalence—1st Order. Here, we assume that each agent n, at each time step, knows the number k_i of their (first order) infectious neighbors. A susceptible agent reduces their infection probability per single contact by $red = exp(-k_i)$, resulting in the following infection probability:

$$1 - (1 - exp(-k_i) \cdot \pi)^{k_i}.$$

Local$_{1and2}$, Reduction Based on Local Prevalence—1st and 2nd Order. We now assume that each agent n, at each time step, knows how many of their first and second order neighbors are *infectious*. Let the number of first *and* second order neighbors be denoted by k_2. The number of first *and* second order neighbors who are infectious is denoted by $k_{i,2}$. A susceptible agent reduces their infection probability per contact according to the health status of their first *and* second order neighbors: $red = exp\left(-\frac{k_{i,2} \cdot \langle k \rangle}{k_2}\right)$ Consequently, their infection probability reads

$$1 - \left(1 - exp\left(-\frac{k_{i,2} \cdot \langle k \rangle}{k_2}\right) \cdot \pi\right)^{k_i},$$

We note that for all three reduction strategies, if the first order local prevalence is equal to the second order prevalence is equal to the global prevalence $\left(\frac{k_i}{\langle k \rangle} = \frac{k_{i,2}}{\langle k_2 \rangle} = \frac{|I|}{|N|}\right)$, then all three reduction factors are equal. Thus, the factors $\frac{\langle k \rangle}{|N|}$ and $\frac{\langle k \rangle}{k_2}$ serve as normalization factors and enable comparability across strategies.

3.3 Iteration Step

In every iteration step, the agents' disease states are checked and potentially adapted. Algorithm 1 shows the no-lag scenario (SEIR model), while Algorithm 2 shows the lag scenario (SEPIR model). The addition of the presymptomatic state is sole difference between the two algorithms; the change can be observed in lines 6 to 11 of Algorithm 2. Susceptible agents only have a chance to move to the exposed state if they have infectious neighbors; the infection chance is reduced by the reduction factor *red*. Agents only remain in the exposed and presymptomatic states for a single time step, before moving on to the next state. Finally, infectious agents have a pre-defined probability of moving to the recovered state.

Algorithm 1. No Lag	**Algorithm 2.** One-Day Lag
1: **for** agent $\in I$ **do**	1: **for** agent $\in I$ **do**
2: **if** rand $< \tau$ **then**	2: **if** rand $< \tau$ **then**
3: agent moves to R	3: agent moves to R
4: **end if**	4: **end if**
5: **end for**	5: **end for**
6:	6: **for** agent $\in P$ **do**
7:	7: agent moves to I
8:	8: **end for**
9: **for** agent $\in E$ **do**	9: **for** agent $\in E$ **do**
10: agent moves to I	10: agent moves to P
11: **end for**	11: **end for**
12: **for** agent $\in S$ **do**	12: **for** agent $\in S$ **do**
13: **if** rand $< 1 - (1 - exp(-red) \cdot \pi)^{k_i}$ **then**	13: **if** rand $< 1 - (1 - exp(-red) \cdot \pi)^{k_i}$ **then**
14: agent moves to E	14: agent moves to E
15: **end if**	15: **end if**
16: **end for**	16: **end for**

4 Results

4.1 No Lag, i.e. No Presymptomatic Phase

For all network topologies, we assume $|N| = 10,000$. Simulations are run for 200 time steps and we consider infection probability per contact $\pi \in [0.1, 0.3]$ (see Table 1 for model parameters). For each combination of network topology, infection probability per contact, and mitigation strategy, we run 100 simulations; in each simulation, the network is newly generated, with newly chosen patient zero, who is infected at the beginning of the simulation. For all parameter combinations, it is possible that the infection will immediately die out. The associated simulation runs are excluded and we only include runs with $|R_\infty| > 1$. All subsequent figures are a result of averaging the remaining seeds.

Table 1. Parameters, notation.

Parameter	Notation	Setting
Set of nodes	$N = \{n_1, \ldots, n_p\}, p \in \mathbb{N}$	$|N| = 10,000$
Set of susceptible nodes	S	At $t = 0$, $|S_0| = 9,999$
Set of exposed nodes	E	At $t = 0$, $|E_0| = 0$
Set of presymptomatic nodes	P	Only exists for extension, then at $t = 0$, $|P| = 0$
Set of infectious nodes	I	At $t = 0$, $|I| = 1$
Set of recovered nodes	R	At $t = 0$, $|R| = 0$
Set of links	L	Depends on network topology
Degree/No. of neighbors	k	$\langle k \rangle = 10$
No. of infectious neighbors	k_i	
No. of first *and* second order neighbors	k_2	
No. of first *and* second order infectious neighbors	$k_{i,2}$	
Infection probability per single contact	$\pi \in [0,1]$	$\pi \in [0.1, 0.3]$
Probability of recovery	$\tau \in [0,1]$	$\tau = 1/5$

The agent-based toy model was written in Julia v1.9.2 [23], and is freely available on GitHub under the GPL-3.0 license [24]. Our software relies heavily on Agents.jl [25], a framework for agent-based models; all packages required for our project, including their respective versions, can be found in the Manifest.toml file in the above-mentioned repository. Instructions are provided to run the software on a local machine, or on a computing cluster.

Random (Erdős-Rényi). We begin by considering an Erdős-Rényi random graph with $|N| = 10,000$, where the edge between each pair of nodes is included in the graph with probability $p = 10^{-2}$. Consequently, the mean degree is $\langle k \rangle = n \cdot p = 10$. Connected networks constructed via this model have an average shortest path length of four, while the average clustering coefficient is $1/1000$.

Exemplary for different infection probabilities per contact π, Panel (a) of Fig. 2 shows the infection curves for the different mitigation strategies for the infection probability per contact $\pi = 0.3$. As the random network has a small average shortest path length, infections spread through the network with exponential speed (note the logarithmic scale). We observe uncontrolled spread in the case of the base strategy, leading to an early and extremely high peak. Consequently, a larger fraction of the agents is infected (and recovers) early in the simulation, letting the infection die out around time step 50. In contrast, the global mitigation strategy is able to decrease the peak height by more than one half, the two local strategies to less than one third. In consequence, all three mitigation strategies lead to a slower decrease of infections after the peak.

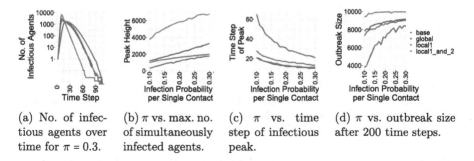

(a) No. of infectious agents over time for $\pi = 0.3$.

(b) π vs. max. no. of simultaneously infected agents.

(c) π vs. time step of infectious peak.

(d) π vs. outbreak size after 200 time steps.

Fig. 2. Simulation results for the random network with $|N| = 10,000$ and $\langle k \rangle = 10$.

Panel (b) of Fig. 2 demonstrates that the three mitigation strategies are able to reduce the peak height. Here, the global strategy is able to halve the peak height, leading to values between around $1,200$ ($\pi = 0.1$) and $3,300$ ($\pi = 0.3$), while both local mitigation strategies prove even more effective, reducing the peak height to less than a third of that of the base strategy. Panel (c) depicts the base infection probability vs. the time step of the peak. Here, we would like to point out that even though the global strategy is able to decrease the peak height, it leads to a very similar time step of peak as the base strategy. The two local strategies, on the other hand, are able to delay the time step of peak. From panel (d) of Fig. 2, we infer that all three mitigation strategies are able to reduce the outbreak size, with the Local$_1$ strategy proving most effective. However, what we find most interesting about the last panel is that even though strategy Local$_{1and2}$ is able to reduce and slightly delay the peak in comparison to the global strategy, both lead to a comparable outbreak size.

Regular Network. Let us consider a regular one-dimensional lattice network, in which each node has exactly $k = 10$ neighbors. This leads to an average shortest path length of 500 and an average clustering coefficient of $2/3$.

Panel (a) of Fig. 3 depicts the infection curves over time for $\pi = 0.3$. For the regular network, the global strategy has almost no visible effect on the infection curve: For the base and the global strategy, the number of simultaneously infectious agents rises to around 35 and plateaus at this level until the end of the simulation. This can be explained by a long average shortest path, which is characteristic for the regular network. The two local strategies, on the other hand, are able to lower the peak of the infection curve to 7, allowing for a very flat example of the classic bell-shape to develop.

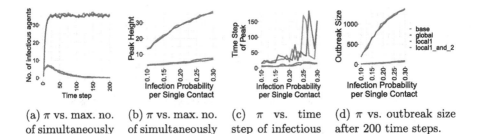

(a) π vs. max. no. of simultaneously infected agents.

(b) π vs. max. no. of simultaneously infected agents.

(c) π vs. time step of infectious peak.

(d) π vs. outbreak size after 200 time steps.

Fig. 3. Simulation results for the regular network with $|N| = 10,000$ and $\langle k \rangle = 10$.

Panel (b) of Fig. 3 shows the peak height for the whole interval of π; all three strategies (Global, Local$_1$ and Local$_{1and2}$) are able to reduce the peak height with respect to the base scenario. The global strategy only slightly reduces the peak, while both local strategies Local$_1$ and Local$_{1and2}$ are able to stifle an outbreak entirely: the peak height lies between 1 and 7 infections (depending on the base infection probability). Panel (c) of Fig. 3 displays the base infection probability versus the time step of the peak. All three strategies lead to an earlier "peak". However, it is interesting to note that for all mitigation strategies (including base), the peak time step is maximal at $\pi = 0.25$, which indicates a threshold point. Panel (d) of Fig. 3 shows that for the base and the global strategy, for small values of π, only around $1/50$ of the agents are infected by the end of the simulation. For both scenarios, the outbreak size steadily increases with π such that when the maximum infection probability per single contact ($\pi = 0.3$) is reached, around $7/50$ agents have been infected at the end of the simulation run. As discussed above, the two local strategies suffice in preventing the outbreak of a wave for small base infection probabilities ($\pi \in [0.1, 0.2]$). For $\pi = 0.3$, only around $9/1,000$ of the agents are infected by the end of the simulation.

Small-World. Third, we consider a Watts-Strogatz network [26] with $|N| = 10,000$ with $\langle k \rangle = 10$. Links are rewired with probability $\beta = 0.01$. For this network, we obtain an average shortest path length of 13.6 and an average clustering coefficient of 0.65.

Panel (a) of Fig. 4 depicts the infection curves for the different mitigation strategies and $\pi = 0.3$. One notes that all three strategies are able to reduce the infection curve compared to the base strategy. For the base strategy, the infection curve grows exponentially, leading to a peak height of more than 2,600. Again, as the small-world network has a small average shortest path length, the infection is able to spread rapidly. This then also implies a rapid decrease in infections after the peak, and that almost every agent gets infected as early as time step 50. The global strategy, on the other hand, leads to a wider infection curve with a peak that is only half as high as for the base strategy. Finally, both local strategies, lead to a slow disease spread: $Local_{1and2}$ displays a peak of around 350; for $Local_1$, we obtain a peak of around 110. The disease does not completely die by the end the simulation at time step $t = 200$ for either strategy.

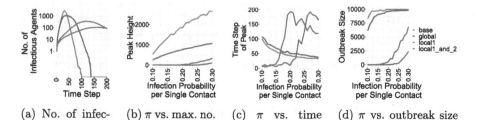

(a) No. of infectious agents over time for $\pi = 0.3$.

(b) π vs. max. no. of simultaneously infected agents.

(c) π vs. time step of infectious peak.

(d) π vs. outbreak size after 200 time steps.

Fig. 4. Simulation results for the small world network with $|N| = 10,000$ and $\langle k \rangle = 10$.

Panel (b) of Fig. 4 is comparable to panel (b) of Fig. 2: The base scenario leads to the highest peak height, the global strategy leads to the second highest peak height, and, until $\pi = 0.2$, both local strategies are able to prevent an outbreak. Starting from $\pi = 0.2$, $Local_1$ is more effective than $Local_{1and2}$, leading to peak heights of 110 and 350 when $\pi = 0.3$. Interesting is the combination of panels (c) and (d): As discussed before, for both local strategie, there exist thresholds below which these strategies are able to prevent an outbreak. The value of this threshold depends on the strategy. However, further examination was beyond the scope of this paper.

Scale-Free. Finally, we use a scale-free network, meaning a network whose degrees follow a power law distribution. Once more, we choose $|N| = 10,000$, $\langle k \rangle = 10$. To generate a scale-free network, we use the Barbási-Albert model [27]. Consequently, we obtain a small average shortest path length of 3.7.

Panel (a) of Fig. 5 depicts the infection curves for the different mitigation strategies when the infection probability per single contact π is equal to 0.3. Once more, the small average shortest path length leads to an exponentially fast spread of the disease. In case of the base strategy, this leads to a peak of almost 7,000, meaning that almost 70% of the agents are infected simultaneously. Consequently, after around 50 time steps, the disease has already infected every agent. The global strategy reduces the peak by less than a half, while both local strategies reduce the peak to less than 1/4 of the base strategy's peak. As seen for multiple networks before, both local strategies lead to a less pronounced and delayed wave. Interestingly, by delaying the peak, $Local_1$ leads to the widest waves: the disease takes 150 time steps to die out.

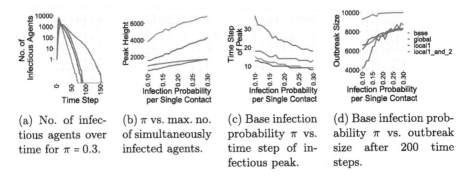

(a) No. of infectious agents over time for $\pi = 0.3$.

(b) π vs. max. no. of simultaneously infected agents.

(c) Base infection probability π vs. time step of infectious peak.

(d) Base infection probability π vs. outbreak size after 200 time steps.

Fig. 5. Simulation results for the scale free network with $|N| = 10,000$ and $\langle k \rangle = 10$.

Panel (b) of Fig. 5 displays the base infection probability π vs. the peak height. We observe that all three strategies perform better than the base strategy. The global strategy leads to a smaller peak height than the base strategy, but is not as effective as either of the two local strategies. $Local_1$ is more effective than $Local_{1and2}$. However, it is interesting to note that the peak height increases faster for $Local_1$ than $Local_{1and2}$, making the difference in peak height for $\pi = 0.3$ less pronounced than for smaller infection probabilities. Panel (c) shows that even though the global strategy is able to lower the peak height, the timing of the peak is very similar to that of the base strategy. $Local_1$ leads to the latest peak, $Local_{1and2}$ to the second-latest peak. Furthermore, it is interesting to note that when it comes to the outbreak size in panel (d), there exists a threshold for π, above which global and the $Local_{1and2}$ strategy become more effective than the $Local_1$ strategy. This contrasts with the other three networks, for which the first-order local strategy always led to the smallest outbreak size.

4.2 One Day Lag, i.e. Including Presymptomatic Phase

We extend our model by introducing the additional disease state "presymptomatic" P (recall Sect. 3.1 and especially Fig. 1 for introduction). While an agent is presymptomatic, they are able to spread the disease to their neighbors. However, their contagiousness cannot yet be detected; since susceptible neighboring agents do not have knowledge of the infection, they will not adapt their behavior to reduce risk. This extension is useful for modeling diseases like COVID-19, where individuals become contagious before showing symptoms and consequently may exhibit a period of uncontrolled transmission. For the purposes of this study, the length of the presymptomatic state is defined to be one day, after which the agent enters the "infectious" state, and is detectable.

Figure 6 shows the resulting infection dynamics, when a presymptomatic phase is introduced; each row shows presents one of the four networks:

Random Network: Looking at the second panel, we note that the base strategy is not influenced by the introduction of the lag. This is to be expected since agents do not adapt their behaviour based on available information in the base case. Since the (unreduced) infection probability per single contact π during the presymptomatic phase is equal to the infection probability per single contact during the infectious phase, the peak is in no way influenced by the introduction of this new disease state. For the global strategy, the introduction of the lag increases the peak height from around 3,300 (see Fig. 2 left panel) to around 5,600. For both local strategies the peak height also increases. It is interesting to note that there exists a threshold of $\pi = 0.15$ above which the $Local_{1and2}$ strategy is more effective in reducing the peak height than $Local_1$. From the right panel, we infer that even though the peak height is higher for the global strategy compared to the no-lag scenario, the outbreak size is hardly affected by the introduction of the lag. The same can be said for $Local_{1and2}$. However, for $Local_1$, the outbreak size increases from around less than 4,000 to 6,000 for $\pi = 0.1$ and from around 8,400 to more than 9,200 for $\pi = 0.3$.

Regular Network: The introduction of the lag does not significantly effect peak height or the outbreak size for either the base or the global strategy. Interestingly, by introducing the lag, none of the strategies are now able to completely suppress an outbreak. The peak height and outbreak size are still relatively low, but, the disease is able to continuously spread slowly through the system.

Small-World Network: Once more, there exist no visible difference for the base and global strategy when compared to the no-lag scenario. For both the peak height (second panel) and the outbreak size (right panel), the $Local_{1and2}$ strategy now proves most effective; at $\pi = 0.3$, the difference in peak height is more pronounced than the difference in outbreak size.

Scale-Free Network: Comparing the first panel of Fig. 6 to the first panel of Fig. 5, we note that the Global and $Local_1$ strategy are most affected by the introduction of the lag. For the global mitigation strategy, the infection curve approximates the infection curve of the base strategy, while the introduction of the lag expedites the infection curve for the $Local_1$ strategy, leading to an earlier end of the disease transmission. Again, for the peak height there exists a threshold of π, above which $Local_{1and2}$ is more effective than $Local_1$. Looking at the last panel, we note that for outbreak size, this threshold is even earlier. Finally, we point out that the right panel is where $Local_{1and2}$ really shines: Without the lag, this strategy led to a similar outbreak size as the global strategy. With the lag, $Local_{1and2}$ clearly leads to the smallest outbreak size. Furthermore, it is also the strategy whose outbreak size is the least increased through the introduction of the lag.

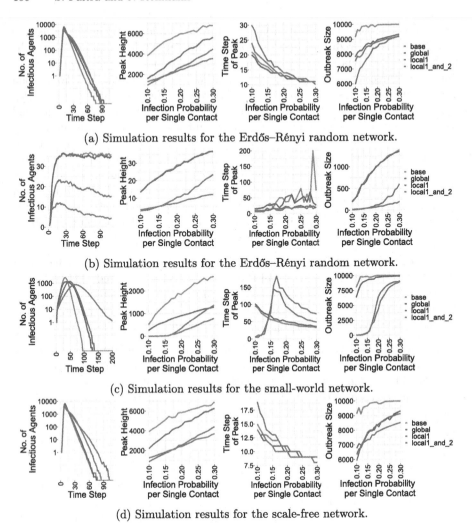

(a) Simulation results for the Erdős–Rényi random network.

(b) Simulation results for the Erdős–Rényi random network.

(c) Simulation results for the small-world network.

(d) Simulation results for the scale-free network.

Fig. 6. Simulation results for the four network topologies with $|N| = 10,000$, $\langle k \rangle = 10$, and a one day lag. In the first column, the infection probability per single contact π is set equal to 0.3

5   Discussion

In this work, we built a toy model to compare different local and global disease mitigation strategies to one another and to a base strategy of uncontrolled disease spread. The toy model is set up on four different network topologies (random, regular, small world, and scale-free) and the parameter space of different infection probabilities is explored.

For most of this work we consider a scenario in which agents have full, correct, and immediate knowledge of their contagiousness and that they communicate this disease state instantaneously. In this no-lag scenario, and for the random, the small world, and the scale-free networks, the global and the two local disease mitigation strategies are able to reduce the peak height of the infection curve, as well as reduce the outbreak size. For the regular network, however, only the two local strategies can reduce the peak height and the outbreak size; the global strategy has a negligible effect. For all four networks, the local strategy $local_1$, where all susceptible agents have immediate knowledge of their first-degree neighbors' contagiousness, proves most effective: It leads to the smallest peak and the smallest outbreak size. We then extended our model by introducing a presymptomatic disease state. During the presymptomatic stage, agents do not know of their contagiousness. This leads to a lag between becoming contagious and becoming detectable; thus, susceptible agents are delayed in reacting to the increased prevalence. In this scenario, the local strategy $Local_{1and2}$ performed as good as or better than $Local_1$ in terms of outbreak size, in all networks except the random network.

In the lag-scenario, $Local_1$ prevalence information becomes less useful; by the time a susceptible agent knows that their neighbor has the disease, there is a sizable chance that the disease has already been transmitted. Strategy $Local_{1and2}$ becomes more interesting; the fact that your second-degree neighbors are "infectious" (and, thus, detectable), increases the chance that your direct neighbors are "presympotomatic", meaning it would be a good idea to mitigate your infection risk. The higher the infection probability per contact π is, the more applicable this dynamic is and the more useful $Local_{1and2}$ becomes. The findings indicate that for diseases that have a "presymptomatic" phase, that disease surveillance of indirect contacts would be useful. This could be incorporated into existing smartphone application infrastructure.

Finally, we would like to point out that, like all modeling studies, our work is based on simplifications and imposes assumptions: First, we assume that the infection and information network are equal. Second, we impose the assumption that even though agents have knowledge of the health status of their neighbors, they do not completely cut ties, but only reduce them. In reality this could be translated to a situation in which an individual knows their local incidence, but is not aware whom of their first/second order neighbors is actually infectious. If they knew which of their neighbors are infectious, it would be more plausible for them to cut these ties, but keep up the ties with their healthy neighbors. Third, we assume that agents are in no way affected by the previous prevalence. Or in other words, they do not have any memory. Finally, we also assume that infectious agent do not curtail their own activities in any way; all risk mitigation stems from susceptible agents. In consequence, this work shall serve as a first exploration of the effect of local vs. global risk perception on infectious disease outbreaks, and we are looking forward to seeing more work in this direction in the future.

Code Availability. All code necessary to reproduce the results of this paper is publicly available on GitHub [24].

Acknowledgments. The work on the paper was in part funded by the Ministry of research and education (BMBF) Germany (grants number 031L0300D, 031L0302A) and TU Berlin. We especially want to thank Kai Nagel, for all the informative discussions that helped shape this paper. We also want to thank the organizers of the 2023 Infodemics Pandemics Summer School (IPSS) in Lübeck, for mentoring us in the theoretical and practical underpinnings for this paper. And a special thank you to IPSS participants Ye Eun Bae, Katharina Ledebur, and Maja Subelj.

Disclosure of Interests. The authors have no competing interests to declare that are relevant to the content of this article.

References

1. Islam, M.S., et al.: COVID-19-related infodemic and its impact on public health: a global social media analysis. Am. J. Trop. Med. Hyg. **103**(4), 1621–1629 (2020). https://doi.org/10.4269/ajtmh.20-0812
2. Zarocostas, J.: How to fight an infodemic. Lancet **395**(10225), 676 (2020). https://doi.org/10.1016/S0140-6736(20)30461-X. ISSN: 0140-6736
3. Pian, W., Chi, J., Ma, F.: The causes, impacts and countermeasures of COVID-19 "Infodemic": a systematic review using narrative synthesis. Inf. Process. Manag. **58**(6), 102713 (2021). https://doi.org/10.1016/j.ipm.2021.102713. ISSN: 0306-4573
4. Rosenstock, I.M.: Historical origins of the health belief model. Health Educ. Monogr. **2**(4), 328–335 (1974). https://doi.org/10.1177/109019817400200403. ISSN: 0073-1455
5. Chen, F.H.: Modeling the effect of information quality on risk behavior change and the transmission of infectious diseases. Math. Biosci. **217**(2), 125–133 (2009). https://doi.org/10.1016/j.mbs.2008.11.005. ISSN: 0025-5564
6. Sarkar, J.: Do disease prevalence and severity drive COVID-19 vaccine demand? Econ. Anal. Policy **75**, 310–319 (2022). https://doi.org/10.1016/j.eap.2022.05.014. ISSN: 0313-5926
7. Litwin, H., Levinsky, M.: Network-exposure severity and self-protective behaviors: the case of COVID-19. Innov. Aging **5**(2) (2021). https://doi.org/10.1093/geroni/igab015. ISSN: 2399-5300
8. Li, S., Feng, B., Liao, W., Pan, W.: Internet use, risk awareness, and demographic characteristics associated with engagement in preventive behaviors and testing: cross-sectional survey on COVID-19 in the United States. J. Med. Internet Res. **22**(6), e19782 (2020). https://doi.org/10.2196/19782. ISSN: 1438-8871
9. Corona-Warn-App Open Source Project. Open-Source Project Corona-Warn-App — coronawarn.app (2020). https://www.coronawarn.app/en/. Accessed 12 Jan 2024
10. Menni, C., et al.: Real-time tracking of self-reported symptoms to predict potential COVID-19. Nat. Med. **26**(7), 1037–1040 (2020). https://doi.org/10.1038/s41591-020-0916-2. ISSN: 1546-170X
11. Menni, C., et al.: COVID-19 vaccine waning and effectiveness and side-effects of boosters: a prospective community study from the ZOE COVID Study. Lancet Infect. Dis. **22**(7), 1002–1010 (2022). https://doi.org/10.1016/S1473-3099(22)00146-3. ISSN: 1473-3099

12. Neuhann, F., et al.: Entwicklung einer Software zur Unterstützung der Prozesse im Gesundheitsamt der Stadt Köln in der SARS-CoV-2-Pandemie, Digitales Kontaktmanagement (DiKoMa). Epidemiologisches Bull. **2020**(23), 3–11 (2020). https://doi.org/10.25646/6923

13. Grüne, B., et al.: Symptom diaries as a digital tool to detect SARSCoV-2 infections and differentiate between prevalent variants. Front. Public Health **10** (2022). https://doi.org/10.3389/fpubh.2022.1030939. ISSN: 2296-2565

14. Kermack, W.O., McKendrick, A.G.: A contribution to the mathematical theory of epidemics. Proc. R. Soc. Lond. Ser. Math. Phys. Eng. Sci. **115**(772), 700–721 (1927)

15. Epstein, J., Axtell, R.: Growing Artificial Societies: Social Science from the Bottom Up. MIT Press, Cambridge (1996). ISBN: 978-0262050531

16. Epstein, J.M.: Agent-based computational models and generative social science. Complexity **4**(5), 41–60 (1999). https://doi.org/10.1002/(sici)1099-0526(199905/06)4:5<41::aid-cplx9>3.0.co;2-f. ISSN: 1099-0526

17. Keeling, M.J., Eames, K.T.D.: Networks and epidemic models. J. Roy. Soc. Interface **2**(4), 295–307 (2005). https://doi.org/10.1098/rsif.2005.0051. ISSN: 1742-5662

18. Danon, L., et al.: Networks and the epidemiology of infectious disease. Interdiscip. Perspect. Infect. Dis. **2011**, 1–28 (2011). https://doi.org/10.1155/2011/284909. ISSN: 1687-7098

19. Menczer, F., Fortunato, S., Davis, C.A.: A First Course in Network Science. Cambridge University Press, Cambridge (2020). https://doi.org/10.1017/9781108653947. ISBN: 978-1-108-65394-7

20. Barabasi, A.-L.: Network Science. Cambridge University Press, Cambridge (2016)

21. Zhao, S., Kuang, Y., Wu, C.-H., Bi, K., Ben-Arieh, D.: Risk perception and human behaviors in epidemics. IISE Trans. Healthc. Syst. Eng. **8**(4), 315–328 (2018). https://doi.org/10.1080/24725579.2018.1464085. ISSN: 2472-5587

22. Herrera-Diestra, J.L., Meyers, L.A.: Local risk perception enhances epidemic control. PLoS ONE **14**(12), e0225576 (2019). https://doi.org/10.1371/journal.pone.0225576. ISSN: 1932-6203

23. Bezanson, J., Edelman, A., Karpinski, S., Shah, V.B.: Julia: a fresh approach to numerical computing. SIAM Rev. **59**(1), 65–98 (2017). https://doi.org/10.1137/141000671

24. Rehmann, J., Paltra, S.: EpiNetSim. Version v0.2 (2024). https://doi.org/10.5281/zenodo.10607229

25. Vahdati, A.R.: Agents.jl: agent-based modeling framework in Julia. J. Open Source Softw. **4**(42), 1611 (2019). https://doi.org/10.21105/joss.01611

26. Watts, D.J., Strogatz, S.H.: Collective dynamics of 'smallworld' networks". Nature **393**(6684), 440–442 (1998). https://doi.org/10.1038/30918. ISSN: 1476-4687

27. Barabási, A.-L., Albert, R.: Emergence of scaling in random networks. Science **286**(5439), 509–512 (1999). https://doi.org/10.1126/science.286.5439.509. https://www.science.org/doi/pdf/10.1126/science.286.5439.509

Digital Publics and the Ukraine Dilemma: Topic Modelling of the Cumulative Twitter Discussion

Anna Sytnik[1,3]([⊠]) [iD], Polina Chernikova[2,3] [iD], Konstantin Vorontsov[2,3] [iD], and Mariia Bazlutckaia[2,3] [iD]

[1] Saint-Petersburg State University, Saint-Petersburg 199034, Russia
anna@sytnik.me

[2] Moscow State University, Moscow 119991, Russia
s02200807@gse.cs.msu.ru, voron@mlsa-iai.ru

[3] Moscow State Institute of International Relations, Moscow 119454, Russia

Abstract. In this study, we explore on what topics and to what extent digital publics – publics that exist on Twitter and share common topics – contributed to the global intensifying information warfare about Ukraine in the world. We use probabilistic topic modelling with time series for 3,676,245 unique tweets with the keyword 'Ukraine' or 100 political or regional hashtags in English or Russian written by 960,422 unique users for the period from 30 August 2021 to 24 February 2022. We reveal 38 politically significant topics (23 persistent topics and 15 event topics) and explore the scope of discussion and its dependency on political events. The application of SNP metric to tweets by topics allow us to carefully study and then describe the political ideas and arguments offered by influential ordinary Twitter users in online information confrontation. We demonstrate the process of cumulative formation of global clusters of digital publics on some important topics with regard to the approaching escalation of the Russian-Ukrainian conflict.

Keywords: Russian–Ukrainian conflict · Digital publics · Information warfare · Topic modelling · Twitter discussion

1 Introduction

The Ukrainian conflict has become the first social media war and a proving ground for multiple actors to test the techniques and tools of information warfare (Mölder and Sazonov 2018; Suciu 2022). Golovchenko et al. (2018, p. 975) considered information warfare in the context of the Ukrainian conflict as 'a number of strategic campaigns to win over local and global public opinion, largely orchestrated by the Kremlin and pro-Western authorities. Even so, both Russian and Western official documents point to the fact that modern information warfare comprises not only foreign influence operations on domestic affairs using information for geopolitical purposes but also democratic activism

---

At the time of writing, Twitter has not yet been renamed to X, so in this paper we are using the old name of the social network.

A. Coman and S. Vasilache (Eds.): HCII 2024, LNCS 14705, pp. 190–207, 2024.
https://doi.org/10.1007/978-3-031-61312-8_13

on social media (Klein 2018). Referring to a quote by Margarita Simonyan, editor-in-chief of the Russian state-controlled media organization (Spiegel International 2013) that 'there is no objectivity – only approximations of the truth by as many different voices as possible', Thornton (2015) made an important argument that it is not the quality so much as the quantity of the information disseminated that is important for the outcome of information warfare operations. All this points to the influence of massive numbers of users shaping the information warfare in the Ukrainian conflict.

According to Wendt's (2015) 'quantum mind' hypothesis, states are projections of the mind of each person, and conversely, the mutual influence of international anarchy and states is reflected in the minds and practices of individuals. In the Russian–Ukrainian 'war of words' or 'war of narratives', social media users are active participants in the information warfare and not just targets. Ordinary users' tweets form narratives, and narratives shape political imaginations or identities, which act as drivers of foreign policies eroding the power and influence of states on the course of world politics. At the same time, personal narratives reflect generalized stories as they are formed inside the absolutized narratives in digitally fragmented political reality (Golovchenko et al. 2018; Lazarenko 2019; Torbakov 2017; Tokarev 2018; Tsvetkova et al. 2022). The aim of this article is to explore the global public cumulative battleground about the contemporary Ukraine of the pre-war period. To achieve it, this study refers to the concept of 'digital publics' by which we mean publics that exist on social media platforms and share common topics. We explore the growing tension in topics of discussion around Ukraine since the summer of 2021, when the first media leaks began to appear, until 24 February 2022.

The article is structured as follows. In the literature review section, we first explain the role of digital publics in shaping narratives about Ukraine. Second, describing the samples and methods for our study, we argue that Twitter data was the most effective choice for this analysis, propose a two-stage data-collection method, and present a brief overview of topic modelling with time series of Russian–Ukrainian information warfare explaining the advantages of the chosen approach.

The key implication of this study is the data-driven explanation of the dynamics of global digital publics' attention to and the interpretation of the Ukraine pre-war dilemma. We closely examined the case of digital publics discursive and quantitative contribution to the global tension surrounding Ukraine in the second half of 2021 and early 2022, thus, adding the growing body of literature on patterns of cumulative deliberation in online communication (Bodrunova 2022). The main added value of our research is that we detected with topic modelling life cycles of narratives 'crowdsourced' by the Twitter publics on 38 political issues and analyzed arguments offered by influential ordinary Twitter users by applying special metrics to tweets.

2   Literature Review

Papacharissi (2015) in a book 'Affective Publics: Sentiment, Technology, and Politics' proved that technology-mediated feelings of connectedness promote broader publics express their point of view on current political issues. Moreover, social media users contribute to the structural transformation of public political sphere by contesting it

(Celikates, 2015). In this article, we understand by 'digital publics' spontaneously formed thematic communities of netizens around shared interests, issues, and identities – topical issue publics (Bruns and Highfield 2015). Unlike 'hashtag publics' that use hashtags to mobilize around certain issues (Rambukkana 2015), digital publics are closer in meaning to general public or online public, which means citizens engaging with political content online (Oswald et. al. 2022). As a rule, digital publics become visible when triggered by specific messages, and do not necessarily refer to particular hashtag campaign in their posts. This is why digital publics are also regarded as 'latent diffused publics' as it is difficult to identify them before something happened (Plowman et al. 2015, p. 274). Such a complex and polarizing political issue as Ukraine pre-war dilemma provides with opportunity to trace the process of cumulative formation and influence of global clusters of digital publics with regard to a major international political issue.

The Maidan protests of 2013–2014 have launched scientific discussions about narratives concerning contemporary Ukraine. Moreover, digital publics have been increasingly shaping the narrative about Ukraine in the world by tweeting in foreign languages, especially in English, and aiming their messages at an international audience (Bolin et al. 2016; Ciuriak 2022; Makhortykh 2018; Makhortykh and Lyebyedyev 2015). In fact, reporting on the conflict, Twitter publics have become elements of information warfare in a new kind of technology-mediated public communication environment (Ojala 2018). Additionally, even the audiences' natural biases customize the narrative in unique ways: for instance, nationalists praise Russia's historic power, while communists scold capitalism (Jaitner and Geers 2015; Makhortykh and Sydorova 2017).

Thus, scholars agree that digital publics are active participants in the 'cycle of narratives' about the Ukrainian conflict in the world, yet to date, these global narratives have not been identified through an analysis of a large number of social media posts. Nevertheless, it is a user-based approach that can shed light on the conditions of modern information warfare. Consequently, the research question for this study took the following form:

RQ: To what extent and on what topics digital publics contributed to the global intensifying information warfare around the Ukraine dilemma according to Twitter data?

3 Sample and Method

3.1 Data Collection

Twitter. The unique degree of transnational communication makes Twitter a medium for exploring the international public debate about contemporary multiple actor conflicts. In the course of the Russian–Ukrainian conflict, Twitter has become an online battleground where multiple actors are attempting to mobilize public support (Golovchenko et al. 2018; see also Chen and Ferrara 2022; Makhortykh and Lyebyedyev 2015; Ojala et al. 2018; Park et al. 2022; Pohl et al. 2022). Twitter is more suitable than other relevant social media networks such as the Russian VKontakte or Meta's Facebook for studying the cross-border discussion about the Russian–Ukrainian conflict for several reasons. First, Twitter is more often used to discuss news agenda. Second, it facilitates global engagement among audiences in Russia, Ukraine and the West with hashtags; and third, a short tweet with 280 characters is more convenient for text analysis. Researchers are already publishing public datasets tracking the Twitter discourse related to the 2022 Russian–Ukrainian war and the support for both sides of the conflict in the context of information warfare (Chen and Ferrara 2022; Park et al. 2022). For instance, Pohl et al. (2022) collected a dataset that covers the period from one week before to one week after the onset of the 2022 war using Twitter streaming API.

A Two-Stage Data Collection Method. The collection of datasets for this study took place in two stages in 2021–2022. For the first stage, a computer program written in the programming language Python with Selenium, an open-source umbrella project for a range of tools and libraries aimed at supporting browser automation, and raw requests from Twitter Advanced Search, an open and publicly available source of information about previously published tweets, was used to collect and analyze data (García et al. 2021). The dataset comprised all accessible public tweets containing the word 'Ukraine' in English and Russian from 30 August 2021 to 24 February 2022. We selected this particular keyword due to the informal rule of using the country's name to convey conflict-related information as this has been used successfully in previous studies (Bruns et al. 2013; Howard et al. 2011; Papacharissi and De Fatima Oliveira 2012). We did not use the keyword 'Russia' because in the analyzed period the conflict was taking place not on Russian territory and for this reason the keyword 'Ukraine' yields more relevant tweets with a large-scale discussion of Russia's actions as well. We also did not use the keyword in the Ukrainian language, assuming that the main information confrontation is conducted in Russian and English, which is also confirmed by a review of the literature. The period for analysis was chosen with a margin that ensured that the intensification of the pre-war discussion about Ukraine, which happened in the autumn, was not missed. At this stage, the collected dataset contained 3,823,153 tweets by 2,358,808 unique users with information related to the discussion about Ukraine.

In the second stage, we expanded this dataset to capture tweets related to the discussion about the Russian–Ukrainian crisis but not including the keyword 'Ukraine' and to make it more closely related to information warfare. To collect additional data, we used the resulting dataset to conduct hashtag analysis for the entire period. The hand-selected hashtags method provides high-relevance scores for increasing a number of relevant tweets in topic-specific dataset from Twitter (Llewellyn et al. 2015). Thus, we classified the top hashtags in the given dataset based on the number of tweets with these hashtags from most used to least. Four independent encoders conducted qualitative content analysis of the received top hashtags about Ukraine for our goal of dataset extension. All four reported that after one-thousand hashtags carried a much smaller semantic load and were often repeated by their counterparts in another language, which was not required for our tasks. Then, of these one-thousand top-hashtags, encoders were asked to choose hashtags based on the following coding frame: (1) spelling in English or Russian and (2) political or geographic significance in relation to the Ukrainian conflict. As a result, 100 top hashtags were selected (Table 1). Thereafter, we repeated the data collection using the method described above and added all available public tweets with 100 highlighted hashtags over the same period to our dataset.

It is important to note that, due to this two-stage data-collection method, some of the tweets in the database are duplicates. Additionally, despite the fact that the keywords

Table 1. Political or Regional Hashtags in English and Russian from the Top 1000 Hashtags in the 'Ukraine' Dataset, 30 August 2021– 24 February 2022. Hashtags are listed from most used to least used. Hashtags in Russian are duplicated in English in brackets.

Political Hashtags	Regional Hashtags
UkraineCrisis UkraineConflict UkraineRussiaCrisis RussiaUkraineCrisis StandWithUkraine RussiaUkraine UkraineInvasion RussiaInvadedUkraine RussiaUkraineConflict Zelensky UkraineWillResist Russianinvasion PutinsWar IStandWithUkraine Maidan worldwar3 ukrainerussia UkraineRussiaConflict Ukraine_StopArmingSAC EuroMaidan PrayForUkraine UkraineRussia UkraineWar StopRussianAggression NoWarWithRussia RussianAggression Зеленский(Zelensky) UkrainiansWillResist MSC2022 Ukrainians CrimeaIsUkraine MH17 SanctionRussiaNow HunterBiden Chernobyl WorldWarIII Russiaukrainewar ВСУ(APU) WeStandWithUkraine RussiaIsATerroristState Zelenskyy StopPutin PutinAtWar Holodomor ww3 PutinIsaWarCriminal Ukrainecrisis агрессияРоссии(Russianaggression) вторжениеРоссии (Russianinvasion) PutinsPuppet MinskAgreements PrayingForUkraine SupportUkraine RussianInvasion russie_ukraine_peco Ukraine_IS_NOT_zelensky SaveUkraine FreeUkraine VolodymyrZelensky Zelenskiy Ukraine_does_not_attack WorldWar3 RussiaCrisis StayWithUkraine PutinIsAKiller UkraineUnderAttack Ukraineinvasion Standwithukraine RussianArmy Nowarinukraine LittleGreenMen UnitedWithUkraine	Donbass Kyiv Donetsk Kiev Lviv Odessa одесса(odessa) Luhansk Odessa Одесса(Odessa) Донбасс(Donbass) WW3 DPR Днепр(Dnieper) ДНР(DPR) LPR Kiev UKR Donestk Крым(Crimea) Donetsk Запорожье(Zaporozhye) Mariupol Днр(Dpr) Crimea DNR Donbas

were only in two languages, the dataset still included many tweets in other languages. We resolved these two issues with data processing.

3.2 Data Processing

Cleaning of Data. To avoid distorting the overall picture due to expanding the dataset with hashtags, we first removed duplicate tweets. Then, we performed the primary cleaning of the tweet texts for the entire dataset by removing the following: hashtags, emojis and newline characters ('\n'); mentions and marks of users; and links to external sources and images. We also built a distribution of tweets by language and deleted tweets belonging to the least frequently used languages, pseudo-languages (for example, characters that are not letters were allocated by Twitter into a separate language), and languages that were defined incorrectly (a mixture of several languages). We present the results in Table 2.

Table 2. Distribution of Languages in the Final Dataset with Public Tweets Containing the Keyword 'Ukraine' or 100 Political or Regional Hashtags in English or Russian, 30 August 2021–24 February 2022

Language code	Transcription	№ of unique tweets
total	All languages	3,676,245
en	English	3,584,527
ru	Russian	55,209
de	German	2,096
fr	French	3,302
uk	Ukrainian	5,978
pl	Polish	8,959
es	Spanish	4,490
it	Italian	1,754
tr	Turkish	3,302
nl	Dutch	2,449
in	Indonesian	2,607
ar	Arabic	1,623
da	Danish	440

For each language, we built a distribution of tweets by length and removed outliers, i.e. all tweets with fewer than four characters or more than 280 (Twitter's official limit) and all punctuation marks in the text of the tweet. Thereafter, the entire dataset was divided into language groups and subsequently translated into English using the deep-translator library and its Google Translator (Google Translate API). The result was a final dataset of 3,676,245 unique tweets written by 960,422 unique users.

Lemmatization. We lemmatized and tokenized English text and removed stop words using the NLTK and spaCy libraries. We selected collocations using the TopMine library with a maximum length of 4.

Considering Ordinary Users' Influence. In order to study how digital publics contributed to the information warfare, we considered the index of Twitter user influence for the subsequent topic modelling results interpretation. We chose a metric 'Social Networking Potential' (SNP), defined as follows (Riquelme and González-Cantergiani,

2016):

$$SNP(i) = \frac{Ir(i) + RMr(i)}{2}$$

where the Retweet and Mention Ratio, RMr(i) is defined as:

$$RMr(i) = \frac{\#tweets\ of\ i\ retweeted + \#tweets\ of\ i\ replied}{\#tweets\ of\ i}$$

and the Interactor Ratio, Ir(i) is defined as:

$$Ir(i) = \frac{RT3 + M4}{F1}$$

where the RT3 is the number of users who have retweeted author's tweets, and M4 is the number of users mentioning the author. Due to the fact that collected data does not allow to build a graph, we used number of replies and number of quotes for counting M4, since these statistics empirically contain a mention of the author.

The SNP statistics were calculated for each of 960,422 Twitter users in the dataset. The application of the SNP metric allowed us to separate ordinary influential users from influential accounts owned by official state representatives or departments, the media and celebrities, whose key differentiating characteristic is the large number of followers (Anger and Kittl 2011). Thus, the number of followers is deliberately omitted in this approach in order to explore narratives produced by ordinary users.

3.3 Time Series Topic Modelling

To date, scholars have rarely employed topic modelling for qualitative studies (Nikolenko et al. 2017). Few studies have successfully applied this method to study public discussions about the Russian-Ukrainian conflict, and most of them relate to the study of Russian information warfare on social media. For instance, Doroshenko and Lukito (2021) combined computational and qualitative content analyses with time series modelling to explore online informational warfare by the Russian Internet Research Agency (IRA) against Ukraine during the military conflict in Donbass.

Nonetheless, there are several studies comparing the narratives about Ukraine on social media. Koltsova and Pashakhin (2020) performed topic modelling coupled with qualitative analysis in order to find quantitative evidence of agenda divergence in the online newsfeeds of Russian and Ukrainian TV channels in the course of the 2013–2014 crisis. They revealed crisis-related topics, their salience and evolution of public attention. Mishler et al. (2015) conducted structural topic modelling (STM) using Russian social media data to model how topics about the Russian-Ukrainian conflict change over time. They showed that STM can be used, first, to detect significant events such as the downing of Malaysia Airlines flight 17, and second, to cluster pro-Ukrainian versus pro-Russian Twitter users as topics vary across a set of authors. Chew and Turnley (2017) adapted a technique for multilingual topic modelling to discover differences between Russian versus English language discussions. They demonstrated that the multilingualism of data may be an advantage as it helps – although in a highly general way – to detect large-scale trends, anomalies, similarities and differences. For instance, they found that the issues discussed by the Twitter public differ depending on which cyberspace it is in, being influenced by national 'master narratives', and that sentiment plays a key role in Russian discourse related to NATO.

Probabilistic topic modelling is widely used as a machine learning technique that decomposes a text-document collection into a set of topics. The model defines each topic by a probability distribution over words and then represents each document by a probability distribution over topics. Unlike typical text-clustering algorithms that assign each document to only one cluster, probabilistic topic modelling performs a 'soft clustering' with a more realistic assumption that a document may cover several topics. Unlike popular neural text-embedding techniques, topic modelling produces sparse and interpretable text embeddings useful for understanding the topical structure of any text fragment from a single word to an entire document.

The additive regularization for topic modelling (ARTM) is a multi-criteria framework that provides a way to identify topic models with given properties (Kochedykov et al. 2017). The idea of combining regularization criteria is implemented in the BigARTM open-source project that we use in this study (Vorontsov et al. 2015). With BigARTM, we identify a topic model regularized by three additive requirements. The first is topic decorrelation, which makes topics more diverse and clears them of common words. The second is making the topical embedding of documents as sparse as possible, based on the assumption that each document contains a small number of topics. This approach has been justified in many previous studies such as exploratory searches, text classifications, and the detection of polarized opinions (Feldman 2020; Kochedykov et al. 2017). Third, we use the requirement of similarity of corresponding topics in adjacent weekly time intervals to achieve the continuity of topics in time and to discover new topics every week. Thus, we obtain a temporal model with the possibility of topic detection and tracking. The use of the ARTM approach in our study improves the interpretability of topics and increases the number of topics suitable for qualitative and quantitative analysis over time.

To build models, we divided the entire dataset into weeks. We built a topic model with 30 topics for each week for the period from 30 August 2021 to 24 February 2022, thus, receiving 780 topics (30 topics for 26 weeks). We used both the concatenation of all tweets of one author for the corresponding week and collocations selected from them with a length of 1 to 4 words as a document for each model. This basic approach allowed us to solve the problem of too short documents to build interpretable topics (Murshed et al. 2022). We used a common dictionary, consisting of individual tokens and phrases extracted from processed and lemmatized tweets. The dictionary was filtered by the frequency of occurrence of tokens. In order to avoid too frequent or too rare tokens, the following restrictions were imposed on the frequency: max_df_rate $= 0.25$, min_df_rate $= 0.0008$. As a result, the dictionary consisted of 21,116 tokens. We built the models sequentially, initializing each successive model of the previous one, so the same topics remained under the same number for each new model. We used the cosine similarity of the phi-matrix for neighboring weeks for the primary visualization of the temporality of topics with a threshold greater than or equal to 0.9 (deduced empirically). For example, if the cosine between the i-th column of the Phi matrix of model 1 and the i-th column of the Phi matrix of model 2 was less than or equal to 0.9, then we considered that the i-th topics in week 1 and week 2 are different. This approach, based on a consistent assessment of the similarity of topic's tokens for each model, allowed us to isolate the lifespan of a topic and evaluate the variability of topics over time. It is important to note that with this approach of sequential construction and subsequent similarity assessment, we did not rigidly set the final number of topics, yet allowed topics to evolve, change their tokens from week to week, while maintaining the overall context. As a result, 116 different topics were found, from which we identified and interpreted 38 unique, politically significant topics.

The interpretation of topics was based on the evaluation of top tokens (separately identified top 25 words and top collocations of length 2, 3, 4) and top tweets. The top tweets of a topic were tweets that met 3 conditions: (1) more or equal 65% probability of matching the topic (column of the theta matrix in the Topic Modeling Matrix Decomposition), (2) tweet text contains the maximum number of top words and collocations, and (3) maximum SNP of tweet author for the topic. In order to improve the interpretability of topics, we used the decorrelator of the phi matrix as regularizer to make topics more 'different'.

4 Results

4.1 Political Events as Digital Publics' Discussion Triggers

To answer our research question, we turned to the analysis of meaningful events, discussion topics, and Twitter users. We first explored which events have potentially provoked digital publics to discuss the Ukrainian dilemma more.

Results visualized as a graph of the intensity of the entire discussion show that the situation began to receive more attention from Twitter publics starting in the second-half of December 2021 (Fig. 1). The visualization of events on the chart provides an opportunity to observe the development of key events about Ukraine over the seven months of the 2022 prelude to war. We matched spike dates with important news from various international media outlets about the escalation of the situation around Ukraine, which provides an understanding of the interdependence of events and the reactions of the digital publics.

The graph reflects the intensity of 3,676,245 unique tweets written by 960,422 unique users by days for the period 30 August 2021–24 February 2022. The x-axis is the days, and the y-axis is the number of tweets. We manually indicated key political events that presumably caused spikes in Twitter public discussion.

In order to assess how these events triggered digital publics in terms of expanding the discussion about the conflict, we built a distribution of different user actions for the entire analysis period. The graph in the Fig. 2 shows that users not only tweeted about political events in their feed, but also responded to other users with almost the same intensity and (less often) used the retweets and quotes feature. At especially significant moments, the number of original tweets and replies to them evened out, which confirms the applicability of the concept of digital publics to global discussion on Ukrainian dilemma.

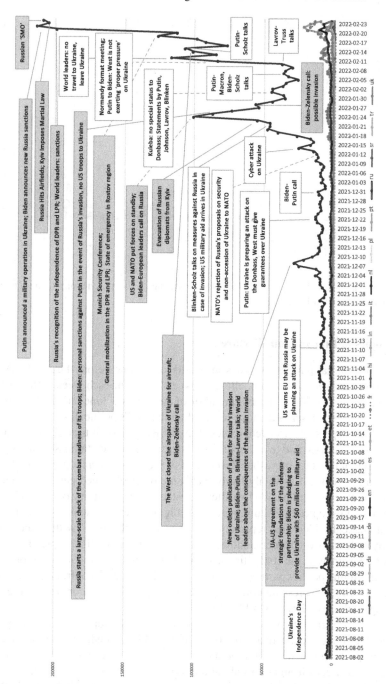

Fig. 1. Tweets, Retweets (Quotes), and Replies Containing the Keyword 'Ukraine' or 100 Political or Regional Hashtags in English or Russian by days, 30 August 2021–24 February 2022

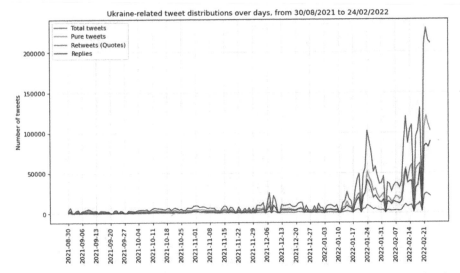

Fig. 2. A more detailed analysis is possible by comparing the events dynamics to the actual topics of discussion and their life cycle.

4.2 Topics of Information Warfare

We mapped digital publics' agendas in regard to Ukraine before the 2022 'SMO' by conducting time series topic modelling of tweets' texts for each week from 30 August 2021 to 24 February 2022. The interpretation of the results of time series topic modelling over the 26 weeks described above revealed a total of 38 politically significant topics: 23 persistent topics and 15 event topics (Fig. 3). By persistent topics, we mean topics that are not necessary tied to a specific event, but rather to a certain issue that worries a large cluster of users for more than 2 weeks. In our case, persistent topics were discussed from 3 to 26 weeks. It is highly likely that some of the revealed persistent topics had appeared before or continued to live after the established time frame of our analysis. The interpretation of topics by examining tokens, bigrams, and n-grams, as well as reading 400 automatically identified representative tweets of influential Twitter users for each topic by at least two encoders, showed that some of the political topics are growing thematic clusters with the conflicting narratives of the intensifying information warfare. Generally, digital publics participated in the global information confrontation by sharing personal feelings, expressing political preferences, pointing to economic interests, and asserting one's own view of world politics.

Firstly, we were interested in political meaning of the topics discussed by digital publics. We found a persistent topic (topic №1 on Fig. 3) dedicated to the discussion about prospects and the timing for the start of the 'big war' in Ukraine. It evolves over the four reviewed weeks from doubts about the seriousness of the talk about the possibility of escalation of the civil war in Ukraine into understanding the inevitability of a Russia–Ukraine war, which may not stop in Ukraine but escalate further to become a third World War. The results of topic modelling with time series allowed us to establish that, the emergence of digital publics discussing the possibility of intervention was preceded by the appearance of 8 event topics related to major political news (topics №5, 6, 8, 12, 17, 27, 29 and 32 on Fig. 3). We explain it by assuming that most of the digital publics in our sample began to express more political interest in Ukraine dilemma after being exposed to a series of media headlines circulated on Twitter in the first week of the analyzed period. In line with previous research on agenda setting through social media, this finding highlights the importance of incidental news exposure (Feezell, 2018). Thus, digital publics who actively spread political news on Twitter presumably contributed to the information confrontation by involving new users and expanding the discussion.

Secondly, the resulting statistics point to several important observations. The most discussed topics in our dataset were 'Ukraine membership in NATO' (18% of users and 25% of tweets) and 'Escalation at the border: Ukraine and Donbass' (14% of users and 23% of tweets). The latter covered the largest audience of almost 2.7 billion users and reached the highest 'Interest rate' (about 26 million reactions). The topics in which users made the most contributions in terms of increasing the potential of the social network (SNP) were 'Cryptocurrency to fund Ukraine's defense and donate to Ukraine', "Russia-US-China geopolitical triangle and Ukraine" and 'Expression of support for Ukraine'. The former and latter obviously came out ahead on this metric due to the call content in the tweets, but the second one contains a discussion about world politics and Ukraine among users. Finally, statistics show that the number of users discussing event topics is relatively small, which tells us that discussions on permanent topics are a key contributor to the spread of information warfare on social networks.

5 Discussion

Our results of topic interpretation and narrative identification, differing in approach and method, are nevertheless consistent with several earlier studies of regional and global narratives about the Russian–Ukrainian conflict (Korostelina 2014; Lazarenko 2019; Musliu and Burlyuk 2019; Smoor 2017). In particular, our topics 'Russia–US–China geopolitical triangle and Ukraine', 'What Putin wants in Ukraine' and 'Ukraine and European or International Security' correspond to Musliu and Burlyuk's (2019) conflicting meta-narratives of this discursive battleground: Ukraine as a liminal category between East and West; Ukraine as (non-)Russian; Ukraine as (non-)European, respectively. A set of conflicting narratives found in topics on Ukraine-Russia escalation with regard to Crimea and Donbass emphasize the point of Korostelina (2014) that Russian actions in Crimea and Eastern Ukraine increased divisions between already-polarized narratives. Our topic 'Alleged Nazis in Ukraine' was discussed earlier by Smoor (2017) as part of a Russian 'nationalist narrative' that appears as a domination of 'extreme right' or 'fascist' and 'foreign powers' in Ukrainian government. Thus, our study continues the scientific discussion about the mapping of narratives of the Ukrainian conflict by applying a methodological approach based on the machine-learning analysis of social media data and offering more topics of concern to a vast number of people worldwide. These topics may be further interpreted as narrative-based political concepts as they include two or more confronting versions of relevant political events (Zhabotynska and Velivchenko 2019).

However, this process of self-clustering on the basis of common interests and political events as discussion triggers is a road with oncoming traffic as various malicious

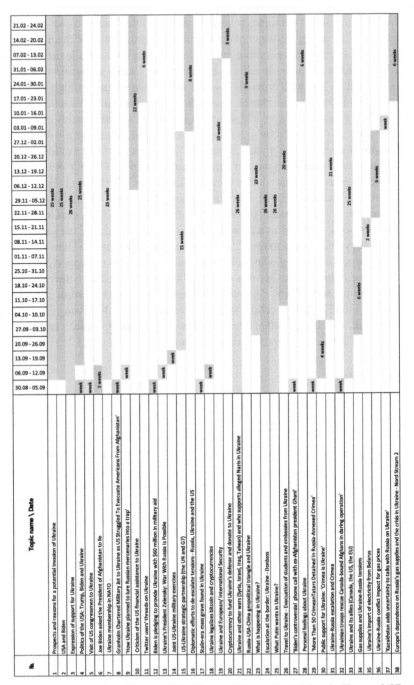

Fig. 3. Results of Topic Modelling with Time Series of Tweets Containing the Keyword 'Ukraine' or 100 Political or Regional Hashtags in English or Russian, 30 August 2021–24 February 2022

actors can effectively target and manipulate specific digital publics (Forestal 2021). This problem should be properly addressed to further identify artificial factors that contribute to the intensification of the discussion on certain especially important topics of the information warfare, such as alleged Nazism in Ukraine.

5.1 Limitations and Directions for Future Research

A number of biases need to be considered as limitations of this study, in particular, those associated with the collection method of using Twitter's advanced search, which doesn't guarantee access to the complete collection of tweets. Data-mining techniques using Twitter's advanced-search functions pose significant challenges as they may miss or exclude important data from the studies. The keyword and hashtags chosen, as well as the languages in which they are written, could not cover a complete discussion about the Ukraine dilemma on Twitter. Moreover, as found by Ojala et al. (2018 p. 14), 'Twitter may paradoxically reinforce the creation of rather uniform interpretations of complex issues, such as the Ukraine conflict'.

It is worth mentioning important computational propaganda trends in this context that can distort the results of topic modelling regarding large amounts of data. The narrative about the Ukrainian conflict in social media is, in part, artificially controlled by state and non-state actors who manipulate social media traffic with the help of so-called bots and trolls (Alyukov 2022; Boyte 2017). Nonetheless, scholars note that foreign countries' opportunities have been gradually reduced due to the 'splinternet', censorship and different measures to combat computational propaganda (Ciuriak 2022; Golovchenko 2022). Given the above and the activity of Ukrainian users in English, we believe that we have created a representative sample as the key 'war of narratives' about the conflict takes place in the Russian- and English-speaking segment of social media.

Nevertheless, the interpreted topics provide opportunities for further research. These might include, for example, building network graphs, applying various statistical methods for causal inference of user influence on the growth of specific topics, the identification of bots and trolls by topics, the enrichment of our results with a comparison of our results with the topics of online discussions about Russia and Ukraine after 24 February and measuring the change in public opinion due to the conflict escalation (Chen and Ferrara 2022; Chen et al. 2022; Doroshenko and Lukito 2021; Stukal et al. 2019; Zhdanova and Orlova 2017).

6   Conclusion

This study explains how digital publics contributed to the global intensifying information warfare around the Ukraine dilemma. We argued that digital publics are active participants in the information warfare surrounding the Ukrainian conflict and explored this phenomenon by using probabilistic topic modelling (ARTM approach) for 3,676,245 unique tweets written with the keyword 'Ukraine' or 100 political or regional hashtags in English or Russian written by 960,422 unique users for the period from 30 August 2021 to 24 February 2022. It should also be noted that our two-stage data-collection method allowed us to collect a dataset related to information warfare. As a result, we revealed 38 politically significant topics: 23 persistent topics and 15 event topics.

The visualization of dependency of discussion on political events and its further comparison with the life cycles of the revealed topics helped us to discover that digital publics contributed to the spread of the information warfare by actively tweeting political news on Twitter in the first week of the analyzed period, thus, expanding the discussion.

Our study shows that controversial political topics are discussed by a wide range of ordinary users, and their tweets are often the reactions in response to some event or someone else's tweet on the topic of interest. Thus, we have added literature about digital publics as thematic communities that arise on some political event, choosing for analysis the information warfare that was flaring up before our eyes. It is indicative which issues related to Ukraine dilemma were the most discussed in the world (on our Twitter sample). Digital publics most extensively reflected on some important strategic dilemmas such as possibility, causes and prospects of NATO intervention in the Ukrainian conflict or escalation of the situation in Donbass and Crimea, as well as numerous diplomatic attempts to resolve the conflict. In terms of global politics, two things are remarkable. Thus, already in 2021-early 2022 the Russian-Ukrainian conflict was not perceived among people in the world as a confrontation only between two countries - Russia and Ukraine, but rather as a crucial moment for the future world balance of power. While one part of the digital publics was actively persuading the Twitter audience by drawing analogies to other proxy wars, criticizing US military aid, and pointing out how Ukraine is becoming a bargaining chip in the global geopolitical race, another part campaigned to donate to Ukraine using cryptocurrencies, called for the Ukraine admission to NATO and reflected on how to effectively resist Russia. Neither has saved the world from a full-scale military escalation of the conflict, but, as the data show, digital publics have expanded the information warfare on Twitter, and therefore potentially influenced the context of what happened next.

We conclude that digital publics in the pre-war period participated in the global public discursive battleground on the Ukraine dilemma, forming special structures (topics) in the online space and, thereby, creating conditions and 'crowdsourcing' the narratives of the intensifying information warfare.

Acknowledgment. The author(s) received no financial support for the research, authorship, and/or publication of this article.

Disclosure of Interests. The authors have no competing interests to declare that are relevant to the con-tent of this article.

References

Alyukov, M.: Propaganda, authoritarianism and Russia's invasion of Ukraine. Nat. Hum. Behav. **6**, 763–765 (2022). https://doi.org/10.1038/s41562-022-01375-x

Anger, I., Kittl, C.: Measuring influence on Twitter. In: Proceedings of the 11th International Conference on Knowledge Management and Knowledge Technologies, pp. 1–4 (2011). https://doi.org/10.1145/2024288.2024326

Bodrunova, S.S.: Practices of cumulative deliberation: a meta-review of the recent research findings. In: Chugunov, A.V., Janssen, M., Khodachek, I., Misnikov, Y., Trutnev, D. (eds.) EGOSE 2021. CCIS, vol. 1529, pp. 89–104. Springer, Cham (2022). https://doi.org/10.1007/978-3-031-04238-6_8

Bolin, G, Jordan, P, Ståhlberg, P.: From nation branding to information warfare: the management of information in the Ukraine–Russia conflict. In: Media and the Ukraine Crises: Hybrid Media Practice and Narratives of Conflict. New York: Peter Lang Publishing Group, pp. 3–18 (2016)

Bruns, A., Highfield, T., Burgess, J.: The Arab spring and social media audiences. Am. Behav. Sci. **57**, 871–898 (2013). https://doi.org/10.1177/0002764213479374

Bruns, A., Highfield, T.: Is Habermas on Twitter? In: The Routledge Companion to Social Media and Politics, pp. 56–73 (2015)

Celikates, R.: Digital publics, digital contestation: a new structural transformation of the public sphere? In: Transformations of Democracy: Crisis, Protest and Legitimation, pp. 159–176 (2015)

Chen, E., Ferrara, E.: Tweets in time of conflict: a public dataset tracking the twitter discourse on the war between Ukraine and Russia. In: Proceedings of the International AAAI Conference on Web and Social Media. 17, pp. 1006–1013 (2023). https://doi.org/10.1609/icwsm.v17i1.22208

Chew, P.A., Turnley, J.G.: Understanding Russian information operations using unsupervised multilingual topic modeling. In: Dongwon Lee, Y.R., Lin, N.O., Thomson, R. (eds.) SBP-BRiMS 2017. LNCS, vol. 10354, pp. 102–107. Springer, Cham (2017). https://doi.org/10.1007/978-3-319-60240-0_12

Ciuriak, D.: The role of social media in Russia's war on Ukraine. Soc. Sci. Res. Netw. (2022). https://doi.org/10.2139/ssrn.4078863

Doroshenko, L., Lukito, J.: Trollfare: Russia's disinformation campaign during military conflict in Ukraine. Int. J. Commun. **15**(28), 4662–4689 (2021)

Feldman, D., Sadekova, T., Vorontsov, K.V.: Combining facts, semantic roles and sentiment lexicon in a generative model for opinion mining. In: Computational Linguistics and Intellectual Technologies (2020). https://doi.org/10.28995/2075-7182-2020-19-283-298

Feezell, J.T.: Agenda setting through social media: the importance of incidental news exposure and social filtering in the digital era. Polit. Res. Q. **71**, 482–494 (2017). https://doi.org/10.1177/1065912917744895

Forestal, J.: Beyond gatekeeping: propaganda, democracy, and the organization of digital publics. J. Politics **83**, 306–320 (2021). https://doi.org/10.1086/709300

García, B., Munoz-Organero, M., Alario-Hoyos, C., Kloos, C.D.: Automated driver management for selenium webdriver. Empirical Softw. Eng. **26**(5), 1–51 (2021). https://doi.org/10.1007/s10664-021-09975-3

Golovchenko, Y.: Fighting propaganda with censorship: a study of the Ukrainian ban on Russian social media. J. Politics **84**, 639–654 (2022). https://doi.org/10.1086/716949

Golovchenko, Y., Hartmann, M., Adler-Nissen, R.: State, media and civil society in the information warfare over Ukraine: citizen curators of digital disinformation. Int. Aff. **94**, 975–994 (2018). https://doi.org/10.1093/ia/iiy148

Howard, P.N., Duffy, A., Freelon, D., Hussain, M., Mari, W., Maziad, M.: Opening closed regimes: What was the role of social media during the Arab spring? Soc. Sci. Res. Netw. (2011). https://doi.org/10.2139/ssrn.2595096

Klein, H.: Information warfare and information operations. J. Int. Aff. **71**, 135–142 (2018)

Kochedykov, D., Apishev, M., Golitsyn, L., Vorontsov, K.: Fast and modular regularized topic modelling. In: 2017 21st Conference of Open Innovations Association (FRUCT), pp. 182–193 (2017)

Koltsova, O., Pashakhin, S.: Agenda divergence in a developing conflict: quantitative evidence from Ukrainian and Russian TV newsfeeds. Media War Confl. **13**, 237–257 (2019). https://doi.org/10.1177/1750635219829876

Korostelina, K.V.: Conflict of national narratives of Ukraine: euromaidan and beyond. Die Friedens-Warte. **89**, 269–290 (2014)

Lazarenko, V.: Conflict in Ukraine: multiplicity of narratives about the war and displacement. Eur. Politics Soc. **20**, 550–566 (2018). https://doi.org/10.1080/23745118.2018.1552108

Llewellyn, C., Grover, C., Alex, B., Oberlander, J., Tobin, R.: Extracting a topic specific dataset from a Twitter archive. In: Kapidakis, S., Mazurek, C., Werla, M. (eds.) TPDL 2015. LNCS, vol. 9316, pp. 364–367. Springer, Cham (2015). https://doi.org/10.1007/978-3-319-24592-8_36

Makhortykh, M.: #NoKievNazi: social media, historical memory and securitization in the Ukraine crisis. In: Strukov, V., Apryshchenko, V. (eds.) Memory and securitization in contemporary Europe, pp. 219–247. Palgrave Macmillan UK, London (2018). https://doi.org/10.1057/978-1-349-95269-4_9

Makhortykh, M., Lyebyedyev, E.: #SaveDonbassPeople: Twitter, propaganda, and conflict in eastern Ukraine. Commun. Rev. **18**, 239–270 (2015). https://doi.org/10.1080/10714421.2015.1085776

Makhortykh, M., Sydorova, M.: Social media and visual framing of the conflict in Eastern Ukraine. Media, War and Conflict. **10**, 359–381 (2017). https://doi.org/10.1177/1750635217702539

Oliveira, A.L.A.M., Miranda, M.V.: "Calling a spade", a spade: impoliteness and shame on Twitter. J. Res. Appl. Linguist. **13**(2), 22–32 (2022). https://doi.org/10.22055/RALS.2022.17800

Mishler, A., Crabb, E.S., Paletz, S., Hefright, B., Golonka, E.: Using structural topic modeling to detect events and cluster Twitter users in the Ukrainian crisis. In: Stephanidis, C. (ed.) HCI International 2015 - Posters' Extended Abstracts: International Conference, HCI International 2015, Los Angeles, CA, USA, August 2–7, 2015. Proceedings, Part I, pp. 639–644. Springer International Publishing, Cham (2015). https://doi.org/10.1007/978-3-319-21380-4_108

Mölder, H., Sazonov, V.: Information warfare as the Hobbesian concept of modern times — the principles, techniques, and tools of Russian information operations in the Donbass. J. Slavic Mil. Stud. **31**, 308–328 (2018). https://doi.org/10.1080/13518046.2018.1487204

Murshed, B.A.H., Suresha, M., Abawajy, J., Saif, M.A.N., Al-Ariki, H.D.E., Abdulwahab, H.M.: Short text topic modelling approaches in the context of big data: taxonomy, survey, and analysis. Artif. Intell. Rev. **56**, 5133–5260 (2022). https://doi.org/10.1007/s10462-022-10254-w

Musliu, V., Burlyuk, O.: Imagining Ukraine: from history and myths to Maidan protests. East Eur. Politics Soc. **33**, 631–655 (2019). https://doi.org/10.1177/0888325418821410

Nikolenko, S.I., Koltcov, S., Koltsova, O.: Topic modelling for qualitative studies. J. Inf. Sci. **43**, 88–102 (2016). https://doi.org/10.1177/0165551515617393

Ojala, M., Pantti, M., Kangas, J.: Professional role enactment amid information warfare: war correspondents tweeting on the Ukraine conflict. Journalism Theory Pract. Criticism **19**(3), 297–313 (2016). https://doi.org/10.1177/1464884916671158

Oswald, L., Munzert, S., Barberá, P., Guess, A.M., Yang, J.: Beyond the tip of the iceberg? Exploring Characteristics of the Online Public with Digital Trace Data (2022). https://doi.org/10.31235/osf.io/yfmzh

Papacharissi, Z.: Affective publics: Sentiment, Technology, and Politics. Oxford University Press (2015)

Papacharissi, Z., De Fátima Oliveira, M.: Affective news and networked publics: the rhythms of news storytelling on #Egypt. J. Commun. **62**, 266–282 (2012). https://doi.org/10.1111/j.1460-2466.2012.01630.x

Park, C.Y., Mendelsohn, J., Field, A., Tsvetkov, Y.: Challenges and opportunities in information manipulation detection: an examination of wartime Russian media. arXiv (Cornell University) (2022). https://doi.org/10.48550/arxiv.2205.12382

Plowman, K.D., Wakefield, R.I., Winchel, B.: Digital publics: tracking and reaching them. Public Relat. Rev. **41**, 272–277 (2015). https://doi.org/10.1016/j.pubrev.2014.12.007

Pohl, J., Seiler, M.P., Assenmacher, D., Grimme, C.: A Twitter streaming dataset collected before and after the onset of the war between Russia and Ukraine in 2022. Soc. Sci. Res. Netw. (2022). https://doi.org/10.2139/ssrn.4066543

Rambukkana, N.: Hashtag Publics: The Power and Politics of Discursive Networks. International Academic Publishers, Peter Lang Incorporated (2015)

Riquelme, F., González-Cantergiani, P.: Measuring user influence on Twitter: a survey. Inf. Process. Manage. **52**, 949–975 (2016). https://doi.org/10.1016/j.ipm.2016.04.003

Smoor, L.: Understanding the narratives explaining the Ukrainian crisis: identity divisions and complex diversity in Ukraine. Acta Univ. Sapientiae Eur. Reg. Stud. **11**, 63–96 (2017). https://doi.org/10.1515/auseur-2017-0004

Spiegel International: Russia Today's Editor-In-Chief: 'The West Never Got Over the Cold War Stereotype' (2013). https://www.spiegel.de/international/world/spiegel-interview-russia-today-editor-in-chief-margarita-simonyan-a-916356.html. Accessed 27 Nov 2023

Stukal, D., Sanovich, S., Tucker, J.A., Bonneau, R.: For whom the bot tolls: a neural networks approach to measuring political orientation of Twitter bots in Russia. SAGE Open **9**, 2 (2019). https://doi.org/10.1177/2158244019827715

Suciu, P.: Is Russia's invasion of Ukraine the first social media war? Forbes (2022). https://www.forbes.com/sites/petersuciu/2022/03/01/is-russias-invasion-of-ukraine-the-first-social-media-war/?sh=3e6d10641c5c. Accessed 27 Nov 2023

Thornton, R.: The changing nature of modern warfare. RUSI J. **160**, 40–48 (2015). https://doi.org/10.1080/03071847.2015.1079047

Tokarev, A.A: Ukrainian elites discourse in respect of the Donbass territory and population of 2009-2018: analysis of the national Facebook segment. MGIMO Rev. Int. Relat. **6**(63), 194–211 (2018). https://doi.org/10.24833/2071-8160-2018-6-63-194-211

Torbakov, I.: Ukraine and Russia: entangled histories, contested identities, and a war of narratives. In: Bertelsen, O. (ed.) Revolution and War in Contemporary Ukraine: The Challenge of Change. Columbia University Press (2017)

Tsvetkova, N., Sytnik, A., Grishanina, T.: Digital diplomacy and digital international relations: challenges and new advantages. Vestnik Saint Petersburg Univ. Int. relat. **15**(2), 174–196 (2022). https://doi.org/10.21638/spbu06.2022.204

Vorontsov, K., Frei, O., Apishev, M., Romov, P., Dudarenko, M.: BigARTM: open source library for regularized multimodal topic modeling of large collections. In: Mikhail, Y., Khachay, N.K., Panchenko, A., Ignatov, D., Labunets, V.G. (eds.) Analysis of Images, Social Networks and Texts: 4th International Conference, AIST 2015, Yekaterinburg, Russia, April 9–11, 2015, Revised Selected Papers, pp. 370–381. Springer International Publishing, Cham (2015). https://doi.org/10.1007/978-3-319-26123-2_36

Wendt, A.: Quantum Mind and Social Science. Cambridge University Press (2015)

Zhabotynska, S., Velivchenko, V.: New media and strategic narratives: the Dutch referendum on Ukraine – EU association agreement in Ukrainian and Russian internet blogs. Eur. Secur. **28**, 360–381 (2019). https://doi.org/10.1080/09662839.2019.1648253

Zhdanova, M., Orlova, D.: Computational propaganda in Ukraine: caught between external threats and internal challenges. In: Working Paper 2017.9, Project on Computational Propaganda, Oxford, UK (2017) https://demtech.oii.ox.ac.uk/wp-content/uploads/sites/89/2017/06/Comprop-Ukraine.pdf. Accessed 27 Nov 2023

Location Information Sharing System on a Virtual Town Map to Enhance a Sense of Connectedness with Group Members

Yui Toshimitsu[✉], Masayuki Ando, Kouyou Otsu, and Tomoko Izumi

Ritsumeikan University, Kusatsu 525-8557, Shiga, Japan
is0568vr@ed.ritsumei.ac.jp, {mandou,k-otsu,
izumi-t}@fc.ritsumei.ac.jp

Abstract. Social isolation and loneliness among people living alone are major social issues that can lead to anxiety and depression. One possible approach to alleviate these issues is to enhance the sense of connectedness and social presence in society and among others. To increase one's sense of connectedness and social presence with others, it is important to increase awareness and the sense of being part of a community by being aware of one's and others' presence, activities, and relevance. This study aims to provide situational awareness by sharing location information and enhancing the sense of connectedness with others. Accordingly, we propose a location information sharing system that visualizes members who live far from each other in real space as if they were living together in a virtual town, reflecting their actual location information. Mapping members on a small-town map is expected to reduce their sense of distance and make it easier for them to notice each other, which may enhance their sense of unity and connectedness as a group. To verify the effectiveness of the proposed system, a comparative experiment was conducted using an application that shares accurate location information on a real map. The results show that the proposed system reduces resistance to sharing location information and increases the sense of unity among group members. In addition, it was confirmed that the proposed system may enhance awareness and a sense of connectedness with continued use.

Keywords: location information sharing · awareness · social presence · loneliness

1 Introduction

1.1 Background

Currently, social isolation and loneliness are major social issues in Japan and around the world. These problems have been pointed out in a study [1] based on data from 113 countries or regions during 2000–2019. Such loneliness can lead to anxiety and depression [2]. Data from a meta-analysis [3] showed that the probability of death increases by 26% for loneliness, 29% for social isolation, and 32% for living alone. Many young people live alone, and even they may experience social isolation and loneliness because of this.

A. Coman and S. Vasilache (Eds.): HCII 2024, LNCS 14705, pp. 208–221, 2024.
https://doi.org/10.1007/978-3-031-61312-8_14

One approach to reduce feelings of social isolation and loneliness is to enhance a sense of connectedness and social presence with society and others. Such an individual's subjective perception of being closely connected to society is termed as "social connectedness" [4]. Social presence is defined as the sense of "being together with another" [5] and it is a factor that enhances social connectedness with society and others. Shen and Khalifa [6] conceptualized social presence into three dimensions: awareness, affective, and cognitive social presence. Awareness refers to being aware of and understanding the activities of others, thereby making relevance to one's and others' activities [7]. Therefore, to increase one's sense of connectedness and social presence with others, it is important to increase one's awareness and sense of being part of a community by being aware of one's and others' presence, activities, and their relevance.

However, it is difficult for a person living in an area geographically distant from family or local friends to be aware of others' activities, presence, and relevance. This could lead to feelings of loneliness. Accordingly, social media, such as a social networking service (SNS), has become a tool for strengthening the sense of social connectedness and presence because it can share the activities and situations of members, even if they live apart or far away geographically. However, the sense of connectedness through activity sharing on social media gradually decreases when actions such as providing common topics and feedback are lost. It is difficult for members who live apart to find common topics related to their daily lives and to provide feedback. Therefore, supporting a sense of connectedness and social presence remains a problem that must be resolved.

1.2 Study Objectives

Enhancing a sense of connectedness among people in remote areas requires them to become aware of each other's life activities and circumstances and relate them to their own lives. Therefore, it is important to naturally support the awareness of others and recognition of relevance in their lives, regardless of distance. In this study, as a potential resolution for this goal, we consider the concept of a location-based sharing system based on a virtual space where the states of users link their actual state in real space, visualizing their lives as if they were connected in one world. We focus on the location information to represent user states. Location information indicates "where each user is right now," but from this information it is also possible to be aware of "what they are doing right now." Therefore, we propose a location information sharing system that presents a virtual town map in which the users' locations are shown in the corresponding town facilities according to their location in real space. The town has one facility for each characteristic, such as a school or library, and users who are far away from each other are visualized as if they were visiting the same facility in the virtual town.

In this study, we verify whether this location-based living-sharing system in a virtual town map can make users feel closer to each other's presence and enhance their sense of connectedness. In the verification experiment, we compared the proposed system to a system that shares detailed location information from three perspectives: awareness, sense of connectedness, and resistance to sharing information. Groups were formed with several experimental participants who were friends, and each group was asked to use each of the two systems for 2.5 days and respond to questionnaires and interviews. Herein, we present the experimental results, which indicate that the proposed system effectively reduces resistance to sharing location information and increases the sense of unity among group members.

2 Related Research

As supporting awareness among people living apart from each other is a critical issue, extensive research has been conducted on this topic. Some propose using a familiar object to display remote people's status to make them naturally aware of others' status. For example, Mynatt et al. [8] proposed a digital photo frame for elderly people and their family members who live apart to share their daily status, such as their health status and the surrounding weather. Itoh et al. [9] proposed a family planter for elderly households living alone, in which the planter's light represented the movements of others. The methods proposed in these studies attempted to enhance awareness of each other's presence and a sense of closeness without burdening users' lives by presenting visible information naturally in their lives. This approach of supporting awareness without burdening the user is also important from the perspective of continuous use; accordingly, we design a system that is potentially less burdensome.

In our proposal, we focus on presenting users' status linked to their actual actions to support their awareness. A similar approach has been adopted in previous studies. Some studies have considered methods for representing and sharing the actual actions of users in real time. Venkatesan et al. [10] proposed a method for viewing a concert with a music player that provides a vibratory sensation created by the artist. It has been shown that listening to music while receiving vibratory tactile sensations not only increases the participant's sense of empathy toward the artist but also decreases the person's sense of isolation. RobotPHONE [11] is a stuffed animal telephone that combines auditory, visual, and tactile transmissions. The stuffed animal changes its movement according to the person's movements so that users can feel the other person's movement through the stuffed animal, according to the appearance and movement of the hand. These studies focused on representing the movement and presence of others using synchronously moving devices. In contrast, we utilize user location information to provide awareness of the presence of others. To the best of our knowledge, no existing study considers location information sharing as a way to enhance awareness and a sense of connectedness to make users aware that they are in the same situation as others or make them feel the presence of others.

Many location information sharing applications [12] are used by friends and family members to communicate with each other. In such applications, detailed and accurate location information is shared on electronic maps. However, sharing location information requires solving issues such as privacy protection or resistance [13]. Therefore, our proposed system indicates the attributes of user locations by mapping them at facilities in a virtual town according to their actual locations rather than sharing real-world detailed location information. This mechanism may reduce the resistance to sharing location information while enhancing the sense of connectedness among users.

3 Proposed Information Sharing System

3.1 Proposed System Concept

In this study, we consider a design for sharing location information that enhances group connectedness and addresses the psychological resistance associated with sharing personal data with family and friends. The proposed system sets up a town where members live in a virtual space, and the members' locations in the virtual space change according to their actual locations in the real space. Detailed location information may not necessarily be required to infer the current activities or status of other members. A group comprising familiar members can imagine each other's activities simply by knowing the attributes of a location such as home, school, or workplace. Therefore, the proposed system does not share detailed information but only the attribute information of the current location. Location attribute information is represented by displaying each member at the corresponding facility on a virtual town map (see Fig. 1). Abstracting the location information provided in this manner can reduce the psychological resistance to sharing personal information.

When detailed location information is shared using a map, users are not likely to notice people who are displayed far away and may feel isolated from distant others. To enhance the sense of connectedness in real space, members must be able to easily sense each other's actions and situations and feel close to each other. For example, in the proposed system, if a user is at school, the system displays the corresponding avatar at the facility "school" in the virtual town. This mechanism also applies to members who live far away. Thus, even if they live in different areas and attend different schools in real space, they will be displayed in the same "school" facility in the virtual town (Fig. 2). For example, if Mr. S is at School A and Mr. T is at School B in real space, then Mr. S and Mr. T are located at the same virtual school in our system. In other words, members who live far from each other in real space can be visualized as if they were living together in a virtual town, reflecting their actual location information. This approach can reduce the sense of distance and make it easier to notice one another, which may enhance the sense of unity and connectedness as a group.

3.2 Prototype System

We developed a prototype system based on the concept of location information-sharing. Figure 1 shows an example of the output of our prototype system. When activated, the system displays a virtual town map where users are mapped to facilities, as shown in Fig. 1. Several predefined facilities with unique attributes exist on the virtual town map. These facilities were selected based on the common characteristics of the locations that group members frequently visit on a daily basis. In the prototype system, three location attributes, namely, "school," "home," and "workplace for a part-time job," are set considering students as users. The system then displays location attributes using facility symbols. In this system, when a user is determined to be at a location with a predefined attribute, the user is displayed at the corresponding facility on the virtual town map (see Fig. 3). Otherwise, the user is shown at a special facility (e.g., a rocket

Fig. 1. Proposed location information sharing system on a virtual town map.

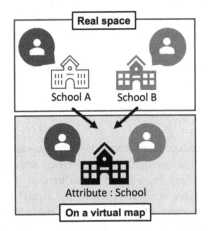

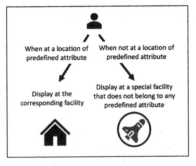

Fig. 2. Users' assignment at the same location attribute on the virtual map.

Fig. 3. Method of presenting a user's location based on location attribute.

in our prototype system) so that other members can notice that the user is not at any of the predefined attribute locations.

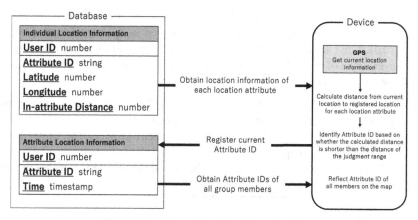

Fig. 4. Data flow of the virtual map database.

The system consists of a smartphone used by the user and a database that stores the locations and location attribute information. The software running on the smartphone was implemented using Flutter's Dart language, which calculates the current location attributes from the GPS location information and registers them to the database, and displays the user's location information obtained from the database on the virtual map.

Figure 4 presents the databases and flow of location information processing in this system. The "Individual Location Information" table in the database holds the location information for each location attribute for each user ID. Specifically, this table stores the IDs of the location attributes and the judgement range latitude, longitude, and distance for each user ID. The judgment range distance is the distance from the location of the registered latitude and longitude within which the user is judged to be at that facility. Information on multiple location attributes can be stored for each user ID and is assumed to be registered in advance. In other words, this prototype system can only judge previously registered location attributes. When the user's device is at startup, the attribute information corresponding to the user ID is obtained from the "Individual Location Information" table. Then, the system on the device calculates the current location attribute at fixed intervals by comparing the judgment range distance to the distance between the registered location and the current location obtained from GPS information for each location attribute. The calculated location attribute is registered in the "Attribute Location Information" table as an Attribute ID. This table contains the current location attributes for each group member. Then, in the prototype system, by periodically obtaining the location attributes of all group members on the device side, their locations are displayed at the facilities corresponding to the location attribute on the virtual map.

4 Verification Experiment

4.1 Purpose

Using a virtual town map, we evaluated the impact of our proposed location information sharing system on users' impressions from three perspectives: resistance to sharing information, awareness of others' status, and sense of connectedness. To evaluate this, we compared our system (hereafter referred to as the virtual map system) with a conventional location information sharing system (hereafter referred to as the real map system) in which detailed and accurate location information is displayed on a real map. Figure 5 shows an example of the real map system output. In this experiment, the following three hypotheses were tested:

- Hypothesis 1 (Resistance to sharing information): The virtual map system reduces resistance to information sharing more than the real map system.
- Hypothesis 2 (Awareness): The virtual map system provides the same level of awareness as the real map system.
- Hypothesis 3 (Sense of connectedness): The virtual map system increases the sense of connectedness and unity with group members.

Fig. 5. Image of the real map system

As the virtual map system does not share the exact location and does not present geographic information on the map, there is likely to be less resistance to sharing location information compared to a detailed map system (Hypothesis 1). Hypothesis 2 relates to a person's awareness of where other members are and what they are doing. While the real map system shares detailed location information, the virtual map system only presents location attributes; therefore, users obtain less information and are less aware of others' situations. However, the virtual map system displays the situations of all members based on their location attributes on a single virtual map, making it easier for users to notice the existence of members and to be aware of others' situations. Therefore, the virtual map system can provide as much or more awareness as the real map system (Hypothesis

2). In addition, even if the members are in different locations, the proposed system gathers members with the same location attributes in the same facility on the virtual map, which is thought to increase the sense of connectedness and unity among group members (Hypothesis 3).

4.2 Experimental Procedures

In this experiment, we set two experimental conditions to compare the two information-sharing systems.

- Real-map condition: Participants use the real map system that provides detailed and accurate location information on a real map.
- Virtual-map condition: Participants use the virtual map system in which their location attribute information is displayed on a virtual town map.

The real-map condition represents the comparison condition, while the virtual-map condition represents the proposed system condition.

In this experiment, each group was composed of three to five participants who were close friends at the same university. However, the participants were only required to be from the same university, while their home areas and part-time jobs differed. The experiment was conducted only on weekdays; therefore, the location attributes in the virtual map system were set to "school," "home," and "workplace for a part-time job," which are location attributes common to college students.

Each group experimented for 2.5 days under each condition. The experimental conditions differed for each group. The experimental procedure is illustrated in Fig. 6. We informed the participants of the experiment and obtained their consent to participate prior to the start of the experiment. In particular, we carefully explained that their location information would be shared with the group members via the experimental system and that if they wanted to decline to participate in the experiment during the experimental period, they could do so. Before using the experimental system, the home, school,

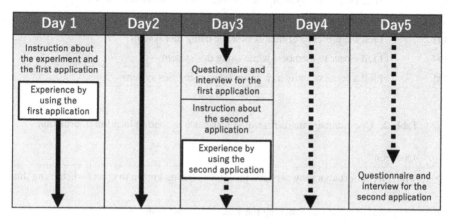

Fig. 6. Experimental work flow

and workplace for part-time job locations were obtained from each participant using a questionnaire and registered in a database.

The following processes were conducted for each experimental condition. The participants were given a device with the application for one of the real and virtual map systems installed and were asked to carry it with them at all times and check the application as much as possible. To encourage participants to view the location information in the application, a message was sent via a messaging application three times a day at 10:00, 12:00, and 18:00, instructing them to use the application. Every evening from the first day of the experiment, the participants were asked to answer a questionnaire about their sense of connectedness and awareness, as mentioned in Sect. 4.3. On the third day, when the use of the first application was terminated, participants were asked to respond to a questionnaire about their resistance to information sharing, as mentioned in Sect. 4.3. The questionnaire was created using Google Forms, and participants answered it on the web via their smartphones.

4.3 Evaluation Items

Questionnaire items about awareness and sense of connectedness are listed in Table 1, which were requested to be answered every night during the experiment. Each participant responded thrice for each experimental condition. Q1 and Q2 are related to the awareness of other members, and Q3–Q5 are related to a sense of connectedness with group members. Table 2 lists the questionnaire items regarding resistance to sharing information. This questionnaire was answered once, after the application was completed for each condition. The participants were asked to rate their answers on a seven-point Likert scale ranging from 1 (not at all applicable) to 7 (extremely applicable).

Table 1. Questionnaire items related to awareness and sense of connectedness.

No.	Question
Q1	When using this system, I was aware of where other members were
Q2	I was able to guess what other members were doing by using this system
Q3	I felt the presence of members while using this system
Q4	I felt closer to members while using this system
Q5	I felt a sense of unity as a group while using this system

Table 2. Questionnaire items regarding resistance to sharing location information.

No.	Question
Q6	I felt discomfort about my personal information being known to others when using this system
Q7	I felt like someone was watching me while using this system

5 Results

5.1 Questionnaire Results

Twenty-three university students (17 males and 6 females) participated in the experiment. First, we present the questionnaire results regarding awareness and sense of connectedness. To investigate the differences in the average values between conditions and over the course of the day, a two-way analysis of variance (ANOVA) with repeated measurements was conducted. Multiple comparisons were performed for those with a significant main effect, and simple main effect tests were conducted for those with observed interactions.

Figure 7 shows a box-and-whisker diagram of the answers to the questionnaire items related to awareness (Q1 and Q2). No significant differences are observed in the ANOVA results for either question. The results for Q1, which asked whether participants were aware of where their group members were, exhibit little difference between conditions for Days 1 to 3. Considering the change in days, while there was a large variation in responses in both conditions on Day 1, the variation decreased on Day 3. In addition, most participants gave positive responses, with a score of 5 or higher on Day 3. In other words, the number of participants with a low degree of awareness decreased as they used the application. The results for Q2, which asked whether participants were able to guess what others were doing, show that the scores under the real-map condition are higher throughout the experimental period. In addition, variations under the virtual-map condition are larger than those under the real-map condition. The real map system exhibits a small difference in the degree in which people feel that they can infer the situations of others; conversely, a difference is observed for each participant in the virtual map system. However, by Day 3 of the virtual-map condition, the variability is smaller, and as the duration of use increases, it may become easier to infer the situation of others.

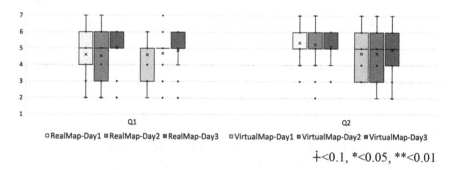

$+<0.1, *<0.05, **<0.01$

Fig. 7. Box-and-whisker diagram for the awareness results

Figure 8 shows a box-and-whisker diagram of the answers to the questionnaire items related to a sense of connectedness (Q3–Q5). According to the ANOVA results, for Q3, there is a marginally significant difference ($p < 1.0$) in the interaction. As the results of the simple main effect tests, for the real-map condition, there are marginally significant differences between Days 1 and 2 ($p < 0.1$) and between Days 2 and 3 ($p < 0.1$). When

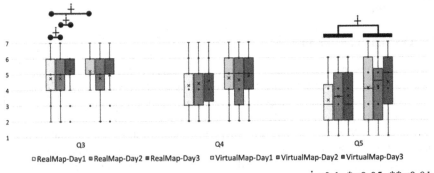

+<0.1, *<0.05, **<0.01

Fig. 8. Box-and-whisker diagram for the resistance to sharing location information results

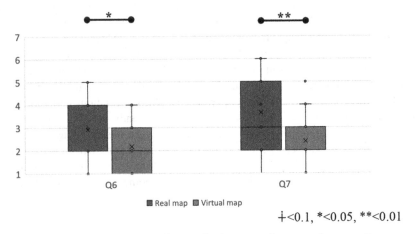

+<0.1, *<0.05, **<0.01

Fig. 9. Box-and-whisker diagram for the sense of connectedness results

comparing the two conditions for each day, Day 1 exhibits a significant trend between conditions. In addition, a main effect of the condition is observed for Q5. The results for Q3, which asked whether the participants felt the presence of members, show that the score significantly tends to be higher under the virtual-map condition on Day 1, indicating that the participants felt the presence of other members more at the time they started using the virtual map system than at the end of the experiment. However, under the real-map condition, the scores increased as the experiment progressed, indicating that the presence of members was felt more with increased system use. The results for Q4, which asked whether the participants felt that other members were close to them, show that there are no significant differences between conditions or between elapsed days; however, the average values tend to be higher under the virtual-map condition for each day. The results for Q5, which asked about the sense of unity as a group, exhibit significantly higher scores under the virtual-map condition than under the real-map condition. Consequently, it can be concluded that the proposed method gives a greater sense of unity as a group than the real map system. However, variations in the feeling are large under both conditions.

Figure 9 shows a box-and-whisker diagram for the answers to the questionnaire items related to resistance to sharing location information (Q6 and Q7). The results are interpreted as more positive when the answer is closer to 1 because the questions asked the participants about the degree of negative perception. A t-test was conducted to examine the differences in means between conditions, and significant differences were found ($p < 0.05$) for both questions. The results for Q6, which asked about discomfort with location sharing, show that the proposed system is significantly less uncomfortable to participants regarding their personal information being known to others. Furthermore, a floor effect was observed under the virtual-map condition, which indicates that most participants experiencing no discomfort. Similarly, in the results for Q7, which asked if participants felt monitored by others compared to the real map system, the proposed system was found to be significantly less likely to lead to such feelings.

5.2 Discussion

First, let us consider Hypothesis 1, which states that the virtual map system reduces resistance to information sharing more than the real map system. The results for the questions related to resistance to sharing information (Q6 and Q7) show that the degree of discomfort and feeling of being monitored were significantly lower for the virtual maps, as shown in Fig. 9. These results support Hypothesis 1. The proposed virtual map system provides only location attribute information and not detailed location information such as GPS information. It can be concluded that this mechanism of sharing location information reduces the resistance to information sharing.

Next, let us discuss Hypothesis 2 regarding awareness (Fig. 7). Although there was no significant difference in the results for Q2, the mean values were higher for the real map system. Detailed location information makes it easier to infer what others are currently doing. Therefore, this result indicates that Hypothesis 2 regarding awareness was not supported. However, for Q2, the variation in responses under the virtual-map condition on Day 3 becomes small, indicating that more participants responded that they were aware of what other members were doing. This indicates the possibility of increasing awareness as the proposed system is used for longer periods. Moreover, the scores for Q1 regarding awareness of others did not differ between the two conditions throughout the experiment. Therefore, it is possible to say that the awareness of where others are could be maintained in the virtual map system, which abstracts the shared location information.

Finally, let us consider Hypothesis 3 regarding the sense of connectedness (Fig. 8). The analysis results for Q3 and Q4 revealed no significant differences between the two conditions. However, except for the responses to Q3 on Day 3, the mean values tended to be higher for the proposed system than for the real map system. This suggests that the proposed system can improve the sense of presence and closeness among group members, although no statistical differences were observed for these questions. Regarding the results for Q5, the participants tended to feel a stronger sense of unity as a group in the proposed system than in the real map system. Therefore, in this experiment, although

Hypothesis 3 regarding a sense of connectedness was not supported, it is possible to say that the proposed system can enhance a sense of group unity.

6 Conclusion

In this paper, an application that aims to alleviate loneliness in people living alone is proposed by focusing on awareness support in location information sharing. The proposed application is presented on a virtual town map, where group members are located in a facility corresponding to the attribute of their actual location in the real world. Considering the resistance to personal information sharing, the application only shares location attributes and not detailed location information. Moreover, in the proposed system, members are assigned to the same facility on a town map when their actual locations have the same attributes, even when they are in distant areas. In other words, the proposed system visualizes members who live far from each other in real space as if they were living together in a virtual town, reflecting their actual location information.

To verify whether the proposed virtual map system can maintain and improve awareness and a sense of connectedness and reduce resistance to sharing information, we conducted a comparison experiment with a real map system that shares detailed location information. The results showed that the proposed system reduced resistance to sharing location information and increased the sense of unity among group members. Although the proposed system was not effective in supporting awareness or a sense of connectedness within the group in the experiment, it was confirmed that the proposed system might enhance these feelings through its continued use.

A group of students from the same university participated in the experiment. However, as our goal is to alleviate the loneliness of people living alone, it is necessary to verify the effectiveness of the proposed system for people who live away from their family or friends and are not connected in the real space.

Acknowledgments. This work was supported in part by Ritsumeikan Global Innovation Research Organization(R-GIRO).

References

1. Surkalim, D.L., et al.: The prevalence of loneliness across 113 countries: systematic review and meta-analysis. In: BMJ, pp.1–17 (2022)
2. Wang, J., Mann, F., Lloyd-Evans, B., et al.: Associations between loneliness and perceived social support and outcomes of mental health problems. BMC Psychiatry **18**, 156 (2018)
3. Holt-Lunstad, J., Smith, T.B., Baker, M., Harris, T., Stephenson, D.: Loneliness and social isolation as risk factors for mortality, a meta-analytic review. Perspect. Psychol. Sci. **10**(2), 227–237 (2015)
4. Lee, R.M., Robbins, S.B.: Measuring belongingness: the social connectedness and the social assurance scales. J. Couns. Psychol. **42**, 232–241 (1995)
5. Biocca, F., Harms, C., Gregg, J.: The networked minds measure of social presence: pilot test of the factor structure and concurrent validity. In: 4th annual International Workshop on Presence, ISPR, pp. 49–59 (2001)

6. Shen, K.N., Khalifa, M.: Design for social presence in online communities: a multidimensional approach. AIS Trans. Hum. Comput. Interact. **1**(2), 33–54 (2009)
7. Dourish, P., Bellotti, V.: Awareness and coordination in shared workspaces. In: Proceedings of the 1992 ACM Conference on Computer-Supported Cooperative Work (CSCW 1992), pp.107–114 (1992)
8. Mynatt, E.D., Rowan, J., Jacobs, A., Craighill, S.: Digital family portraits: supporting peace of mind for extended family members. In: Proceedings of the SIGCHI Conference on Human Factors in Computing Systems (CHI 2001), pp.333–340 (2001)
9. Itoh, Y., Miyajima, A., Watanabe, T.: 'TSUNAGARI' communication: fostering a feeling of connection between family members. In: CHI 2002 Extended Abstracts on Human Factors in Computing Systems (CHI EA 2002). Association for Computing Machinery, pp.810–811 (2002)
10. Venkatesan, T., Wang, Q.J.: Feeling connected: the role of haptic feedback in VR concerts and the impact of haptic music players on the music listening experience. Arts **12**(4), 148 (2023)
11. Sekiguchi, D., Inami, M., Tachi, S.: RobotPHONE: RUI for interpersonal communication. In: CHI 2001 Extended Abstracts on Human Factors in Computing Systems (CHI EA 2001). Association for Computing Machinery, pp.277–278 (2001)
12. Life360 Homepage. https://www.life360.com/intl/. Accessed 29 Jan 2024
13. Spreitzer, M., Theimer, M.: Scalable, secure, mobile computing with location information. Commun. ACM **36**(7), 24 (1993)

Author Index

Printed in the United States
by Baker & Taylor Publisher Services